The
Newspaper Publishing
Industry

The
Newspaper Publishing
Industry

Robert G. Picard
California State University/Fullerton

Jeffrey H. Brody
California State University/Fullerton

Allyn and Bacon
Boston   London   Toronto   Sydney   Tokyo   Singapore

Vice President, Humanities: Joseph Opiela
Editorial Assistant: Kate Tolini
Marketing Manager: Karen Bowers
Editorial Production Service: Chestnut Hill Enterprises, Inc.
Composition/Prepress Buyer: Linda Cox
Manufacturing Buyer: Suzanne Lareau
Cover Administrator: Suzanne Harbison

Copyright © 1997 by Allyn & Bacon
A Viacom Company
Needham Heights, MA 02194

Library of Congress Cataloging-in-Publication Data

Picard, Robert G.
     The newspaper publishing industry / Robert G. Picard,
Jeffrey H. Brody.
          p.   cm.
     Includes bibliographical references (p.   ) and index.
     ISBN 0-205-16145-6 (pbk.)
     1. Newspaper publishing—United States.   2. Newspapers—
United States.   I. Brody, Jeffrey H., 1952-   .   II. Title.
Z479.P53   1996
070.5'722—dc20   96-19616
                                                            CIP

Printed in the United States of America

10 9 8 7 6 5 4 3   05 04 03 02

For Marc Alan Brody,

who died too young of AIDS

Contents

5   A Day in the Life of a Newspaper   99

PART III

6   Technology and Labor Issues   109

7   Contemporary Editorial Issues and Problems   126

Preface

This book has been written at a time when those in and about the newspaper industry are expressing significant anxiety about its future and the future of news. Although profits for newspaper companies have rebounded in the mid-1990s with rates of return reaching well into double digits, worries persist about the long-term prognosis for newspapers. It appears that the print medium is caught between the Scylla of television news and the Charybdis of the information age. The question in many publishers' and journalists' minds is whether and how newspapers will survive in the next century. Fears generated by the closing of afternoon newspapers and the financial troubles of some large-city dailies have led many observers both within and outside the industry to conclude that the newspaper industry is dying. The dominance of the broadcast industry and the rush to electronic delivery of the news have raised concerns that the print medium may become obsolete. It is our intention to dispel some of the many misconceptions that have arisen about the industry, and we intend as well to analyze the issues and problems that editors and publishers must resolve to assure continued growth in the twenty first century.

We believe that many misconceptions about the news industry have been fueled by misperceptions about the nature and scope of the business. The nation's largest and most well-known newspapers—*New York Times, Wall Street Journal, Los Angeles Times, USA Today*—have circulations that are more than twenty times that of the average newspaper. The market forces and financial pressures that these and other metropolitan newspapers face are far from representative of the market forces and financial pressures confronted by most newspapers, yet they are the issues that focus on the industry and its observers. Unlike the larger, more visible newspapers that reach a national audience or serve huge metropolitan areas, the average newspaper is small, serving a local market of about 160,000 people. It has no other local daily newspaper competition and is financially sound. Furthermore, the average newspaper faces far less competition from broadcast news and threats posed by new commercial technology than its larger counterparts. The average daily newspaper is the dominant source of information and advertising within its circulation area, usually in small cities and suburbs.

Although critics since A. J. Liebling have lamented the trend toward one-newspaper towns because of its unfortunate effects on information and idea competition, the trend toward monopoly has created profitable newspapers. In fact, this book will demonstrate that newspaper publishers have prospered by acquiring and operating monopoly newspapers and have suffered in head-to-head competition.

Discussions of the newspaper industry have also traditionally suffered from a narrowness that has focused only on daily newspapers, ignoring the overwhelmingly higher number of newspapers that do not publish daily, and those that do not target general audiences but serve minorities and foreign language groups, as well as those with other interests not well served by general dailies. We have tried to overcome those limitations by including information on these significant publications in our exploration of the industry.

The entire newspaper industry is clearly being affected by social, technological, and economic changes and we attempt to place those changes and effects into context to help those working in the industry, as well as those individuals observing and studying it, to gain insight into the industry's current situation and prospects for the future. We have approached our task by dividing this book into three major sections.

The first part of this book presents an overview of the nature, scope, and roles of the newspaper industry. It covers such subjects as the parts of a newspaper, formats, multiple editions, competition between newspapers, and newspapers as employers and financial institutions. Insights are offered into the peculiar economics of newspapers as a product that delivers both advertising and information in an easy-to-read, easy-to-handle format. We explore the competitive advantages of newspapers that make them important and desirable carriers of news, information, and advertising. To provide perspective on the evolution of American newspapers, we present historic milestones within the newspaper industry, discussing how they changed content, audiences, and operations of papers and their implications.

The second part of the book offers an overview of the operations of a daily and weekly newspaper, focusing on the realities of the business and the processes of putting out a product that recreates itself everyday. We look at the editorial, advertising, business, circulation, and production activities of papers and how they are coordinated to create and distribute the newspaper product.

In the third part, we address issues that affect the newspaper industry's future. While we firmly believe newspapers still have a future and that the industry is fundamentally healthy, we cannot ignore how editorial, labor, technological, business/management and legal issues are currently affecting the industry and the important roles they will play in the industry's future developments.

Given data that suggest that the best strategy for success is for publishers to carve out a circulation area with no competition from a competing daily and with a different type of competition from the broadcast media, one may be surprised at the level of anxiety that led newspaper managers to make significant changes in the editorial philosophy of newspapers in the 1980s and the real effect these changes have had on papers. Editors have made great efforts to rely on marketing to attract and appeal to new readers in ways that are fundamentally altering the content of some papers, changing their relations with audiences, and affecting their market positions.

Technological changes have also altered newspapers. The last twenty years have not only seen the rise of computers in the newsroom, but also the rise of color printing, increasing packaging of news stories with graphics and photographs, and new types of reporting. The introduction of computers for word processing, layout, photography, and graphics has had a profound effect on newsroom and backshop operations. Whereas it once took scores of people all day to typeset classified ads, computers can do the job in less than an hour. Many newspapers design pages by computer pagination, and photographers use them to crop and reproduce photographs for layout. Graphic programs allow artists to develop charts, maps, and illustrations in very short periods of time. Reporters use word stations and light-weight laptop computers with modems that have almost eliminated the need to call in stories to the rewrite desk, and made it possible to do significant amounts of research on stories in a short period of time.

But the same computer technology has given rise to the information age and the fear that print newspapers will become obsolete. We discuss how the industry has made inroads in developing fax newspapers and on-line newspapers—but so far has been unsuccessful in generating significant advertising revenue from these ventures. Answers to questions of how to make profits on the Internet have so far eluded publishers who would like to use its potential to eliminate the high cost of newsprint and gain more control over the reporting, production, and distribution aspects of the business.

We also explore business and management issues ranging from increasing diversity to developing telecommunications-based information services that enable readers to retrieve information over phone lines. Demographic trends indicate that American society will become more diverse in the next century and that the non-Hispanic Caucasian population will become a minority in this country as the number of Asians, Blacks, Hispanics, and other minorities increase. To increase readership of newspapers we show how newspapers will have to broaden their coverage of people of color and hire staffs that are representative of American society.

We then explore how telecommunications technology has enabled newspapers to expand their operations to include new types of information services. Restaurant guides and reprints of important stories are available for sale. Classified advertising dating services using 900 numbers appeal to single readers. We show how newspapers hope to create on-line networks that provide ticket services, home shopping, travel guides, world-wide weather reports, stock quotes, food booklets, sports packages, including biographies and statistics on players and background information on major sporting events, entertainment guides, restaurant reviews, and listings of community activities. This is done to increase profit by packaging information rather than discarding it the day after it appears in print. Information for a single news article may be recycled electronically in many different versions, depending on reader preference.

Many of the legal and regulatory issues that deal with technological changes are evolving. This book concludes with an examination of these developments and other issues that are drawing newspapers into conflict with government agencies and into courtrooms across the country. The question of whether writers should be reimbursed for the electronic dissemination of their work and what copyright protection is available on the Internet are explored. We discuss major legal issues currently being wrestled with in the industry, including libel, distribution regulations, employment questions, environmental problems, taxation, and antitrust problems.

We hope that the book will provide a broad context that will give a better understanding of the industry and its situation, whether they work in newspapers or study them. The newspaper industry is a vibrant and exciting industry that serves important social and economic functions and provides significant opportunities for employment and investment. We believe that this book will clarify many of the questions surrounding the industry and help reduce the misconceptions and misperceptions that many observers have about its current situation and its future.

We would like to acknowledge the contributions of the followng reviewers: Mary Alice Shaver, University of North Carolina/Chapel Hill; Stephen Trosley, Editor, Inland Valley Daily Bulletin; Sandra Haarsager, University of Idaho; and Conrad Fink, University of Georgia.

Finally, we would like to thank our families for their support and patience as we wrote this book. Forgive us our prolonged absences for research and the hours we spent at the keyboard.

1

The Nature and Scope of the Industry

The growth of broadcast and other electronic media and the increasing linkage of computers and telecommunications has for several decades led futurists to make prognostications about the imminent demise of the newspaper industry. Those technological changes, along with changes in the circulation and advertising markets, have led newspaper industry personalities, associations, and publications to emphasize the idea that the industry is in serious difficulty by accepting and using the language of crisis. Michael Crichton, a futurist and author of *Jurassic Park*, has fueled the fears of the future by calling newspapers "mediasaurs,"[1] and *Washington Post* media critic Howard Kurtz says the industry is now permeated with "the smell of death."[2]

Speeches made before industry conferences have emphasized the need "to alter our image problem," "to defend our turf," and "to fight back" with marketing strategies for advertising and circulation sales. Industry publications have been filled with news about newspapers suffering "sales slides" and "economic stress," of the industry "reeling," and of publishers "fearful of the future." Task forces, committees, and conferences have sought and promoted strategies to overcome and respond to "obstacles" and "challenges" in the industry. And numerous publications have offered advice to newspaper owners and managers on how to "survive" the current environment.[3]

Publishers and editors have used existing organizations and founded dozens more to serve as industry support groups to address the crises and needs of the modern newspaper industry. Newspaper managers could easily spend a week each month attending conferences aimed at improving circulation and advertising practices, marketing, and editorial content and newspaper design to make papers more desirable in the face of the perceived threats to their existence.

Newspaper industry associations and specialty reporting organizations have responded with programs and seminars aimed at saving the newspaper and making it more desirable to advertisers and audiences. Industry associations and organizations—whose purposes are to educate members, help members respond to contemporary problems, and represent member interests—have wrestled with perceived threats to their continued existence in national, state, and regional meetings.

Newspapers themselves have banded together to meet the challenges of the Information Age, with publishers establishing cooperative ventures to share technology and create networks of newspapers for the electronic era. The largest of these networks was created in 1995 when eight major newspaper companies announced they were establishing The New Century Network that would help smaller papers start on-line service, link them to other newspapers' services, and tie electronic newspaper editions together on the Internet. This highly significant move by competing newspaper groups is evidence of how fears for the future have led the industry to band together to ensure its fiscal health and a profitable future. [4] The eight organizing companies, Cox Newspapers, Gannett Co., Hearst Co., Knight-Ridder Inc., Times Mirror Co., Tribune Co., and Washington Post Co., together own 196 daily newspapers, about 13 percent of the nation's total.

Despite the nearly overwhelming impression that it is a declining industry whose future is in great doubt, the newspaper industry is today vibrant, lively, and fundamentally sound. Although the environment in which the industry operates is being altered, thus inducing change in newspaper operations and management, newspapers are still one of the most stable of all business enterprises. The newspaper remains the primary medium used by audiences and advertisers for in-depth news, features, and commercial information. Newspapers are well distributed throughout the nation to serve every economically viable town and city.

Although some newspaper managers and casual media observers project rapid decline for the industry, investors and serious researchers of the industry recognize the fundamental strengths and condition of the industry and do not accept or convey the same sense of fear. "Newspapers remain the cheapest way to get mass amounts of any kind of information," says John Morton, newspaper analyst for the Wall Street firm Lynch, Jones & Ryan. "And this will probably remain true well into the time when the so-called electronic information superhighway into the home becomes widely available." Papers should survive even if the traditional print form becomes no longer desirable or possible at a point in the distant future, he says, because "newspapers are already producing through digital electronic systems right up to the printing press. This makes newspaper information already compatible with whatever kind of electronic transmission system is developed to reach most consumers."[5]

Morton's views are echoed by others. Standard & Poors' investment report on the newspaper industry, for example, indicates that the high level of concern about the impact of on-line services is premature. "The threat from on-line services, as well as future services from cable television, which is expected to add digital interactive capabilities that will result in the availability of hundreds of channels, has had in our opinion a minimal impact on newspapers thus far," it said its 1995 report.[6]

Part of the reason that investors and newspaper industry researchers exhibit less anxiety about the industry is that they place it in a broader context. By comparison to other manufacturing industries, the newspaper industry is about the same size as the textile products, lumber and wood products, and petroleum and coal products industries in the U.S. It is larger than the tobacco, furniture and fixtures, and petroleum refining industries. Newspapers account for more than $45 billion in activity each year. More than 60 million newspaper copies are purchased every day, and 55 million copies of paid and free circulation weekly newspapers circulate each week.

Most people conceive of the newspaper industry as being comprised of relatively large-circulation daily newspapers that are experiencing declines in circulation, household penetration, and advertising. They describe an industry in which most owners are large public newspaper companies. They envision a product that consists of dozens of pages each day, a product that increasingly uses large photographs and color printing, and a product that is being overwhelmed by and finding it increasingly difficult to compete with television and new information delivery systems.

Such conceptions of the industry are erroneous, however, because they ignore the scope and breadth of the industry, fail to distinguish the great differences in purposes, size, frequency, and scope among newspapers, and accept trends affecting some highly visible papers and industry segments as exemplary of the industry as a whole. This book will explore the broader context and operations of the industry to show the far greater scope and health of the industry and why such general conceptions of the industry are in error.

NEWSPAPERS AS MANUFACTURING AND SERVICE COMPANIES

In simple manufacturing terms, newspaper firms create an editorial and advertising product, manufacture copies of that product, and then sell and distribute those copies to customers. The process involves the acquisition and creation of content (both advertising and editorial), selection and editing of content, design and layout of the newspaper, production preparation and printing, collation of various sections and inserts and bundling of groups of papers, and distribution of the papers. Circulation marketing and sales operate concurrently (Figure 1.1). The life cycle of that product is short—only twenty-four hours for a daily and seven days for a

FIGURE 1.1   Stages in the Creation and Production of a Newspaper

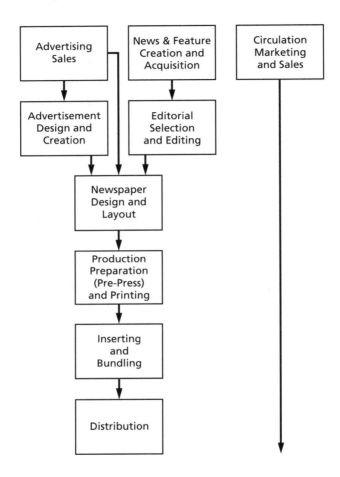

weekly—so companies are constantly engaged in the creation, manufacture, sales, and distribution processes.

That brief description belies the complexity of the operation, however, because the economics and operations of the newspaper industry differ significantly from other types of manufacturing due to the unique nature of the creation and production of newspapers, their marketing, their distribution, and their social functions. A major difference arises from the fact that newspaper firms are not merely manufacturers of a single product, but simultaneously produce a manufactured product and provide a service.

Newspapers operate in two markets at the same time. They create, manufacture, and sell the physical product—a newspaper copy—to readers while simultaneously selling a service—access to those readers—to advertisers. The two separate markets are interdependent and the performance in each affects the performance of the other. The success of a newspaper in attracting readers with news and information makes it more attractive to advertisers, and its success in attracting advertisers provides financial resources and advertising information that help attract readers.[7]

In the creation of the content for each issue, newspaper firms acquire a wide variety of information and features from scores of news and feature services and syndicates, as well as produce information and features on their own. These activities create a large pool of information and features from which newspapers select, edit, and rewrite editorial materials. Although some of the material from news and feature services is increasingly available to readers through other means, it is the reading and selection of materials from scores of sources, the creation of original materials, and the packaging of materials that is the value added by newspapers for which readers are willing to pay and can be used to provide competitive advantages over other information providers. Although there are some general similarities, each newspaper's emphasis and packaging of materials is somewhat different, giving it an institutional personality through the types of materials, tone, general appearance, and perspectives it conveys. Editors and publishers who play close attention to the interests and values of readers in their local markets can emphasize those elements in their news and information choices to help create the newspaper's personality and develop strong bonds between the reader and the paper.

Concurrent with the development of these editorial materials is the sale of advertising access to companies, organizations, and individuals. When sales are made, advertising materials are provided by the advertisers or its advertising agency, or newspaper personnel are used to design and create the material. This advertising material is critical because it provides the primary source of revenue for newspapers. U.S. daily newspapers are among the most dependent upon advertising for revenue among newspapers throughout the world (Figure 1.2). Advertising is also crucial because it provides the majority of the content for the newspapers (Figure 1.3).

After the editorial and advertising material is complete for an issue, the reproduction of that material takes place through preparation and printing. After printing, the copies are then distributed to subscribers and made available for single-copy purchase. Issues relating to methods of distribution and access to distribution systems are increasing as technology provides new opportunies for conveying information and advertising to readers.

There are great differences in the types, functions, and operations of newspapers within the industry. Understanding these differences and the nature and scope of the industry are crucial for understanding the variety of operational issues and

**FIGURE 1.2   Advertising Income as a Percentage of Newspaper
Revenue in Selected Nations**

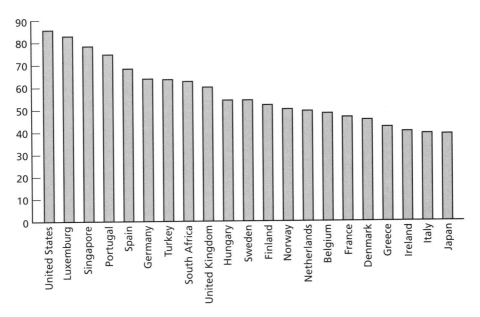

Source: International Federation of Newspaper Publishers, 1995

**FIGURE 1.3   Advertising as a Percentage of Content of
Daily Newspapers, 1950–1990**

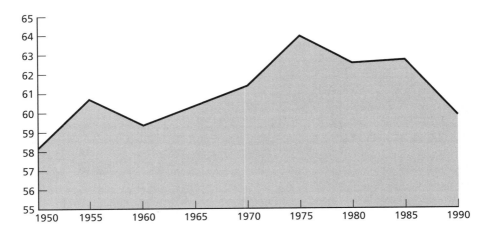

problems facing different branches of the industry as well as individual newspaper companies.

DEFINITION OF A NEWSPAPER

The definition of a newspaper has always been and will undoubtedly remain nebulous because there is no single industry-wide agreement on elements such as publication frequency, size dimensions of pages, the average number of pages and stories produced, and the format that makes a publication fall within the scope of the term. As a result, in the United States and in other nations, there are wide differences in frequency, size, and format of publications that call themselves newspapers.

Although the newspaper industry itself has never established a single agreed-on definition, a variety of government bodies and agencies, including the postal service, legislatures, courts, and city councils, have established criteria defining newspapers for a variety of purposes. A generally agreed-on definition for legal purposes describes a newspaper as "a publication, usually in sheet form, intended for general circulation, and published regularly at short intervals, containing intelligence of current events and news of general interest."[8]

The postal service definition must be met in order to receive the fiscal advantages of reduced postal rates offered under a second-class mail permit. The United States Postal Service defines a newspaper as a publication that is published at regularly stated intervals, in which editorial content averages at least 25 percent of the total content, and that more than 50 percent of the publication's circulation is paid.[9]

Legislatures have established definitions for regulation and tax purposes. And many government bodies and agencies have established definitions of "official" newspapers for the purpose of establishing the locations in which public acts, resolutions, and other legal and official notices should be published. The U.S. Congress, in writing the Newspaper Preservation Act in 1970, defined the newspaper as "a publication produced on newsprint which is published in one or more issues weekly. . . and in which a substantial portion of the content is devoted to the dissemination of news and editorial opinion."[10]

Numerous private efforts have been made to forge a clear definition of a newspaper, but all have failed to gain universal acceptance. Some definitions have included the ideas that a newspaper is linked to a specific geographic location (such as a city, county, or state) or that it is printed on newsprint, but these elements have tended to disappear from definitions in recent years as regional, national, and international newspapers have strongly developed and as many firms have begun using types of paper other than newsprint for some or all of their newspapers. Although newspapers have traditionally focused on a wide range of news and information intended for a general audience, the definition has been expanded in the past century to include some publications emphasizing special topics, especially publications that focus on business and finance.

If one reviews the various definitions, however, several elements are universal: the publication should contain news, it should be produced using a printing press, the publication should appear regularly, and it should be available to the general public. The newspapers under discussion in this book are based on those universal elements and encompass a wide variety of the newspapers available.

TYPES OF NEWSPAPERS

When considering the many differences in newspapers, nine general categories of papers are clear: (1) international and national daily papers; (2) metropolitan and/or regional daily papers; (3) local daily papers; (4) non-daily general audience papers; (5) minority papers; (6) papers published in secondary languages; (7) religious papers; (8) military papers; and (9) other specialty newspapers.

International and national papers are the types of papers that most often generate intense public discussion. These are papers intended for broad distribution and are not as clearly linked to a single location in terms of the news and advertising that they carry. Such newspapers maintain bureaus in many cities in the nation and throughout the world and usually publish several editions of the newspaper designed for distribution in different parts of the nation or the world. This category includes publications such as *USA Today*, *Wall Street Journal*, *New York Times*, and *Washington Post*. These papers emphasize reporting on national and international topics and are written in a way that accounts for the fact that readers may be unfamiliar with local personalities, locations, and issues when they cover events involving specific states or cities. Only about a half dozen such papers are found in the United States.

Large metropolitan and regional newspapers represent a second tier of daily newspapers that tend to be published in major cities and whose content is highly influenced by events in those cities and their surrounding metropolitan areas. In some cases, these papers serve readers well beyond the boundaries of the metropolitan area. The *Boston Globe*, for example, provides coverage of and is circulated throughout New England and the *Des Moines Register* dominates the entire state of Iowa. In recent years, however, many such metropolitan newspapers have reduced their circulation areas to cut unprofitable circulation and thus reduced the influence they once had over larger areas surrounding their place of publication. Major metropolitan and regional newspapers tend to maintain news bureaus in Washington, DC, and sometimes New York City, Chicago, and other major regional cities in the United States, as well as in the capital and other major cities of the state in which they are located. They often operate their own advertising sales offices in New York City and other major financial and advertising locales. Metropolitan/regional newspapers tend to be published seven days per week, with especially large circulation sales on Sundays. About fifty of the slightly more than 1,500 daily newspapers in the nation fall into this category.

Local daily newspapers are those tied to smaller metropolitan areas, specific cities and towns, whose primary purpose is to provide local news coverage and local advertising service. This group includes papers such as the *News-Journal* in Pensacola, Florida, and the Wichita (Kansas) *Eagle*. Local papers tend to publish only one edition daily and to maintain only a local reporting and sales staff, obtaining statewide, national, and international coverage from news services and using the services of nonstaff sales representatives or advertising networks that represent many papers throughout the nation to achieve some national advertising sales. This type of paper accounts for about 95 percent of the daily newspaper segment of the industry. Such papers normally publish at least five days per week and in larger cities are available six or seven days per week. Readers of newspapers in this group that are not published on Sunday tend to purchase the nearby metropolitan/regional newspaper on that day.

The nondaily general audience newspaper category covers the largest group of newspapers, those published less than five days per week. These traditionally include papers that appear once per week or several times each week. Such papers tend to serve counties, small communities, neighborhoods of a larger city, or as a complementary paper to a daily newspaper by providing coverage and advertising services that are not available from the daily. Nondaily papers include publications such as the *Forsyth County News* in Cumming, Georgia, and alternative newspapers such as the *Bay Guardian* in San Francisco. The circulation sizes of nondailies range from a few hundred copies to hundreds of thousands of copies, but their total circulation is rapidly approaching the same level as total daily newspaper circulation. The number of papers in the nondaily press is more than five times as large as the number in the daily newspaper categories.

Minority newspapers are intended to service the needs of specific English-speaking minority groups in the nation's population. Most minority newspapers are nondailies. The largest and most active minority newspaper category includes papers that identify themselves as serving the black community, such as the Chicago *Daily Defender* and the Birmingham, Alabama, *World*. Few other racial or ethnic minority groups maintain as active an English-language press as blacks, although a few newspapers exist to serve the needs of other minority ethnic groups, such as the national *Indian Country Today*, which serves Native Americans, and the *American-Arab Message*, which serves Americans of Arab descent. Gays and lesbians are served by an active nondaily press including such papers as the New York *Native* and the *Bay Area Reporter*.

An important and often ignored segment of the newspaper industry includes papers published in languages other than English. This segment includes both daily and nondaily newspapers published at the national, metropolitan/regional, and local levels. These secondary language papers provide news and advertising in languages ranging from German to Vietnamese, from Spanish to Korean, from Russian to

Chinese. Papers in this group include the local and regionally oriented *El Diario-La Prensa* in New York and the *Chinese Times* in San Francisco. Other papers, such as the German-language *Wochen-Post* and the Norwegian *Nordisk Tidende,* serve readers nationwide. These papers are designed to serve not only the information needs of immigrants but also those of citizens who have been born and live in communities in which English is a minority language. They also serve English speakers who wish to preserve the languages of their ancestors for cultural or other reasons.

Papers intended for minorities are not typically major players on the national scene but are important for the the service they provide to their communities. In metropolitan areas with large minority populations, these papers sometimes wield considerable influence on the political and social life of the community.

Religious organizations and individual members of a number of religions publish newspapers, usually nondailies, intended to provide coverage about activities and issues associated with the religions, as well as general news reported from the perspectives of those religions and their members. Among the largest and best-known segments of this portion of the newspaper industry are Jewish and Catholic newspapers, which are published and widely available throughout the United States. These papers include both national and local publications such as the *National Catholic Register* and the *Jewish Times* in Baltimore. This segment of the newspaper industry also includes papers such as the *Baptist Record* in Jackson, Mississippi, and the *Adventist Review* in Silver Spring, Maryland.

Another major category of newspapers, primarily nondailies, is comprised of papers associated with military bases. These papers are operated either by military personnel or private parties and cover base activities and provide news and advertising for surrounding communities. Such papers include the *Hawaii Navy News*, which serves U.S. Navy personnel from Pearl Harbor, the *Quantico Sentry,* which serves the U.S. Marine Corps base in Quantico, Virginia, and the *Fort Leavenworth Lamp*, which serves the U.S. Army facilities at Fort Leavenworth, Kansas. Although some papers have longer histories, most of these papers developed during and after World War II and were strongest during the Cold War when the number of military personnel was at its highest point.

Other specialty papers focus on topics including law, business, labor, sports, and fashion. This category includes both daily and nondaily publications. Well-known examples of this type of paper include *Investor's Business Daily*, *Women's Wear Daily*, *Chicago Daily Law Bulletin*, *Daily Variety*, and the *Daily Racing Form*.

NUMBER OF PAPERS

No single, accurate figure exists for the number of all types of newspapers in the United States, because federal and state governments do not require official registration of publications and because private organizations tracking newspapers normally include only those that fit into a few of the eight general categories of newspapers discussed above. Between 9,500 and 10,000 newspapers are published in the United States, and fewer than 15 percent are daily papers. Privately compiled, regular counts of daily and weekly newspapers have been maintained only for the past four decades, but they reveal that the segments of the industry that they track have undergone significant changes over time.

Daily Newspapers

Despite the perception that the number of newspapers has dropped dramatically in the past five decades, the total number of daily newspapers published in this country remained relatively stable from 1950 to 1980, declining by less than 2 percent (Figure 1.4). The distorted perception of newspaper mortality was fueled by the deaths of a large number of competing secondary papers in mid- and large-sized cities as populations moved to new suburban communities. But concurrent with the development of those communities came the establishment of new dailies to serve their needs, so the aggregate number of newspapers remained relatively stable. The 1980s, however, brought about a significant and rapid decline in the number of daily newspapers, with the number decreasing from 1,745 in 1980 to 1,611 in 1990, a drop of nearly 8 percent. Although that number is dramatic, the decline did not leave communities without newspapers, nor did it indicate a dramatic decrease in competition nationwide, because the majority of the closures came in second editions or "sister publications" of newspapers that did survive. The primary closures occurred in afternoon editions published by morning newspapers.

FIGURE 1.4   Number of Daily and Sunday Papers

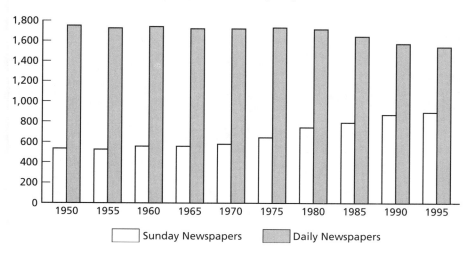

There are a variety of explanations for the declining interest in these second newspapers, including the extension of urban areas that began requiring readers to commute by auto rather than traditional public transportation systems that earlier spurred afternoon readership. In addition, many metropolitan afternoon papers had established a working-class orientation and personality, and did not adjust when the type of workers commuting to metropolitian cities began shifting to the professional and managerial classes.

Because many of the newspapers that died between 1950 and 1980 were afternoon newspapers, many observers of the newspaper industry came to believe that afternoon papers could not survive. This belief was underscored in the title of a popular book about newspaper closures called *Death in the Afternoon.*[11] The belief gained credibility despite the fact that about 80 percent of all newspapers were afternoon newspapers throughout most of the second half of the twentieth century (Figure 1.5). Although a significant number of large metropolitan afternoon newspapers were closed, it was not merely because they were afternoon papers but because they were secondary papers in their markets and unable to withstand the population shift to the suburbs and advertiser preferences for the newspaper with the largest circulation in a metropolitan area. In fact, as suburban papers were established, they were usually afternoon papers. It was not until the 1980s, when publishers of morning newspapers began a wave of closures of their afternoon editions and a significant number of publishers of afternoon papers converted to morning publication, that the number of afternoon papers declined significantly. Even today, however, about two-thirds of all newspapers are published as afternoon papers.

FIGURE 1.5 A.M. and P.M. Papers as Percentage of Dailies

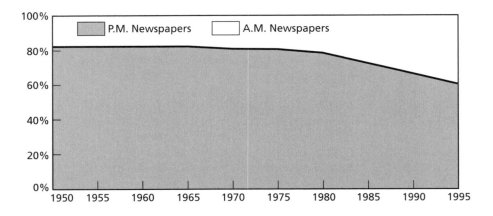

Sunday Newspapers

Only about half of the nation's newspapers publish on Sundays, but that number has increased by about 50 percent since 1960, growing from 563 papers to 863 in 1990 (Figure 1.4). Sunday papers typically have larger circulations than their daily counterparts because they are popular among readers who do not believe they have time to read during the week and because metropolitan Sunday papers are often used by readers of local papers that do not publish a Sunday edition of their own. The larger readership of Sunday papers and the greater amount of time spent with Sunday papers by readers results in greater advertising placement, so Sunday editions typically contain a far greater amount of advertising material than weekday papers.

Other Categories

The number of weekly and non-daily newspapers published has fluctuated greatly in the past three decades with a peak of more than 8,000 in the 1960s. Today the number stands at approximately 7,500 newspapers (Figure 1.6).

The number of papers in other categories is not regularly tracked but various directories list approximately 250 religious newspapers (of which 185 are Catholic), 150 military newspapers, 80 papers serving the black community, 50 foreign language papers, and over 24 gay and lesbian newspapers.

FIGURE 1.6   Number of Weekly Newspapers, 1960–1990

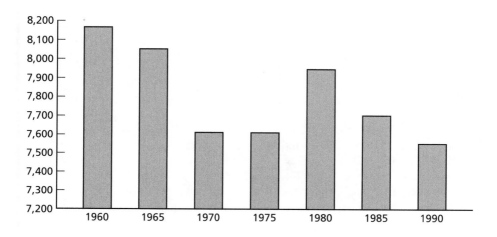

LOCATIONS OF DAILY NEWSPAPERS

The existence of newspapers is influenced by a variety of geographic and demographic factors, including distribution, size, and proximity to other newspapers.

Newspapers are well distributed throughout the nation, ranging from two in Delaware and the District of Columbia to 111 in California, but Delaware and the District of Columbia both have a statistically lower than average number of daily papers per state or district (Table 1.1). California, Illinois, Indiana, New York, Ohio, Pennsylvania, and Texas have statistically larger than average numbers of papers. Together these seven states with a larger than average number of newspapers contain almost 40 percent of all newspapers in the country. California alone accounts for about 7 percent of all daily papers, almost half of all the papers found in the western states. Clearly, the populations of these seven states create the potential for a larger number of readers, as will be discussed below.

The daily newspaper industry is concentrated in the central and eastern U.S. Considering the geographical distribution, one finds that about 40 percent of the papers are located in eastern states, nearly half are located in central states, and about 15 percent in western states.

The number of newspapers in a state is influenced both by its physical size and its population. If the number of papers is considered using a state size measure (total area in square miles), the number of square miles per paper ranges from thirty five in the District of Columbia and 202 in Rhode Island to 14,150 for Utah and 84,429 for Alaska. Only Alaska falls outside the statistical norm (Table 1.2). Because Alaska is the nation's largest state in terms of square miles and is the third smallest state in terms of population, only ahead of Wyoming and Vermont, its presence highly skews the statistical analysis. If Alaska is removed, seven other states have an unusually large number of square miles served by each newspaper: Idaho, Montana, Nevada, New Mexico, North Dakota, Utah, and Wyoming.

The differences shown here are important because they influence the number of competitors and potential competitors faced by the papers, the sizes of their coverage and circulation areas, and the sizes of the audiences they serve. The figures also quickly reveal some of the major differences faced by urban and rural publishers that significantly affect their operations and costs.

Nationwide, the average daily paper serves about 2,972 square miles, an area slightly larger than the state of Delaware and a little more than twice the size of Rhode Island.

If one considers the distribution of daily newspapers based on state populations, the range is from 1 paper for every 47,000 persons in Wyoming to 1 for every 345,000 persons in Delaware. The nationwide average is 1 paper per 163,000 persons in a state. This means that the average paper serves a population about the size of the cities of Orlando, Florida, Salt Lake City, Utah, or Syracuse, New York. A statistically lower than average population per newspaper is found in Arkansas,

TABLE 1.1   Number of Newspapers by State

	Number of Dailies	Location
Alabama	27	E
Alaska	6	O
Arizona	19	W
Arkansas	31	C
California	111^{+3}	W
Colorado	23	W
Connecticut	19	E
Delaware	2^{-1}	E
District of Columbia	2^{-1}	E
Florida	42	E
Georgia	34	E
Hawaii	6	O
Idaho	11	W
Illinois	69^{+1}	C
Indiana	72^{+1}	C
Iowa	37	C
Kansas	46	C
Kentucky	23	E
Louisiana	26	C
Maine	7	E
Maryland	15	E
Massachusetts	41	E
Michigan	52	C
Minnesota	25	C
Mississippi	22	E
Missouri	44	C
Montana	11	W
Nebraska	20	C
Nevada	8	W
New Hampshire	9	E
New Jersey	20	E
New Mexico	18	W
New York	68^{+1}	E
North Carolina	49	E
North Dakota	10	C
Ohio	84^{+2}	C
Oklahoma	46	C
Oregon	18	W
Pennsylvania	88^{+2}	E
Rhode Island	6	E
South Carolina	16	E
South Dakota	13	C
Tennessee	27	E
Texas	95^{+2}	C
Utah	6	W
Vermont	8	E
Virginia	30	E
Washington	24	W
West Virginia	23	E
Wisconsin	36	C
Wyoming	10	W
Total	1555	
Mean	30.5	
Median	23	
Mode	6	
Standard Deviation	25.6	

Based on 1992 data.

Superscript indicates number of standard deviations above or below average.

Location: E = eastern states, C = central states; W = western states; O = other.

TABLE 1.2   Average Number of Square Miles and Population per Daily Newspaper by State

	Sq. Miles	Adj. Sq. Miles*	Population
Alabama	1,915	1,915	153,000
Alaska	84,429+6	——	98,000
Arizona	5,700	5,700	202,000
Arkansas	1,662	1,662	77,000-1
California	1,368	1,368	278,000+1
Colorado	3,589	3,589	151,000
Connecticut	239	239	173,000
Delaware	1,023	1,023	345,000+2
District of Columbia	35	35	295,000+1
Florida	1,364	1,364	321,000+1
Georgia	1,636	1,636	199,000
Hawaii	1,079	1,079	193,000
Idaho	6,964	6,964+1	97,000
Illinois	817	817	169,000
Indiana	489	489	79,000-1
Iowa	1,521	1,521	76,000-1
Kansas	1,788	1,788	55,000-1
Kentucky	1,757	1,757	163,000
Louisiana	1,705	1,705	165,000
Maine	4,158	4,158	176,000
Maryland	697	697	327,000+2
Massachusetts	207	207	146,000
Michigan	1,126	1,126	181,000
Minnesota	3,376	3,376	179,000
Mississippi	2,168	2,168	119,000
Missouri	1,584	1,584	118,000
Montana	13,368	13,368+2	75,000-1
Nebraska	3,868	3,868	80,000
Nevada	13,820	13,820+3	166,000
New Hampshire	1,031	1,031	123,000
New Jersey	339	339	339,000+2
New Mexico	6,755	6,755+1	88,000
New York	692	692	266,000+1
North Carolina	994	994	140,000
North Dakota	7,070	7,070+1	64,000-1
Ohio	475	475	131,000
Oklahoma	1,428	1,428	70,000-1
Oregon	4,854	4,854	165,000
Pennsylvania	498	498	136,000
Rhode Island	202	202	168,000
South Carolina	1,830	1,830	225,000
South Dakota	6,426	6,426	55,000-1
Tennessee	1,505	1,505	186,000
Texas	2,723	2,723	186,000
Utah	14,150	14,150+3	302,000+1
Vermont	1,068	1,068	71,000-1
Virginia	1,199	1,199	213,000
Washington	2,621	2,621	214,000
West Virginia	2,373	2,373	79,000-1
Wisconsin	1,560	1,560	139,000
Wyoming	9,781	9,781+1	47,000-1
Mean	4,569	2,972	163,000
Median	1,636	1,610	163,000
Standard Deviation	11,916	3,482	83,000

Based on 1990 data.

*Removing Alaska from statistical calculation.

Superscript indicates number of standard deviations above or below average.

Indiana, Iowa, Kansas, Montana, North Dakota, Oklahoma, South Dakota, Vermont, West Virginia, and Wyoming (Table 1.2). A statistically higher than average population per newspaper is found in California, Delaware, District of Columbia, Florida, Maryland, New Jersey, New York, and Utah.

NEWSPAPER CIRCULATION

The circulation of weekday newspapers grew steadily until about 1970 when it reached a plateau. Today the figure is slightly less than 60 million copies sold daily (Figure 1.7). Between 1950 and 1990, daily circulation overall increased 15.8 percent, but during the period from 1970 to 1990 circulation increased by only 216,629, representing only 2.5 percent of the total growth from 1950 to 1990.

Consideration of the average (mean) circulation per newspaper, however, presents a more positive picture of the health of newspaper circulation. It rose 27.4 percent between 1950 and 1990 (Table 1.3), almost at twice the rate of total daily circulation, and it experienced 9 percent growth between 1970 and 1990 (Figure 1.8). Between 1990 and 1995 the figure declined, primerily due to publishers' decisions to reduce unprofitable circulation in outlying areas and to cease publishing afternoon editions of morning pepers, as well as closures of secondary papers in a few communities.

The growth in total circulation and average circulation has clearly been affected by the decline in the total number of daily newspapers, but it also indicates that surviving daily papers benefited from the decline in competition and that, despite

FIGURE 1.7   Daily and Sunday Circulation, 1950–1995

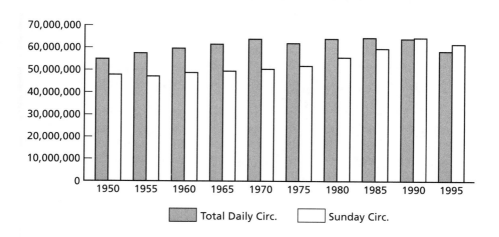

TABLE 1.3   Average (Mean) Circulation of Daily and Sunday Newspapers, 1950–1995

	Daily	Sunday
1950	30,378	84,849
1955	31,902	85,855
1960	33,339	84,722
1965	34,370	84,722
1970	35,531	93,987
1975	34,542	79,963
1980	35,646	74,383
1985	37,450	73,717
1990	38,687	72,578
1995	38,020	69,081

mistaken beliefs to the contrary, the average newspaper has tended to gain rather than lose circulation.

Although the average circulation per newspaper has risen, its circulation size (38,020 in 1995) indicates that most daily newspapers are relatively small. This is underscored when one categorizes daily newspapers by their circulation size. More than half of daily newspapers have circulations under 25,000, and more than two-thirds have circulations below 50,000. Only about a quarter have circulations between 50,000 and 500,000, and fewer than 5 percent of the nation's dailies exceed 500,000.

Population changes need to be taken into account when reviewing the growth of circulation over time. If one adjusts changes in daily newspaper circulation using a circulation per 1,000 population figure, a rapid decline in overall use of newspapers is readily apparent (Table 1.4). The figure dropped 34 percent, from 356 per 1,000 population to 234 per 1,000 population, between 1950 and 1995. This development is significant because it indicates that the penetration of newspapers—the degree to which they are reaching audiences—is declining.

TABLE 1.4   Daily Newspaper Circulation Per 1,000 Population 1950–1995

Year	Circ/Pop
1950	356
1960	328
1970	305
1980	275
1990	251
1995	234

FIGURE 1.8   Daily Circulation Per 1000 Population

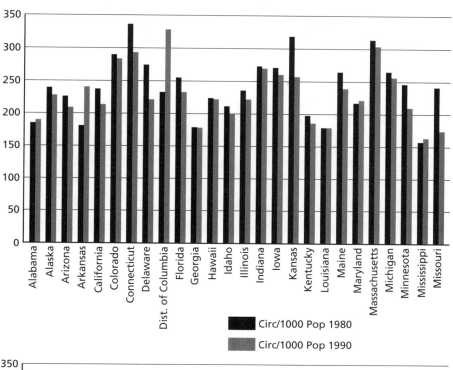

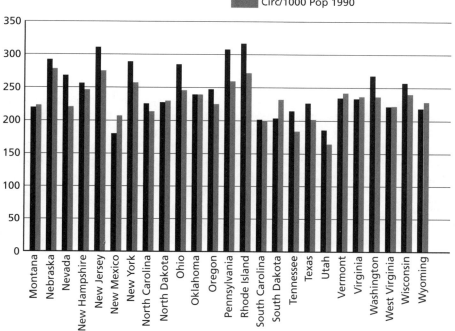

These aggregate trends are not indicative of the situation in all states and the District of Columbia, however. Between 1980 and 1990, for example, twenty-nine states showed increases in daily newspaper circulation within their borders, while twenty-two states had decreases. Daily circulation changes during the period ranged from a decline of 15.6 percent in Kansas to an increase of 37 percent in Arkansas (Table 1.5).

Important differences are also found in terms of daily circulation per 1,000 population. In 1990, for example, the figure ranged from a high of 333 in the District of Columbia (Connecticut had the state high of 295) to a low of 163 in Utah.

Between 1980 and 1990, a decline in circulation per 1,000 population occurred in thirty-five states, while fifteen experienced increases and one remained the same (Figure 1.8). The change ranged from a 40.5 percent increase in the District of Columbia (Arkansas had the highest percentage increase for any state at 34.6) to a 27.3 percent decrease in Missouri (Table 1.6).

The percentage of households in the states and the District of Columbia covered by daily newspaper circulation declined in forty-six of the fifty-one cases between 1980 and 1990. Like the circulation per 1,000 population figure reported above, household coverage also provides a measure of penetration. The four cases in which increases per household occurred include Arkansas, District of Columbia, South Dakota, and Wyoming (Figure 1.9). By 1990 the percentage of households covered by daily circulation ranged from a low of 46 percent in Mississippi and Missouri to a high of 81 percent in the District of Columbia and Massachusetts (Table 1.7). The average state had a household coverage of 62 percent in 1990 and experienced a decline of 7.8 percent between 1980 and 1990.

The decline in newspaper circulation per 1,000 population and in terms of household penetration needs to be considered in light of lost circulation from competing secondary newspapers and evening editions of morning papers that disappeared in recent decades, as well as the fact that many newspaper readers purchased both papers in such towns. The statistics of circulation per household and household coverage have never accounted for these issues, so these figures can only be expected to decline with the disappearance of those papers.

The circulation of Sunday newspapers has risen steadily, concurrently with the increase in the number of Sunday papers, and it is now at about the same level as weekday papers (Figure 1.7). From 1950 to 1995 Sunday circulation increased 32.6 percent (Table 1.3). Because that circulation was being spread among an increasing number of Sunday papers, however, the average circulation of Sunday papers declined by 18.6 percent in the same period (Figure 1.10). Nevertheless, the circulation of Sunday newspapers increased in forty-seven states and declined only in Delaware, Michigan, Missouri, and West Virginia between 1980 and 1990 (Table 1.5). Changes in that decade ranged from a decline in Sunday circulation of 3.6 percent in Missouri to an increase of 154 percent in Alaska.

TABLE 1.5   Change in Newspaper Circulation by State, 1980–1990

	Daily Circulation			Sunday Circulation		
	1980	1990	% Change	1980	1990	% Change
Alabama	722,217	772,184	-6.9	675,033	771,140	14.2
Alaska	97,202	126,022	29.6	55,086	140,014	154.2
Arizona	619,894	769,306	24.1	595,048	848,341	42.6
Arkansas	414,642	568,043	37.0	451,060	696,224	54.4
California	5,652,386	6,393,497	13.1	5,338,903	6,638,934	24.4
Colorado	84,7301	943,696	11.4	917,854	1,118,706	21.9
Connecticut	1053,233	973,490	-7.6	877,304	980,737	11.8
Delaware	164,709	147,352	-10.5	178,271	176,086	-1.2
District of Columbia	149,345	201,325	34.8	159,083	168,403	5.9
Florida	2,505,214	3028,873	20.9	2,636,463	3,759,720	42.6
Georgia	982,783	1,159,180	17.9	966,057	1,249,140	29.3
Hawaii	217,399	247,557	13.9	234,514	264,530	12.8
Idaho	201,036	201,642	0.3	191,159	227,311	18.9
Illinois	2,726,647	2,555,705	-6.3	2,811,028	2,849,835	1.4
Indiana	1,514,860	1,511,712	-0.2	1,253,829	1,373,435	9.5
Iowa	802,603	713,280	-11.1	718,245	724,304	0.8
Kansas	7,52,035	634,482	-15.6	624,098	650,588	4.2
Kentucky	724,427	688,757	-4.9	616,876	663,561	7.6
Louisiana	759,176	761,738	0.3	783,488	834,303	6.5
Maine	301,100	296,366	-1.6	137,035	297,198	116.9
Maryland	919,896	1,063,148	15.6	994,557	1,163,924	17.0
Massachusetts	1,790,394	1,819,587	1.6	1,468,398	1,635,504	11.4
Michigan	2,440,473	2,374,103	-2.7	2,394,885	2,333,785	-2.6
Minnesota	1,011,263	925,016	-8.5	972,837	1,139,924	17.2
Mississippi	39,,173	422,480	5.8	357,484	430,349	20.4
Missouri	119,,263	903,187	-24.6	1,111,418	1,071,354	-3.6
Montana	17,,815	178,268	2.6	174,490	181,904	4.2
Nebraska	460,035	439,000	-4.6	385,883	405,093	5.0
Nevada	216,582	264,901	22.3	214,501	297,104	38.5
New Hampshire	236,119	273,144	15.7	167,315	243,469	45.5
New Jersey	2,262,444	2,140,318	-5.4	2,453,331	2,558,066	4.3
New Mexico	235,122	313,051	33.1	229,723	297,689	29.6
New York	5,087,520	4,642,759	-8.7	4,680,462	4,852,155	3.7
North Carolina	1,320,265	1,413,435	7.1	1,101,748	1,391,657	26.3
North Dakota	148,947	146,648	-1.5	83,713	140,265	67.6
Ohio	3,099,114	2,673,270	-13.7	2,519,888	2,833,608	12.4
Oklahoma	729,266	756,625	3.8	756,184	895,124	18.4
Oregon	654,032	639,559	-2.2	571,545	645,854	13.0
Pennsylvania	3,681,491	3,106,415	-15.6	2,938,749	3,028,980	3.1
Rhode Island	302,836	275,912	-8.9	241,901	286,983	18.6
South Carolina	631,465	69,7941	10.5	541,589	752,895	39.0
South Dakota	140,962	162,194	15.1	128,074	130,372	1.8
Tennessee	979,373	899,877	-8.1	88,4228	984,212	11.3
Texas	3,255,750	3,426,136	5.2	3,578,158	4,333,092	21.1
Utah	273,948	283,936	3.6	272,744	325,718	19.4
Vermont	121,307	137,883	13.7	103,705	115,768	11.6
Virginia	1,273,210	1478,103	16.1	1,145,969	1,389,655	21.3
Washington	1,118,778	1155,879	3.3	107,3625	1,179,415	9.9
West Virginia	434,140	400,144	-7.8	367,471	36,2144	-1.4
Wisconsin	1,227,000	1,186,659	-3.3	1,054,287	1,185,478	12.4
Wyoming	103,427	104,591	1.1	85,469	91,469	7.0

TABLE 1.6   Daily Newspaper Circulation Per 1,000 Population by State

	1980	1990	% Change
Alabama	184	190	3.3
Alaska	236	227	-3.8
Arizona	221	206	-6.8
Arkansas	179	241	34.6
California	236	211	-10.6
Colorado	288	284	-1.4
Connecticut	272	295	8.5
Delaware	275	219	-20.4
Dist. of Columbia	237	333	40.5
Florida	250	229	-8.4
Georgia	177	176	-0.6
Hawaii	222	221	-0.5
Idaho	209	200	-4.3
Illinois	238	223	-6.3
Indiana	274	272	-0.7
Iowa	274	258	-5.8
Kansas	316	255	-19.3
Kentucky	196	187	-4.6
Louisiana	179	181	1.1
Maine	266	239	-10.2
Maryland	217	220	1.4
Massachusetts	312	301	-3.5
Michigan	263	255	-3.0
Minnesota	246	210	-14.6
Mississippi	157	164	4.5
Missouri	242	176	-27.3
Montana	218	224	2.8
Nebraska	291	278	-4.5
Nevada	263	213	-19.0
New Hampshire	252	242	-4.0
New Jersey	307	276	-10.1
New Mexico	177	204	15.3
New York	290	257	-11.4
North Carolina	223	211	-5.4
North Dakota	227	231	1.8
Ohio	287	246	-14.3
Oklahoma	238	241	1.3
Oregon	244	223	-8.6
Pennsylvania	310	261	-15.8
Rhode Island	318	274	-13.8
South Carolina	200	198	-1.0
South Dakota	203	233	14.8
Tennessee	211	183	-13.3
Texas	225	200	-11.1
Utah	183	163	-10.9
Vermont	234	243	3.8
Virginia	236	236	0.0
Washington	267	234	-12.4
West Virginia	221	225	1.8
Wisconsin	259	242	-6.6
Wyoming	213	233	9.4

**FIGURE 1.9   Household Penetration of Daily Circulation,
1980 and 1990 (Percentages)**

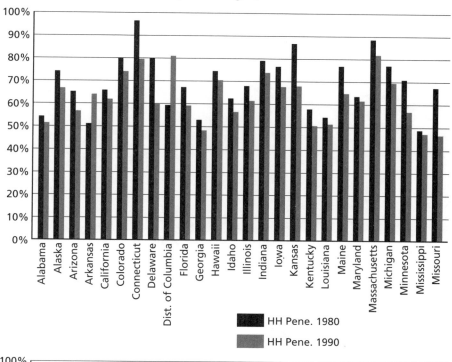

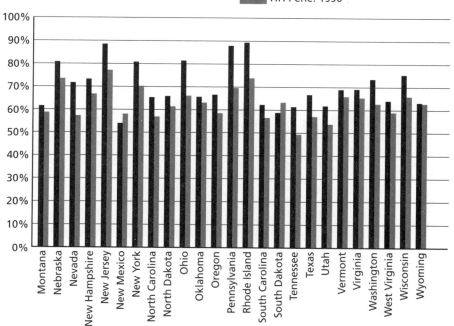

TABLE 1.7   Household Coverage of Daily Newspaper Circulation by State

	1980	1990	% Change
Alabama	53	51	-3.8
Alaska	71	66	-7.0
Arizona	62	55	-11.3
Arkansas	50	64	28.0
California	64	60	-6.3
Colorado	78	73	-6.4
Connecticut	95	79	-16.8
Delaware	78	59	-24.4
Dist. of Columbia	59	81	37.3
Florida	65	58	-10.8
Georgia	51	48	-5.9
Hawaii	72	69	-4.2
Idaho	60	56	-6.7
Illinois	67	61	-9.0
Indiana	78	73	-6.4
Iowa	75	67	-10.7
Kansas	85	67	-21.2
Kentucky	56	50	-10.7
Louisiana	53	51	-3.8
Maine	75	63	-16.0
Maryland	62	60	-3.2
Massachusetts	87	81	-6.9
Michigan	75	69	-8.0
Minnesota	69	56	-18.8
Mississippi	47	46	-2.1
Missouri	66	46	-30.3
Montana	60	58	-3.3
Nebraska	79	73	-7.6
Nevada	68	55	-19.1
New Hampshire	71	65	-8.5
New Jersey	88	76	-13.6
New Mexico	52	57	9.6
New York	80	70	-12.5
North Carolina	63	56	-11.1
North Dakota	64	61	-4.7
Ohio	80	65	-18.8
Oklahoma	64	63	-1.6
Oregon	64	58	-9.4
Pennsylvania	86	69	-19.8
Rhode Island	88	73	-17.0
South Carolina	60	55	-8.3
South Dakota	57	63	10.5
Tennessee	59	48	-18.6
Texas	64	56	-12.5
Utah	59	52	-11.9
Vermont	67	65	-3.0
Virginia	67	64	-4.5
Washington	71	61	-14.1
West Virginia	62	59	-4.8
Wisconsin	73	65	-11.0
Wyoming	60	62	3.3

FIGURE 1.10   Change in Average Newspaper Circulation, 1950–1995

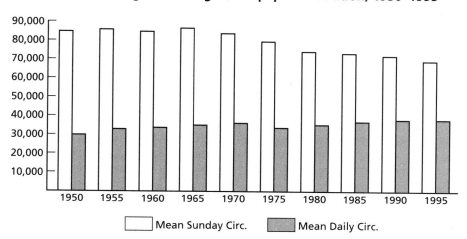

The circulation of weekly newspapers has also increased steadily during the past thirty years and there is no indication that the growth in those numbers has begun to diminish (Figure 1.11). Circulation for weekly papers rose from 20.9 million in 1960 to 55.2 million in 1990. The average (mean) circulation of weeklies rose from about 2,500 in 1960 to 7,300 in 1990.

FIGURE 1.11   Total Circulation of Weekly Newspapers, 1960–1990

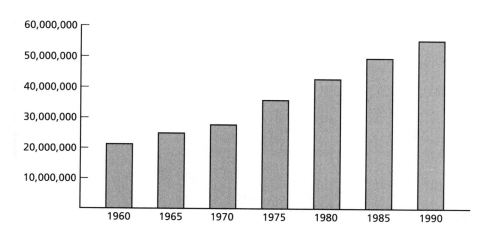

NEWSPAPER REVENUE

Newspapers can obtain revenue from the sales of both advertising and circulation (subscriptions and single-copy sales). Some nondaily general circulation newspapers, minority papers, and military papers are distributed at no charge to readers and are fully dependent on advertising sales for revenue, but the greatest bulk of papers charge for circulation and receive revenue from both sources.

Data on advertising and circulation revenue is incomplete for most segments of the newspaper industry because government statistics, industry associations, and advertising researchers typically do not report more than aggregate data or data mixed with nonnewspaper publications. Available data often exclude large segments of the newspaper industry. The most reliable and available statistics cover only daily newspapers and primarily involve advertising. These data reveal, however, that industry advertising revenues have risen strongly over time and that daily newspaper advertising continues to account for the bulk of total advertising expenditures.

Advertising sales by dailies rose from $2 billion in 1950 to more than $36 billion by 1995 (Figure 1.12). By 1994, daily newspapers had $34.2 billion in advertising sales. The dollar value of sales grew 78 percent during the 1950s, 55 percent during the 1960s, 159 percent in the 1970s, and 188 percent in the 1980s. The per-

FIGURE 1.12   Advertising Revenues for Daily Papers, 1950–1990 (Millions of Dollars)

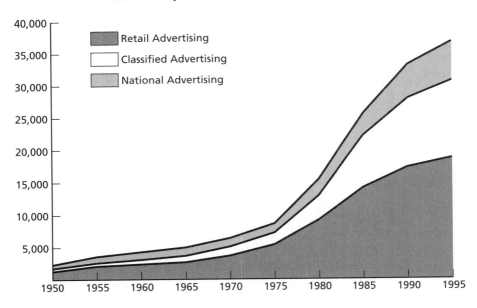

centage of total sales resulting from advertising sales is 85 percent, well above that of other industrialized countries with well-developed newspaper industries. In Japan, for example, the figure is 40 percent; in the United Kingdom, 63 percent; and in Germany, 65 percent.[12]

If one considers newspaper advertising expenditures in relation to population, one sees that per capita spending increased from $13.68 in 1950 to $136.63 in 1995 (Table 1.8). Accounting for inflation, newspapers today receive almost three times the amount of advertising per capita that they received in 1950.

Newspapers continue to gain the largest share of advertising expenditures of any medium, currently about 23 percent of total advertising expenditures. The share of advertising dollars used to purchase newspaper advertising declined from 29 percent to 22.4 percent between 1970 and 1995, a trend evident throughout most of the last half of the twentieth century as more choices became available to advertisers. Although some wish to blame the maturation of television and cable television advertising for the decline in advertising share, changes in the shares over time indicate that the shift to the electronic media was greatest in the 1970s and that much of the gain for television was at the expense of magazine advertising shares. In the 1980s the advertising share for television clearly stabilized at about 20 percent, but the newspaper advertising share continued to drop because advertisers shifted shares to direct mail (Figure 1.13), which has become the primary print competitor for traditional newspaper advertisers.

Despite shifts in advertising shares among media, newspaper advertising revenue has increased in the three different advertising submarkets in which it operates: classified, national, and retail. During the past four decades classified advertising revenue grew at an explosive rate, increasing nearly 3,000 percent, more than twice the growth rate of retail ad revenue and four times the rate of national advertising revenue (Table 1.9). Classified advertising was the third source of revenue in 1950 and had become second by 1960. It has provided an increasingly larger share of revenue. Classified advertising provided less than one-fifth of total revenue in 1950 but by 1995 it provided more than 36 percent of all income (Table 1.10). This increase was due, in large part, to the growing use of classifieds by automobile

TABLE 1.8   Per Capita Spending for Daily Newspaper Advertising

Year	Amount
1950	$13.68
1960	20.53
1970	28.07
1980	65.30
1990	129.79
1995	136.63

FIGURE 1.13   Shares of Advertising Expenditures by Medium (Percentages)

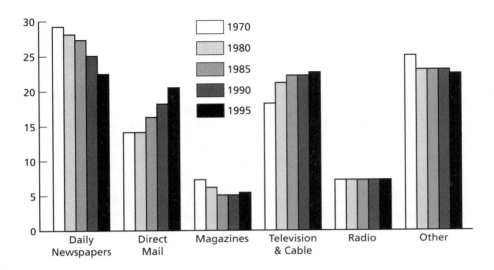

dealers and real estate agents. The increasing importance of classified advertising as a revenue source can also be seen in the fact that the percentage of advertising revenue contributed by national advertising was cut in half during that same period.

Statistics on circulation revenue are not as readily available in government and industry reports as are statistics on advertising, but in 1994 circulation sales provided approximately $9.5 billion in revenue, about 15 percent of the total revenue of daily newspapers in the U.S. Available data indicate that circulation revenue rose from $1.6 billion in 1960 to approximately $19.7 billion in 1995 (Figure 1.14). Circulation revenue per capita rose from $8.95 in 1960 to $24.14 in 1980, and to an estimated $37 in 1995 (Table 1.11).

TABLE 1.9   Rate of Increase in Revenue by Advertisement Category

Source	1950–1970	1970–1990	1950–1990
National	.72	3.63	6.96
Retail	1.80	4.06	13.17
Classified	3.04	6.57	29.52
Total Ad Revenue	1.76	4.66	14.59

**TABLE 1.10   Percentage of Daily Newspaper Advertising
Revenue by Category**

Category	1950	1960	1970	1980	1990
National	25.0	21.1	15.6	13.3	12.8
Retail	56.8	57.1	57.7	58.2	51.6
Classified	18.2	21.8	26.7	28.5	35.6

Taken as a whole, these revenue figures indicate that the average newspaper in 1994 had a mean annual turnover (income from advertising and circulation sales) of $28.4 million. The total annual turnover value of each copy of paid circulation was thus approximately $740.[13]

FIGURE 1.14   Circulation Revenue (in $ billions)

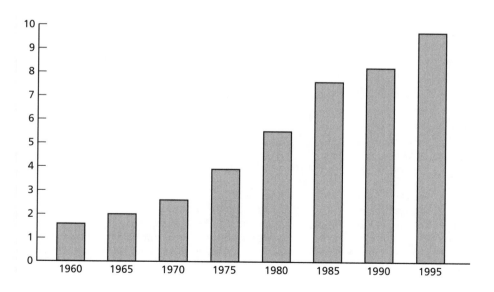

TABLE 1.11   Per Capita Spending for Daily Newspaper Circulation

Year	Amount
1960	8.95
1970	13.96
1980	24.14
1990	35.00
1995	37.43

SUMMARY

Despite concerns among some observers that the newspaper industry is troubled, this overview has shown that the industry is much broader and much healthier than is generally believed. It has also shown that the average daily newspaper is small, serving a market of about 163,000 persons within 2,972 square miles, and that the overwhelming majority of newspapers are nondaily papers, many designed to serve the needs of subgroups in the population.

The data show that the general perception of daily newspapers as being large and suffering from economic ills is highly distorted. The average daily newspaper has a daily circulation of only about 40,000, and its circulation has been growing slowly and steadily at about .50 percent per year. The average daily has no other local newspaper competition and has been experiencing growth in both advertising and circulation revenues.

ENDNOTES

1. "Silicon Valley Nerds Herald Newspapers of Tomorrow," *South China Morning Post*, 2 March 1994, Media Supplement.

2. Michael Moran, "Downcast News," *Evening Standard*, 23 November 1994, 62.

3. Two well-known book titles that have helped fuel the impression of a struggle to keep papers alive are Philip Meyer's *The Newspaper Survival Book: An Editor's Guide to Marketing* (Bloomington: Indiana University Press, 1985) and Jim Willis's *Surviving in the Newspaper Business: Newspaper Management in Turbulent Times* (New York: Praeger, 1988).

4. Kara Swisher, "Post Co., 7 Media Firms Enter On-Line Alliance," *Washington Post*, 20 April 1995, B10.

5. John Morton, "Worried Publishers Enter the Information Age," *San Francisco Examiner*, 24 April 1994, A15.

6. "Newspaper Industry Making Headlines With Comeback in 1994 and 1995," *Standard and Poor's Emerging & Special Situation*, No. 4, 17 April 1995, 3.

7. For economic discussions of these phenomena see Robert G. Picard, *Media Economics: Concepts and Issues* (Newbury Park, CA.: Sage Publications, 1989).

8. 4 Op. Attys. Gen. 10; *Black's Law Dictionary* (St. Paul, MN: West Publishing, 1968).

9. Public Law 233, 65 Stat. 672.

10. Public Law 91-353, 84 Stat. 466, 15 U.S.C. sections 1801–1804 (1970).

11. Peter Benjaminson, *Death in the Afternoon: America's Newspaper Giants Struggle for Survival* (Kansas City, MO: Andrews, McNeel and Parker, 1984).

12. International Federation of Newspaper Publishers, *World Press Trends* (Paris: International Federation of Newspaper Publishers, 1995).

13. Average (mean) annual turnover per newspaper is calculated by dividing total turnover (i.e., revenue) by the number of newspapers. Annual turnover value of each copy of paid circulation is calculated by dividing total turnover by total circulation.

2

The Roles of Newspapers as Products and Institutions

Newspapers are in the unusual position of acting as an economic entity and a social institution at the same time. As such, they must constantly balance the interests of the two roles. In their economic role, they produce and provide products and services and market these to consumers. In their institutional role, they are transmitters of information needed for the operation of society and they help create and convey the elements of culture.

The pressures, forces, and elements that comprise and affect both roles differ. A clear understanding of both is needed to comprehend the complexities of the industry and the functions of individual newspapers.

NEWSPAPERS AS PRODUCTS AND SERVICES

As indicated in Chapter 1, newspapers are unique because they operate in two markets simultaneously—the market for the physical newspaper product and the service market providing advertisers access to audiences.

Because the term *market* is often used imprecisely, it is important to understand how it specifically and precisely applies to the newspaper industry.

Markets are defined as groups of buyers and sellers wishing to engage in trade. The relationships between the two groups are based on the sellers' products or services and the geographical locations of sellers and buyers. Descriptions of markets in precise analyses include both the product and service element and the geographic element. A product market consists of sellers that provide the same product or service, or closely substitutable products and services, to the same group of consumers. The geographic market represents the boundaries in which sellers offer the same products or services to the same buyers.

Newspaper Goods/Services Market Elements

In economic terms the newspaper industry is unusual because it operates in dual product markets. That is, it produces one tangible product but participates in two separate product and service markets (Figure 2.1). A paper's performance in one market affects its performance in the other.

The tangible product is information that is packaged and delivered in the form of the printed newspaper. Information in this context includes news, features, and advertising. This product is marketed to newspaper consumers. If a newspaper produces more than one edition, its separate editions are considered as separate products. Performance in this goods/services market is measured by circulation statistics for two primary subproduct markets of subscribed and single-copy sales or revenue from that circulation. Daily (weekday and Saturday) newspapers and Sunday newspapers are also considered subproduct markets. Some daily papers consider their Wednesday or Thursday grocery and major retail advertising editions to be separate editions and charge different rates for inclusion in that edition. In the case of free-circulation papers, performance is measured by papers distributed.

FIGURE 2.1   Interplay of the Dual Product Markets of Newspapers

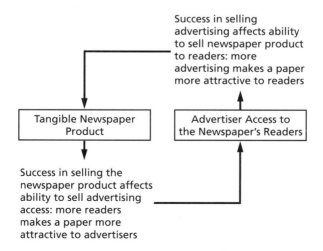

The second market in which newspapers participate is the advertising market. Although some observers may conclude that papers sell space to advertising purchasers, a more precise and descriptive explanation is that newspapers sell *readers* to advertisers. The amount charged for bringing readers into contact with advertisers' messages is more dependent upon the sizes and characteristics of audiences than the sizes of the advertisements themselves. Performance in this market is measured by sales of advertising lineage for national, display/retail, classified, legal, and insert/preprint subproduct markets or revenue from sales in those subproduct markets.

Newspaper Formats

There is no single industry standard for the format and size of a newspaper, but most fall within standard ranges that result from similarities in capabilities of pre-press, printing press, and post-press equipment made by different manufacturers.

Newspapers are primarily found in two formats: broadsheet and tabloid. Broadsheets are the traditionally formatted newspaper, usually 21 to 22-1/2 inches long and about 13-1/2 inches wide, whereas tabloids—such as the Chicago *Sun-Times* or New York *Post*—are a smaller format, usually 14 to 14-1/2 inches long by 11 inches wide. In the mid-1990s, a number of broadsheets began reducing the size of their pages as the result of purchasing smaller width webs—the rolls of newspapers used in printing—for cost-saving purposes. Tabloids were designed as reduced-size papers with easy readability that targeted mass audiences. As a result, there is a tendency for tabloids to emphasize popular topics and use sensational headlines and layouts, although these are not requirements of the smaller format.

Broadsheet papers normally consist of more than one section. Although these sections are often divided by subjects (for example, international and national news, state and local news, sports, lifestyle, and so on) the primary reasons for sections are that the printing capabilities of most presses in use have traditionally limited the number of pages that could be incorporated into a single section. Tabloids, which typically have a smaller number of pages, are configured slightly differently and normally are incorporated into a single section with loose pages or their pages saddle-stitched or glued at the fold.

The lack of an absolute industry standard creates significant differences in the number of columns found on a newspaper page. Some newspapers use a four-column format and others employ a nine-column format, while others employ the entire range in-between. The most common is a six-column format. Because the differences in column formats created order, production, and cost-calculation difficulties for advertisers using multiple newspapers, the newspaper industry created the standard advertising unit (SAU), which is acceptable in papers regardless of their column format. SAUs will be discussed further in Chapter 4.

Parts of the Newspaper

Different parts of the newspaper are created by establishing sections that are used to separate editorial content by subject matter. This is accomplished by using the separate groups of pages available through the printing process for different types of subjects. Because of the number of categories of subject matter traditionally grouped as sections, most newspapers include more than one subject area in the group of pages and highlight their differences by creating visually identifiable sections rather than completely separated groups of pages. Typical sections include international and national news, state news, local or metropolitan news, editorials/commentary and letters, sports, business and finance, and features/lifestyle sections. Papers also employ sections to serve the particular needs and interests of their readers. *La Opinión*, the primary Spanish-language daily of Southern California, publishes a "Latinoamérica" section that provides significant news coverage of Mexico, Central America, and South America for the large immigrant population from those areas.

Through sectionalization, readers are able to rapidly locate the material in which they are most interested. Editors try to maintain the general location of sections within papers from day to day and week to week so readers will be able to locate sections consistently and easily.

Although all newspapers differ somewhat in their appearance and the order of sections and materials, professional standards dictate that certain elements appear in newspapers. These elements have their own terminology. The first page carries the *nameplate* of the paper, sometimes called the *flag*, above the fold. It is traditionally, but increasingly less often for design reasons, found at the top of the first page. Inside the paper—usually on the editorial page—one finds the *masthead*, which generally includes the name and address of the newspaper, its publisher and main editors, and subscription information. Papers use *headlines* to summarize and attract reader interest to stories and are increasingly using *drop heads*—second layer headlines—and *subheads* within stories for visual and organizational purposes. The primary headline on page one is called the *banner*. Stories carry the *bylines* of their writers. Stories from news and feature services carry the byline of their writers, plus an indication of the service providing the material, and *datelines* indicate from where (and less often when) the story was transmitted. When stories are continued on other pages, *jumplines* indicate the page on which the story is continued.

Multiple Editions

Although smaller newspapers tend to publish only one newspaper each day, larger newspapers often publish multiple editions. These editions use the same name but are typically targeted to readers at a different time of day or in distinct geographical areas. Although there are some differences in content, these differences typically involve only a few pages or one section of the paper.

Many papers, for example, publish separate home delivery and news rack (single-copy) editions. Although the bulk of the paper is the same, the front page is traditionally altered to make the primary headline more visible and to tout or move headlines for stories that appear below the mid-page fold that are not visible without removing the paper from a news rack. These editions may also differ in the currency of the information contained in the major stories and the types of advertising and insert materials they carry. Papers with different home delivery and single-copy editions typically print the home-subscribed papers first (because of the extra time required in the home delivery process) and then the presses are stopped to replace the home delivery front-page plates with the news rack front-page plates.

Some papers publish throughout the day, using the first edition for home delivery and initial news rack sales but then updating the front page and other pages in the first section once or twice during the day to reflect news that has become available since the first edition was sent from the newsroom to the production department. Thus, a paper may have a midmorning and/or afternoon edition that is slightly different from the primary edition. *All-day papers* were typically larger metropolitan-based publications and are becoming less common for economic reasons. Some papers that do not regularly publish all-day editions occasionally adopt the practice in times of local, national, or international crises when breaking news is of particular interest to readers.

Metropolitan newspapers and smaller newspapers that serve large geographic areas or several communities often publish separate or zoned editions to serve readers in different areas. A newspaper, for example, may have a local and statewide edition, with the primary differences being more local news in the local edition and more news of other communities in the statewide edition. This difference is usually accomplished by dropping or diminishing the local news section and replacing it with the state edition material. In other cases the changes may occur only on the front page of the edition. A similar process is followed by papers that serve different communities with separate *zoned editions*. The *El Paso Times*, for example, publishes a "West Side" edition that includes a special section of enhanced coverage of events and news in the downtown, western, and upper valley portions of El Paso, Texas. Where larger groups of readers are involved, these separate editions usually appear daily, but zoned editions with separate editorial matter also appear less frequently—often weekly or two or three times a week—to serve readers in smaller communities where less news occurs each week. When it is economically feasible, and the decision usually involves demand for advertising in zoned editions, some larger metropolitan newspapers alter more than merely the local section for high-circulation zoned editions and may alter some of the content of entertainment, sports, lifestyle, and business sections as well as news sections.

Total Market Coverage/Non-Duplicating Coverage Products

For the past two decades, *free circulation* papers have been one of the most rapidly growing segments of the publishing industry. The development of such papers has introduced competition in some categories of advertising that were formerly dominated by daily and weekly paid newspapers. Because of the growth of independent free circulation papers, especially advertising sheets, many daily and weekly newspapers began publishing such papers, which are distributed through home delivery and free distribution racks.

Shoppers—papers designed primarily to convey advertising, but which may carry some news and feature material—and high-penetration free nondaily papers are attractive to many advertisers because they normally offer better market coverage than daily or nondaily paid newspapers. The higher penetration levels are useful to advertisers, especially in markets in which daily newspaper readership is low and penetrates less than 40 to 50 percent of households.

Nondaily free circulation publications have several names. Some are called shoppers or advertising sheets to distinguish them from publications that carry news. The term *total market coverage* (TMC) paper is used to indicate publications that reach nearly all households in a market. These publications are especially popular among discount chain stores and other retailers that use preprint inserts. Daily and weekly newspapers have aggressively entered this market to gain additional revenue from a subsidiary operation and to slow or halt the development of nondaily free newspapers and shoppers in their markets.

Some newspapers have chosen to use *nonduplicating coverage* (NDC) publications as a means of accomplishing the same goals but at a lower cost. In these cases, the publication is distributed only to those who do not subscribe to the daily newspaper, thus providing them preprint and other advertising that is provided in the daily newspaper and giving those advertisers who wish more coverage the overall market penetration they desire.

Newspaper Geographic Market Elements

Several recognized standards are used to designate the geographic market area for the dual product markets of newspapers: *Metropolitan Statistical Area,* ABC (*Audit Bureau of Circulation*) Retail Trading Zone, County, ABC (Audit Bureau of Circulation) City Zone, *Newspaper Designated Market Area.* It is possible to operate in a nationwide market, but only a few papers do so.

The applicable geographic market descriptors are specific to individual newspapers and can differ for circulation and advertising even for a single newspaper. Subproduct markets of circulation and advertising may involve several or different geographic market areas.

Metropolitan Statistical Area (MSA)

MSAs are officially designated economic and social regions in which a nucleus city(ies) and adjacent communities have achieved a significant degree of economic and social integration. MSAs are created by the U.S. Office of Management and Budget. To be designated a MSA, a region must have at least one city of 50,000 population and a total population exceeding 100,000 in one or more counties. Other criteria include elements of population density, distances traveled to work, economic activity, and other characteristics of metropolitan character. As of 1994, there were 262 MSAs designated in the United States.

When a newspaper operates within a MSA, the MSA may be considered a relevant geographic designation.

ABC Retail Trading Zone

The ABC Retail Trading Zone (RTZ) is a designation given the area surrounding a community from which business customers are drawn to the city. It represents the commercial extension of the central business zone. This is the area within which the primary trading for retail and classified advertising lineage and circulation is typically conducted by a newspaper. The RTZ often consists of one or more counties.

The designation of an ABC Retail Trading Zone is made jointly by newspapers and the Audit Bureau of Circulation (ABC), with the definitions approved and coordinated by the ABC. For most market situations, the RTZ is recognized as the relevant geographic market.

County

County geographic designations are weak tools for market analysis because they are politically rather than economically determined. Nevertheless, they are sometimes used to define newspaper markets if the markets are not recognized as MSAs and are used for certain types of analysis that do not require greater economic accuracy. This market definition is important in terms of some legal advertising—an important source of income for many smaller papers—that is required to be published within specific county markets.

ABC City Zone

ABC City Zone designates the geographic area that includes the central portion of a city and its contiguous suburbs. It is a standard geographic region recognized in the newspaper and advertising industries for circulation study purposes. ABC City Zone is always a relevant market measure for newspapers.

The designation of an ABC City Zone is made jointly by newspapers and the Audit Bureau of Circulation (ABC), with the definitions approved and coordinated by the ABC.

Newspaper Designated Market Area

A newspaper designated market area is a geographic market area specifically designated by a newspaper that does not correspond to predetermined, standardized measures such as MSA, RTZ, city zone, or county zone. The area is the primary commercial and residential region in which the newspaper operates. The designation is most often used by larger daily newspapers operating in very large metropolitan areas or papers with unusual geographic distribution of their newspapers. A similar designation is sometimes made by weekly newspapers whose distribution areas do not correspond with traditional descriptions.

DEMAND AND SUBSTITUTABILITY OF THE NEWSPAPER PRODUCT AND SERVICE

The demand for the products and services in the information and advertising product markets of newspapers differs, and the availability of substitutable products and services affects that demand in some situations.

Despite publishers' worries to the contrary, media consumers' demand for newspapers is relatively inelastic—that is, consumers do not respond to reasonable changes in price by significantly changing their newspaper purchasing patterns. And, the number of papers purchased remains relatively stable over time. This general rule applies to more than 99 percent of all geographic newspaper markets, where only one daily paper is produced locally. In metropolitan areas, where more than one daily may be competing for the same audience with substantially similar products, more elasticity is found.

Demand for advertising purchases varies greatly, however. Days of the week, seasons, general business climates, and changes in the demographics of readers affect demand, even when price is not a factor. Demand for space by retail advertisers is relatively inelastic with regard to price, however, except in large markets where competing media are most prevalent. The same is generally true for national advertising. Most daily newspapers, then, do not induce significant changes in advertising consumers' purchasing decisions by raising or lowering their prices reasonably, because most papers are located in relatively small and moderately-sized markets and do not experience much intermedia or intramedia competition.

In larger markets, demand for space is somewhat more elastic, especially that of national advertisers. Demand is especially sensitive to price changes when there is another competing daily available and its audience demographics are similar and the disparity in circulation between the two papers is not great.

In the newspaper market, a directly substitutable product for a local daily newspaper exists only when another daily newspaper *produced and distributed primarily in the same geographic market* is present. Newspapers are inherently local products, identified with a specific geographical market by the information they provide about that locality.

Daily newspapers from outside the locality provide some substitutability if they are available within the geographic market, but that substitutability is limited. In such cases the interchangeability involves information originating outside the local area, such as state, national, and international news, features, and national advertising. Because of a relatively small number of sources for such information, papers from separate geographical markets are substantially similar in these regards. Papers from separate geographical markets differ substantially in terms of the provision of local information, however.

Local daily newspapers can be replaced in a limited way by weekly or other nondaily papers that also provide local, but not national and international, information. In cases where a local daily exists, however, it is rare for consumers to substitute the nondaily as an information source. Instead, it is usually used for supplementary information.

More substitutability is evident in the market for advertising than in the information product market, but the substitutability is highly limited. All media and communication services that offer access to audiences for advertising messages compete in the broadest sense for a share of the 2 to 3 percent of gross national product devoted to advertising. The different media provide different access to audiences; however, that limits their ability to be interchangeable and directly compete with each other.

Newspapers have a number of competitive advantages regarding advertising compared to other media. These advantages limit the interchangeability of newspaper advertising with other types.

- Newspapers provide advertisers great ability to target specific geographic markets because they are able to concentrate their activities in designated areas to a greater degree than broadcasters and other media.
- The amount of information and detail possible in newspaper ads far surpasses other media. A fleeting thirty-second television advertisement must contain very little information, but a printed newspaper advertisement can contain a great deal of information because interested readers are able to use it at their own pace. This factor is particularly important to advertisers that wish to include information on a variety of items offered for sale or need to include a great deal of specific information about the qualities of products or the terms for their acquisition.
- The speed and flexibility of newspaper advertising makes it different from other media. Magazines often require two to three months lead time in the placement of advertising, and television requires a minimum of several days for the production and post-production of advertising. Newspapers can produce advertising within one or two days, which gives them advantages in selling advertising in rapidly changing retail and service markets.
- Newspapers are able to coordinate advertising of manufacturers and retailers through co-op advertising, a type of advertising in which the manufac-

turers and retailer split the cost of advertising. A major appliance retailer such as Maytag, for example, may pay half of the cost of an advertisement for a local appliance store if the ad contains only Maytag appliances. By using co-op advertising strategies, a small retailer can increase their advertising presence without necessarily increasing their own ad budget.

- Newspapers provide greater penetration per ad because of the patterns of use of media by audiences. Although one ad in a newspaper will typically gain 40 to 60 percent household penetration in a market, one ad on television will typically gain only 10 to 20 percent penetration, and one advertisement on a cable network will typically gain 2 to 5 percent penetration.
- Cost factors also give newspapers advantages. For example, a half-page advertisement will cost about $1,000 at an average-sized midwestern newspaper, whereas one thirty-second ad will cost about $500 on television and $50 on radio. In addition, many television and radio ads require financial investments in production of the ads that are not required when newspapers are used. Although some newspapers are charging fees for photography and creative services, these charges typically remain far below the costs of electronic media production.

The following specific examples illustrate why all advertising outlets cannot be considered directly competitive.

- An individual whose dog has puppies and who wishes to sell the puppies will not buy an advertisement in the phone book.
- A fast-food restaurant wanting to distribute coupons to attract customers will not buy an ad on cable television.
- A county soliciting bids for road construction will not use radio advertising for the solicitation.
- A shoe repair shop whose customers are drawn from a five-square-mile area will not advertise on television stations that serve a 100-square-mile market.
- An auto dealer who wishes to showcase ten different models and to describe their options and prices will not use a billboard.
- A furniture store with a sale on five models of sofas and the different fabrics available will not advertise the sofas and fabrics in an ad on the side of a bus.
- A grocery store that wishes to advertise one hundred specially priced items each Thursday will not place the ad in a monthly magazine.

This is not to indicate that there is no competition in the advertising market between newspapers and other media. Newspapers face their strongest competition in the advertising market from media that can provide higher market penetration, such as total market coverage papers and postal delivery of advertising. Direct mail is increasingly useful for some advertisers because the Postal Service rate structure and delivery zones are favorable to direct mail materials and can be targeted to specific Zip Codes and delivery zones of as few as 200 households. Studies of shifts in advertising shares accounted for by various media have shown that, in the past twenty-five years, direct mail has drawn ad share from newspapers and television and cable have drawn ad share from magazines. This indicates that direct advertising competition does not exist among all media but is limited to those who provide similar uses to advertisers.

Another indication that competition is limited is that some media firms own combinations of newspapers, television stations, cable systems, radio stations, and weekly newspapers in the same geographic markets. No reasonable firm would do so if they directly competed for advertising because the only result of competing with itself would be increases in the firm's costs and a reduction of its own profits.

Media firms are willing to own different media in the same markets because they provide complementary rather than competing access to audiences for advertisers. This type of complementary access leads advertisers to seek an effective "ad mix," that is, the placement of different styles, types, and amounts of advertising in different media. Thus, K-Mart does not choose to advertise only in newspapers but also adopts advertising budgets that place ads on television and radio, and in other media as well.

The dependency of media on different sources of advertising is also an important factor that reduces competition. Television stations typically receive only 30 percent of their advertising revenue from local sources, and cable systems typically receive only 20 percent of their income from the location in which they operate, thus having a greater dependency on national and regional advertisers. Newspapers and radio have nearly the opposite situation. Newspapers get about 85 percent from local sources and radio about 75 percent from the area surrounding the locale in which they operate.

Differences that keep media from directly competing for advertising are well recognized in the newspaper industry and among those who study the newspaper industry and competition among media. The differences between media and how these give strengths to each that keep them from being substitutable are widely recognized by both scholars and practitioners. "Because each medium has comparative advantages in some types of advertising, businesses tend to do two things. First, they target certain types of media for certain types of advertising. Second, they tend to use several media for an advertising campaign."[1] As a result, the "enlightened newspaper management team is well aware that advertising media tend to complement rather than compete with each other."[2]

The pricing of newspaper advertising is also indicative of the lack of direct competition with other media. Most newspapers set their prices using industry average or target-return price policies. The industry average policy is one in which the average of what other papers are charging is used. Target-return policy uses a level of return (normally return on sales) as the determinant of pricing and sets the price based on estimates of revenues needed to cover costs and achieve the targeted return. In addition, in situations in which a competing local daily newspaper disappears, or competition between two newspapers is ended with a joint operating agreement, advertising prices immediately rise 15 to 30 percent. This could not occur if other media were in direct competition for advertising.

COMPETITION BETWEEN NEWSPAPERS

As shown above, newspapers are in relatively enviable positions when it comes to marketing themselves. Unlike the automobile industry, in which a particular model of car may face one hundred other competitors in its size and price range, or the soap market, in which a particular brand may face hundreds of competitors, newspapers face relatively few direct competitors. Even when other papers do exist, as in major metropolitan areas such as New York, Chicago, and Los Angeles, true competition does not exist in the economic sense because two or three daily competitors do not create a perfectly competitive market. This is not to say that the papers do not vigorously compete for circulation and advertising, only that the number of direct competitors is limited and that the market shares controlled by each paper are envied by marketers of other products.

Although the number of directly competing daily newspapers is limited, the growing number of dailies outside the core of metropolitan cities and the rise of weekly newspapers has contributed to what has been called "umbrella competition" by James Rosse, who is now president of Freedom Newspapers.[3] In metropolitan markets, particularly, it is recognized that different layers of competition exist and that competitive pressures are different between them. According to Rosse, newspapers exist in four layers, each acting as an umbrella covering the cities in the layers below (Figure 2.2). The first layer consists of large metro dailies that cover an entire region or state. The second consists of dailies located in satellite cities surrounding the metropolitan center but whose coverage is typically focused on local rather than metro news. A third layer is comprised of suburban dailies with very narrowly focused coverage and, under that, a fourth layer of weeklies and shoppers compete.

Under umbrella competition, newspapers compete within their layers and between layers for circulation, advertising, and content. In the two decades since the model was introduced it has been observed that the directions and amount of competition between and within layers differs, depending on the size of markets involved and the number of competitors present at each level. It has been generally observed, however, that competition tends to be heavier between layers for readers than for advertising because lower-level papers tend to carve out niches that attract local and smaller advertisers that would not normally use the metropolitan level paper or papers.

When competition exists in any industry, producers engage in market strategies designed to make their product different and more desirable to a portion of con-

FIGURE 2.2   Umbrella Competition Model

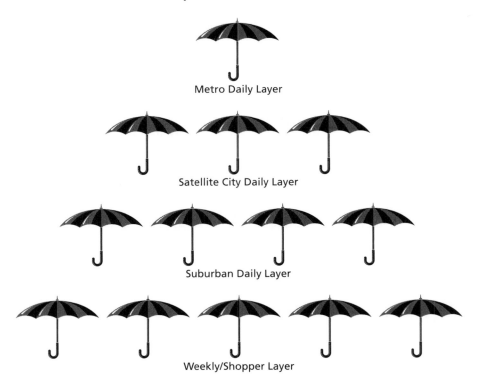

Metro Daily Layer

Satellite City Daily Layer

Suburban Daily Layer

Weekly/Shopper Layer

sumers. In the newspaper industry, two primary market strategies are used: product differentiation and audience differentiation. Because professional norms and reader expectations about newspapers are strong, the number and types of differentiation strategies are limited but newspaper managers can still make a variety of market decisions about their product. Because of the dual product nature of newspapers, these strategies involve choices about the product as well as choices about the audience (Figure 2.3).

Product differentiation in newspapers involves choices about distribution or publication time, the news–editorial orientation of the paper, and production techniques. Thus, one paper may choose a product strategy of being a morning publication with strong national and state coverage, providing general news in a tradition-

FIGURE 2.3   Market Strategies for Newspapers

Product Differentiation	Audience Differentiation

DISTRIBUTION TIME
–a.m., p.m., all-day
EDITORIAL ORIENTATION
–coverage emphasis
  *international
  *national
  *state/regional
  *local
–news focus
  *general
  *political
  *business/finance
–presentation tone
  *neutral
  *sensational
–readability level
–graphics/photo use
PRODUCTION CHOICES
–size
  *broadcast
  *tabloid
  *special size
–inks
  *single color
  *multicolor
–paper
  *newsprint
  *colored newsprint
  *glossy
	TARGET READERS
	–mass
	–specialized
	  social/economic class
	  *education
	  *employment
	  *other demographics
	PLACE OF USE
	–home
	–office
	–commuting
	SALES METHOD
	–subscription
	–single use copy
	–both

←——————→
Product differentiation influences
audience differentiation and vice versa

al, neutral fashion, written at the college level, making only nominal use of graphic devices and photos, and having a broadsheet format using only black ink on traditional newsprint. A second paper may choose evening publication, with local emphasis, a sensational tone, written at the ninth-grade level, make heavy use of photos and graphic devices, and publish in a tabloid format with multiple colors and tinted newsprint to give extra color to the paper. These differentiation choices will produce very different kinds of newspaper products.

Managers can make audience differentiation choices as well, to attract different types of readers. The first choice involves identifying the type of reader to be targeted. Some may choose to reach a mass audience or some may choose to emphasize segments based on demographic criteria, although this is seen more often in specialized newspapers rather than general circulation newspapers. Others may attempt to differentiate their readers by making choices about where the primary place of use will be. These choices then affect the distribution and marketing efforts of the paper. Finally, papers can differentiate the audience by their sales methods. A paper that relies on single-copy sales will generate a different type of audience than one that provides its product by both subscription and single-copy sales.

By using such market strategies, managers in competitive situations can create differences in their products that result in different consumer or reader demographics and thus create different types of readers to whom access can be provided to different advertisers. Because of the dual product nature of the newspaper industry, product and audience market strategies occur simultaneously. Choices made in product differentiation influence choices made in audience differentiation and choices made in audience differentiation will lead to specific choices in product differentiation.

NEWSPAPERS AS EMPLOYERS

As of the mid-1990s, newspapers employed more than 500,000 individuals in the United States. Although newspapers were a white male-dominated industry in the past, the employment patterns of the industry have changed significantly.

Women have made great strides in employment in the newspaper industry during the last four decades (see Figure 2.4), partly because of the decline in employment in the traditionally male-dominated areas of production and printing, and partly because of the increased employment of women in advertising, business, circulation, and news editorial departments. Women made up 43 percent of the total newspaper work force in 1994 and 39 percent of news editorial employees as of 1989. According to a 1992 study by the National Federation of Press Women, about 18 percent of executive editors and 9 percent of publishers were female.[4]

The industry has been slow, however, to mirror those gains in the top management of newspaper companies. A 1995 study found that women are not well represented at the top of publicly traded newspaper companies and that their placement in corporate and executive management positions diminishes as the significance of the position increases. The study found that only 12.4 percent of board members were women and 5.3 percent of the board chairs were female. No chief executive officers or corporate presidents of the public firms were women, although 4 percent of the subsidiaries of the these companies had women as presidents. The study found that 5 percent of the executive and senior vice-presidential positions were

FIGURE 2.4   Newspaper Employment by Gender (in thousands)

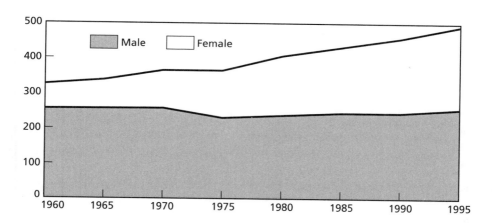

filled by women and that 17.4 percent of the vice-presidential positions were filled by women.[5]

Superficially, these data would seem to indicate that an increasing percentage of senior/executive vice presidents and vice presidents are now women and that their advancement to the highest levels may be possible. A closer look at these levels, however, reveals that the majority of women with these titles are not in positions that typically advance to positions as divisional chairs or presidents, corporate presidents, or CEOs.

Employment of minorities continues to be a concern as the industry works to reflect the diversity of American society, but its sucess at attracting and keeping minorities has been limited. Nevertheless, minorities represent 11 percent of the newsroom employees in 1994, according to a study by the American Society of Newspaper Editors and represent only 8 percent of supervisory personnel in newsrooms. The study found, however, that 21 percent of new hires are minorities. In the population as a whole, minorities account for about one in every five persons.

Newspapers in areas with high minority populations are more likely to emphasize minority hiring, the study found. For example, 62 percent of the *El Paso Times* newsroom employees are minorities, 44 percent of the Honolulu *Advertiser*, 40 percent of the *Miami Herald*, and 37 percent of the *Oakland Tribune*.

The wages and salaries of newspaper employees vary widely, depending on the type of job, the size of paper, and its location. A journalist for a small weekly in Kansas, for example, may receive only $200 a week, whereas a journalist for a New York daily may receive $1,200 a week.

The majority of individuals employed in U.S. newspapers are not unionized, but newspaper unions continue to play important roles in some parts of the country and in some job classifications. The Newspaper Guild, which originally represented only journalists, now represents employees in a number of newspaper departments. The guild represents about 30,000 workers nationwide and recently began a merger with the Communications Workers of America, which also represents newspaper employees. Other important unions representing newspaper employees include the International Brotherhood of Teamsters (which primarily represents truck drivers, helpers, and mechanics in the industry), and the Graphic Communications International Union (which represents about 100,000 press operators).

NEWSPAPERS AS FINANCIAL ENTITIES

Newspapers are regarded as excellent investments because of their financial stability, the general lack of competition from other newspapers, the strong cash flows they produce, and their relatively stable and forecastable revenues and costs.

Average newspapers currently have operating margins (profit) of 15 to 20 percent, compared to about 7 percent for an average manufacturing firm. In highly profitable papers and newspaper firms that margin has risen to as high as 30 percent during good economic times. Because of differences in circulation and advertising, differences in costs of doing business in various cities and regions, differences in technologies employed, and differences in economies of scale, variations occur in the operating costs of newspapers. Nevertheless, newspapers exhibit similarities in the ranges of revenues and costs. Typical ranges of revenues and expenses for newspapers are illustrated in Table 2.1. The ranges reveal the heavy dependence of newspapers on advertising revenues and the extensive costs contributed to newspapers by the production and distribution aspects of newspaper enterprises.

Because newspapers are noted for high profit margins in comparison to other investments, and because they produce strong cash flows, the economic value of newspapers is high. When papers are sold they bring high prices, especially when they are in growing, monopoly markets.

Each newspaper's market is unique and the condition and value of its assets vary, but some "rules of thumb" have been applied to determining the basic value of a newspaper. Some rely on revenue- and earnings-based formulas such as 3 to 4 times gross revenue, 30 to 40 times operating profit or 10 to 12 times earnings before interest and taxes. Occasionally a circulation-based measure will be used. On a per-subscription basis, $500 is at the low end of the spectrum and $2,500 is at the upper end for daily newspapers. The broad range in circulation-based valuation occurs because circulation provides so little of a newspaper's revenue and the real measure of value is its performance in terms of advertising sales, which are reflected in revenue- and earnings-based valuation formulas.

TABLE 2.1   Revenues and Expenses as Percentages of Newspaper Operating Budgets

Operating Revenues

Advertising	% of Operating Revenue
	70-85%

	% of Advertising Revenue
Local/Retail	55-60%
Classified	20-35%
National	10-15%

Circulation	% of Operating Revenue
	15-30%

	% of Circulation Revenue
Subscriptions	80-90%
Single Copies	10-20%

Operating Expenses

	% of Operating Expenses
Editorial	8-12%
Advertising	5-6%
Circulation	9-12%
Promotion	1-3%
Mechanical	13-15%
Newsprint	20-35%
Administration	8-12%
Land and Building	1-3%

Operating Margin (before interest and taxes)	15-20%

NEWSPAPER GROUPS

Newspaper groups, sometimes called chains, develop when a company owns two or more newspapers that operate separately in different locations. Historically, groups were created when the owner of a newspaper had an opportunity to purchase or start a complementary paper in a nearby town. As a result, most groups have tended to be regional, often based on a flagship paper in a county seat or metropolitan area with subsidiary papers located in surrounding areas. Such groups tend to involve only a few papers and have existed throughout the history of modern newspapers. Most of the newspaper groups in the nation are of this type.

The development of deliberately organized, geographically diverse newspaper groups is a much newer development that has occurred for about 100 years. The phenomenon began in the United States at the end of the nineteenth century as major press barons such as Scripps, Hearst, and Pulitzer began to establish nation-wide groups. The development of public companies that gained access to large amounts of capital through sales of shares on stock markets, especially during the 1970s and 1980s, led to the development of the largest and most recognized news-paper groups such as Dow Jones, Gannett, Knight–Ridder, New York Times, Times Mirror, and Tribune. Many of these large groups are now diversified, with sub-sidiaries or divisions operating in broadcasting and cable, multimedia, book pub-lishing and other related industries (information on specific major newspaper groups is found in Appendix I).

A significant factor in the growth of newspaper groups has been the sale of newspapers or smaller newspaper groups owned by families. When the will or abil-ity to continue operating individual newspapers and family groups diminishes, or estates are not appropriately structured to reduce the pressures of taxes, families typically choose to sell their papers and large groups have been able to provide the most attractive bids. Among large and mid-sized newspapers today, few newspapers owned by families remain and their numbers are diminishing rapidly. In 1995 it was calculated that only 77 of the papers above 30,000 circulation were family owned.[6]

The tax issue is, and has been, an important factor in the sale of papers to groups for many years. Because estate taxes are based on the value of a newspaper if it is sold, and because newspaper groups can deduct the price of purchasing a paper from their income taxes as a cost of doing business, the value of a newspaper is heightened to the point that many families cannot afford to pay the estate taxes and keep a paper in the family even if they wish to do so.

About 130 newspaper groups exist in the United States today. The top twenty-five groups own about 43 percent of the daily newspapers (see Table 2.2). This accounts for about 54 percent of all daily newspaper circulation (see Table 2.3). No one group controls more than 10 percent of the total number of daily newspapers or daily circulation. At the turn of the century, newspaper groups owned less than 2 percent of all dailies, today groups own about 75 percent of all dailies (see Figure 2.5). There is a tendency to think of groups as only involving daily newspapers. Many groups, however, include both dailies and weeklies and some groups are made up only of weeklies or alternative papers.

An impetus for the creation of groups is that they produce a variety of benefits for companies. Groups create economies of scale of purchasing supplies, especially newsprint, because discounts are typically available to those who purchase larger amounts. Groups also provide access to less expensive capital because larger, more stable companies receive lower interest rates for borrowed capital and they can

TABLE 2.2   Largest Newspaper Groups in the United States by Percent of Papers Owned, 1994[1]

Rank (by percent)	Newspaper Group	Number	% Total Newspapers
1	Thomson Newspapers	108	7.0%
2	Hollinger International (American Publishing)	96	6.2%
3	Gannett	82	5.3%
4	Donrey Media Group	51	3.3%
5	Morris Communication	31	2.0%
6	Park Communications	29	1.9%
7	Knight–Ridder	27	1.8%
8	Freedom Newspapers	26	1.7%
9	Newhouse Newspapers	26	1.7%
10	New York Times	25	1.6%
11	Dow Jones	22	1.4%
12	Lee Enterprises	19	1.2%
13	Cox Enterprises	19	1.2%
14	E. W. Scripps	18	1.2%
15	MediaNews Group	16	1.0%
16	McClatchy Newspapers	12	0.8%
17	Hearst	12	0.8%
18	Times Mirror	11	0.7%
19	Multimedia	11	0.7%
20	Copley Newspapers	10	0.7%
21	Central Newspapers	9	0.6%
22	Harte–Hanks Communications	9	0.6%
23	Capital Cities/ABC	8	0.5%
24	Tribune	6	0.4%
25	Media General	3	0.2%
26	Chronicle Publishing	3	0.2%
27	Washington Post	2	0.1%
	Pulitzer Publishing	2	0.1%
	Total Top 25	**690**	**44.9%**

[1]Includes groups that own at least 1 percent of total dailies, produce 1 percent of total circulation, or are publicly traded companies.

more easily sell shares and issue other financial instruments to raise capital. Small regional groups can create centralized printing facilities that make it much less expensive to produce all the papers at one site.

Groups can also gain benefits by creating advertising sales networks through which an advertiser can purchase space in all the papers in the group more efficiently and often at a preferential rate. In addition, groups can provide advice and support to group papers in the form of employment services, accounting services, management information services, and training.

TABLE 2.3   Largest Newspaper Groups in the United States by Circulation, 1994[1]

Rank (by % circulation)	Newspaper Group	Total Circulation	% Total Circulation
1	Gannett	5,831,000	9.9%
2	Knight–Ridder	3,606,000	6.1%
3	Newhouse Newspapers	2,960,000	5.0%
4	Times Mirror	2,624,000	4.4%
5	New York Times	2,435,000	4.1%
6	Dow Jones	2,366,000	4.0%
7	Thomson Newspapers	2,071,000	3.5%
8	Tribune	1,348,000	2.3%
9	Cox Enterprises	1,315,000	2.2%
10	E. W. Scripps	1,295,000	2.2%
11	Hearst	1,231,000	2.1%
12	Hollinger International (American Publishing)	1,080,000	1.8%
13	MediaNews Group	1,066,000	1.8%
14	Freedom Newspapers	940,000	1.6%
15	Washington Post	851,000	1.4%
16	Central Newspapers	821,000	1.4%
17	McClatchy Newspapers	819,000	1.4%
18	Donrey Media Group	765,000	1.3%
19	Capital Cities/ABC	731,000	1.2%
20	Morris Communication	723,000	1.2%
21	Copley Newspapers	719,000	1.2%
22	Chronicle Publishing	673,000	1.1%
23	Lee Enterprises	648,000	1.1%
24	Media General	568,000	1.0%
25	Pulitzer Publishing	437,000	0.7%
26	Multimedia	321,000	0.5%
27	Harte-Hanks Communications	288,873	0.5%
28	Park Communications	279,535	0.5%
	Total top 25	**37,923,000**	**64.2%**

[1]Includes groups that own at least 1 percent of total dailies, produce 1 percent of total circulation, or are publicly traded companies.

Groups also make it possible to pool and exchange news and feature stories among papers in each group. This provides low-cost editorial material to smaller members of the group and makes it possible for the group to establish correspondents in major news centers to cover news of specific interest to members of the group. As a result, the development of groups has played a major role in the establishment of news and feature services competing with and supplementing the services of national and international news services.

FIGURE 2.5   Number and Percentage of Group-Owned Dailies

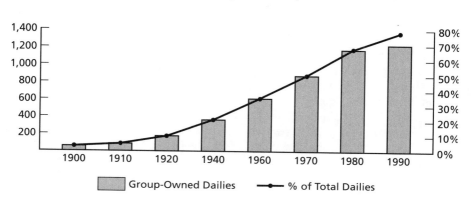

The creation of newspaper groups can occur for a variety of business and economic reasons. Some develop as the results of mergers in times of financial instability when firms want to combine their strengths and improve their finances. Others occur when some firms are weak and must sell to a superior company in order to ensure survival or financial benefits for their original owner. At other times, the development of groups is part of a deliberate business strategy to reduce risk. By operating newspapers in more than one locality, a company becomes less vulnerable to changes in the economy of one town or city and thus spreads its investment risk and may stabilize its revenues.

Group Differences

Although there are similarities in newspaper groups, the companies vary greatly in their structures, the manners in which they operate, their purposes, and their values and cultures. As a result, one cannot think of groups as uniform, parallel entities because the differences are often more striking than their similarities.

Groups, for example, have great differences in terms of their ownership: some are private companies and others are public firms with shares traded on various stock exchanges. Some private firms are owned or controlled by single individuals, others by large groups of persons. Some private firms are family owned, some by partners. Some public firms are controlled by their shareholders, other public firms are controlled by families or a select group of investors.

Newspaper groups vary widely in terms of their financial strength and activity. The largest has assets of almost $7 billion, while others have assets of only a few hundred million (see Table 2.4). Their revenues also vary widely, with the largest exceeding $6 billion annually (see Table 2.5).

Even among the largest firms, the groups vary widely in the number of papers they own (see Table 2.2). In 1994, for example, Thomson Newspapers owned 108 daily newspapers in the United States and Pulitzer Publishing owned only two. Groups also differ widely in terms of the number of readers they service. Daily papers belonging to Gannett, for example, sold more than five million papers every day in 1994, while papers in the Harte–Hanks group sold only about 290,000 papers every day (see Table 2.3).

Newspaper groups also vary widely in their methods of operation. Some provide full autonomy to each newspaper and its managers. Others centralize control and make decisions at the group level and give directions to the manager of each paper. Some groups strive to keep managers and employees at one of the group's papers during their entire careers, other groups regularly move managers and employees among papers in their group.

Newspaper groups also place different emphases on objectives and goals. Some place greatest emphasis on profit, others on quality. Some have a strong community orientation, some have a strong national orientation. Some pursue public awareness of the group, others prefer anonymity.

Newspaper groups also vary in term of their business strategies. Some pursue a strategy of focusing on the newspaper business, other diversify their activities by purchasing or establishing other media and industries. The degree to which they

Table 2.4 Assets of Publicly Traded Companies, 1994

Rank	Newspaper Group	Assets (millions of dollars)
1	Capital Cities/ABC	6,766
2	Times Mirror	4,265
3	Gannett	3,707
4	New York Times	3,138
5	Tribune	2,786
6	Knight–Ridder	2,447
7	Dow Jones	2,446
8	E. W. Scripps	1,723
9	Washington Post	1,697
10	Media General	787
11	Multimedia	684
12	Hollinger International (American Publishing)	636
13	McClatchy Newspapers	587
14	Central Newspapers	500
15	Harte–Hanks Communications	497
16	Lee Enteprises	475
17	Pulitizer Publishing	468

Table 2.5 Revenue of Major Newspaper Groups, 1994[1]

Rank	Newspaper Group	Revenue (millions of dollars)
1	Capital Cities/ABC	6,379
2	Thomson Newspapers	5,849[2]
3	Gannett	3,825
4	Times Mirror	3,357
5	Cox Enterprises	2,939
6	Knight–Ridder	2,649
7	New York Times	2,358
8	Tribune.	2,155
9	Dow Jones	2,091
10	Hearst	*1,800*[3]
11	Washington Post	1,614
12	E. W. Scripps	1,220
13	Multimedia	630
14	Media General.	626
15	Central Newspapers	520
16	Harte–Hanks Communications	514
17	Pulitzer Publishing	486
18	McClatchy Newspapers	471
19	Hollinger International (American Publishing)	423
20	Newhouse Newspapers	*421*
21	Lee Enterprises	403
22	Freedom Newspapers	*294*
23	Donrey Media Group	223
24	Chronicle Publishing	*188*
25	Park Communications	*159*
26	Morris Communication	*144*
	MediaNews Group	
	Copley Press	

[1] Includes groups that own at least 1 percent of total dailies, produce 1 percent of total circulation, or are publicly traded companies.
[2] 1993 data.
[3] Italicized figures are Dun & Bradstreet estimates.

remain newspaper based varies widely as is seen in publicly traded companies in the United States (see Table 2.6). Companies such as McClatchy Newspapers receive all of their revenue from newspapers, whereas companies such as Capital Cities/ABC get less than 20 percent of their revenue from newspaper operations.

Criticism of Newspaper Groups

The growth of large newspapers groups, from those established by the press barons of the late nineteenth century to those developed by public newspaper com-

Table 2.6 Percentage of Revenue from Newspaper Operations for Newspaper Groups Publicly Traded in the United States, 1994

Rank	Newspaper Group	Percentage
1	McClatchy Newspapers	100.0[1]
2	Central Newspapers	99.5
3	Hollinger International (American Publishing)	98.5
4	New York Times	83.5
5	Knight–Ridder	80.6
6	Gannett	78.5
7	Pulitzer Publishing	62.7
8	Times Mirror	61.4
9	Tribune	60.0[1]
10	Lee Enterprises	59.9
11	Dow Jones	53.3[1]
12	Media General	51.8
13	E. W. Scripps	49.4
14	Washington Post	44.4
15	Harte-Hanks Communications	27.4
16	Multimedia	23.8
17	Capital Cities/ABC	17.3

[1]Includes all publishing and printing activities, including some non-newspaper revenue.

panies at the end of the twentieth century, has resulted in a great deal of concern and criticism.

Today, the top twenty-five firms alone own 45 percent of the nation's newspapers and control 64 percent of all newspaper circulation (see Tables 2.2 and 2.3). No single firm owns more than 10 percent of the nation's daily newspapers or accounts for more than 10 percent of total circulation, although Gannett is very close to the latter figure.

Primary criticisms have focused on the bottom-line orientation of some newspaper groups, the cost effects of group ownership, homogenization of content, and lack of continuity in management and staff.

The bottom-line orientation criticism has focused on how some groups have sacrificed good coverage or behaved in other ways that serve profit interests but harm public interests. Arguments of this type include charges that the quality of content is harmed by groups, that group papers take on a strong marketing and management orientation that serves corporate needs rather than social needs, and that the needs of advertisers rather than the needs of readers receive priority.[7] There is, indeed, evidence that public ownership affects financial performance and that public newspaper companies put more emphasis on profit than private firms.[8]

Although there is a great deal of evidence linking such behavior to some newspaper groups, the criticisms cannot be universally applied, because some groups have maintained high levels of reporting standards and worked to improved standards in papers they have acquired, balancing corporate needs with social and reader needs. Research has found no significant differences in quality between group and nongroup owned papers as a whole. This occurs because both group and independent owners choose to emphasize or deemphasize quality and also because there are differences in quality among newspapers owned even by the same group.

A study of newspaper quality recently ranked groups using quality indicators suggested by editors themselves, including items such as amount of locally produced material, editorial versus advertising content, number of in-depth stories, story length, reporter workload, and so on.[9] The study found that Times Mirror and Newhouse Newspapers topped the list and that Stauffer (now part of Morris) and Ottaway were at the bottom of the quality ranking of fifteen newspaper groups (see Table 2.7).

The cost-effectiveness criticism has argued that consumers suffer economic harm from newspaper groups because such newspapers charge higher prices for circulation and advertising. Research on this criticism has shown that it has merit. Group-owned papers tend to be industry price leaders and charge appreciably high-

TABLE 2.7   Rankings of Newspaper Groups Based on a Quality Index Suggested by Newspaper Editors

Rank	Newspaper Group
1	Times Mirror
2	Newhouse
3	Hearst
4	Scripps Howard[1]
5	Capital Cities/ABC
6	New York Times
7	Gannett
8	Donrey Media
9	Harte–Hanks
10	Clay
11	Scripps League[1]
12	Thomson
13	Lee
14	Ottaway[2]
15	Stauffer

[1]Now part of E. W. Scripps.
[2]A subsidiary of Dow Jones.
Source: Stephen Lacy and Frederick Fico, "Newspaper Quality and Ownership: Rating the Groups," *Newspaper Research Journal*, 11 (Spring 1990):42–56.

er prices than nongroup papers. Studies have also found that the growth of large companies has had an effect on managerial goals and decisions.[10]

Charges that group ownership negatively affects newspaper content have received less support from research than other complaints. Studies of content effects have found that group- and nongroup-owned papers resemble each other in national and international reporting and vary only slightly in editorial page material. Research has also shown that locally owned independent papers tend to do a better job of covering community controversies, but that group-owned papers are less affected by, and less willing to be swayed by, adverse local reactions to stories. Interestingly, group papers tend to take more editorial positions on local issues than do locally owned papers.

The criticism of lack of continuity in coverage and relations within the community has been shown to have merit. This is especially true for some of the largest newspaper groups because they tend to move personnel from one paper to another for promotions and career development. This tends to reduce ties to the community that the papers cover and to minimize deep personal knowledge of the community that leads to better coverage and depth of coverage. On the positive side, however, it has been shown that the lessening of community roots tends to insulate journalists and newspaper managers from some social pressures that develop with long residence in a community.

Concerns have also been raised about the increasing reliance on capital from stock markets by some companies and the loss of independence that occurs when the majority of capital comes from those markets and protective mechanisms, such as classified stock, are not in place. A recent study showed that institutional investors are now the primary owners of more than half of the public newspaper companies and that there is growing cross-ownership of newspaper groups among these investors.[11]

ENDNOTES

1. Stephen Lacy and Todd F. Simon, *The Economics and Regulation of United States Newspapers* (Norwood, NJ: Ablex Publishing, 1993), 42.

2. International Newspaper Promotion Association. *Promoting the Total Newspaper* (Reston, VA: International Newspaper Promotion Association, 1984, 42).

3. James N. Rosse, "Economic Limits of Press Responsibility," discussion paper (Palo Alto: *Stanford University Studies in Industry Economics*, No. 56, 1975).

4. Carolyn Terry, "Breaking Through. Or Are They? Women in Newspaper Management Assess their Progress," *Presstime* (March 1995) 17, No. 3: 31-36.

5. Robert G. Picard, "Gender Representation in Corporate Management of Public Newspaper Companies," Research Report (Fullerton: California State University,1995).

6. John Morton, "Farewell to More Family Dynasties," *American Journalism Review* (October 1995), 17: 68.

7. Ben Bagdikian, *The Media Monopoly*, 4th ed. (Boston: Beacon Press, 1992); Robert G. Picard, James P. Winter, Maxwell McCombs, and Stephen Lacy, eds. *Press Concentration and Monopoly: New Perspectives on Newspaper Ownership and Operation* (Norwood, NJ: Ablex Publishing, 1988); Robert G. Picard, *The Press and the Decline of Democary: The Democratic Socialist Approach in Public Policy* (Westport, CT: Greenwood Press, 1985); Herbert I. Schiller, *Who Knows? Information in the Age of the Fortune 500* (Norwood, NJ: Ablex Publishing, 1981).

8. William B. Blankenburg, and Gary W. Ozanich. "The Effects of Public Ownership on the Financial Performance of Newspaper Corporations," *Journalism Quarterly* (Spring), 70 (1993):68–75.

9. Stephen Lacy and Frederick Fico, "Newspaper Quality and Ownership: Rating the Groups," *Newspaper Research Journal* 11(Spring 1990):42–56 .

10. David P. Demers and Daniel Wackman, "Effect of Chain Ownership on Newspaper Management Goals," *Newspaper Research Journal* 9 (Winter 1988):59–68; P. Meyers and S. T. Wearden, "The Effect of Public Ownership on Newspaper Companies: A Preliminary Inquiry," *Public Opinion Quarterly*, 48 (1984):564–577; and John Soloski, "Economics and Management: The Real Influence of Newspaper Groups," *Newspaper Research Journal* 1 (November 1979):19–28.

11. Robert G. Picard, "Institutional Ownership of Publicly Traded U.S. Newspaper Companies," *Journal of Media Economics*, 7 (1994):49–64.

3

Milestones in the Development of the U.S. Newspaper Industry

GENERAL HISTORICAL DEVELOPMENTS

Although the history of publications carrying news can be traced as far back as the Chinese and Roman empires, the appearance of publications recognizable as newspapers began early in the seventeenth century, apparently appearing first in Germany and then spreading to cities in the countries that are now Switzerland, Austria, the Netherlands, and the United Kingdom.

Although colonization of North America began about the time that newspapers spread throughout Europe, it was not until the following century that newspapers appeared in the colonies. Colonists, particularly those in the northern colonies, tended to have British ties, embraced puritan religious philosophy, and generally had higher levels of literacy and education. Despite their literacy and ties to a country that began use of newspapers in the seventeenth century, the northern colonists' need for newspapers was low because they tended to live in small, tightly knit communities in which news could easily be disseminated verbally and because they had no real history of newspaper reading prior to immigration. As newspapers developed in Europe during the seventeenth century, copies were brought to the colonies on ships and served the need for information from the European continent.

In the mid-Atlantic colonies, colonists tended to come from Britain, the Netherlands, Germany, and Scandinavia, and were more diverse in terms of religion and social class. They tended not to live in such tightly knit groups as in the more northern colonies, and they developed cities more rapidly than their northern counterparts. Although the southern colonies preceded northern colonies by more than a decade, their development was slower because they tended to be more agrarian, with fewer and smaller cities. Although some colonies were noted for intellectual contributions, the educational level of colonists in the south as a whole tended to be lower than that for the northern and mid-Atlantic states.

By the eighteenth century, the economic and population growth in the colonies, and an improved standard of life by comparison to the first colonies at the beginning of the seventeenth century, led to the development of commerce between colonies. The growth of the colonies led to debates over their future and governance, and disputes between European nations changed control of and threatened the status of various colonies, particularly in the mid-Atlantic states.

These developments created a demand for more information and discussion of events. In addition, the growing population and travel between colonies reduced the ability to exchange information and ideas informally and created conditions in which demand for a more formal means for exchanging news, commercial information, and ideas emerged. Initially, there was a need for commercial information, such as the need for and availability of goods, shipping schedules, and so on to serve the interests of the small merchant class. Over time, however, the need for political information and discussion, as well as general news and information, expanded the audience.

The first effort to meet informational needs in the colonies with a newspaper was made by Benjamin Harris, a fugitive wanted by London authorities for operating a seditious newspaper there, in Boston. In 1690 he published *Publick Occurrences, Both Foreign and Domestick*, a publication that he intended to be the first newspaper in North America, modeled after European papers. The publication was banned for violating Massachusetts laws requiring a license to print newspapers and never appeared a second time, so it cannot be considered a newspaper, because regular periodicity is a crucial element in the definition of newspapers.

Although Harris's venture failed, it underscored the need for newspapers and for regular exchange of information. The development of a postal service in the colonies in 1692 led to the appointment of postmasters, who soon became centers of information from other colonies and Europe and who regularly exchanged information on events and developments in letters exchanged among themselves.

In 1704, the postmaster of Boston, John Campbell, used his position to obtain permission to print the Boston *News-Letter*, which became the first true newspaper in North America. It carried official news of the colony, information about activities in the community, information received from postmasters in other colonies, and news copied from European papers. The paper maintained close ties to the colonial government. Each issue was reviewed prior to publication in the governor's office, and at times the paper received government funds. Because there was little advertising, the publication was dependent on circulation sales that ultimately reached only 300, although Boston had a population of 7,000 people at the time.

The survival of the paper and its acceptance by the colonial government led to the establishment of similar papers in other colonies by their postmasters. These postmasters began exchanging their papers, creating a news exchange system that allowed papers to receive regular information on events and developments in other colonies.

The first newspaper to break this pattern and be successfully produced by a publisher who was not a government-appointed official was the New England *Courant*, established in 1721 by James Franklin. In addition to information about events, the paper began challenging the control of the puritan clergy and questioning the effectiveness of the colonial government in dealing with emerging problems and issues. In a dispute over smallpox inoculation, the *Courant* conducted the first editorial crusade in the U.S. newspaper industry, a contribution that continues to this day.

The development of official and private newspapers spread through the colonies, with Philadelphia becoming the nation's second most important center for the industry. *American Weekly Mercury*, established there in 1719 by Andrew Bradford, was the first paper published outside of Boston. In 1729 Benjamin Franklin took over the Pennsylvania *Gazette* and made it one of the best-known papers in the colonies. By the 1730s, important colonial cities such as New York, Annapolis, and Williamsburg all had notable newspapers of their own.

The first paper to be published daily was the Pennsylvania *Evening Post*, a Philadelphia-based weekly that was converted into a daily in 1783 by Benjamin Towne. Within twenty years daily papers were available in most port cities and there was competition among dailies in major cities such as New York, Philadelphia, and Baltimore.

Although newspapers served all major cities by the nineteenth century, the interests of the residents of those cities were not equally served. To provide for the needs of the black community in New York City, John Russwurm and Samuel E. Cornish established *Freedom's Journal* in 1827, making it the first black paper in the nation. In that same year a special audience paper, the *Journeyman Mechanic's Advocate*, was established in Philadelphia as the first labor paper in the country.

The distinction as the first national newspaper goes to the *New York Tribune*, a daily that started a weekly edition in 1841 intended for distribution in the Midwest and Western parts of the U.S., which was at that time roughly the areas along the Ohio and Mississippi rivers, respectively. The paper, established by Horace Greeley, was distributed via railroad and post and became one of the most sought-after and influential papers in the country.

The *New York Herald* became the first newspaper to achieve 100,000 daily circulation in 1862 as demand for news and casualty lists from the Civil War pushed its circulation upward. Which paper first achieved the one million daily circulation mark is unclear because heavy competition and false circulation reporting just prior to the turn of the twentieth century obscure the truth. That achievement either goes to the *New York World* or the *New York Journal*, both of which had surpassed that mark by 1900.

The growth of these and other newspapers during the latter half of the nineteenth century was spurred by urbanization, changing economics that created new middle and working classes, increasing literacy and educational levels, and the development of technologies that made it possible for publishers to meet the increasing demand for newspapers.

This chapter will not attempt to trace the development of individual newspapers and the role of newspaper personalities beyond the important milestones already discussed because several classic histories of the press in the United States have already done so.[1] Instead the remaining portions of this chapter will focus on major changes in the technology, content, and business of newspapers, and the persons and papers involved in those developments that have influenced the evolution of the newspaper industry.

TECHNICAL DEVELOPMENTS

In the 300-year history of the newspaper industry in the United States, the technology used to produce papers has been remarkably stable. Unlike other manufacturing industries, in which technological revolutions radically and more frequently changed the methods and means of production, the newspaper industry has not faced the issue of continuing and rapid reinvestment in manufacturing equipment.

Although there have been important developments in production technology that have made newspaper production easier and quicker, the first 250 years of the industry's technical history can be characterized by relative stability and evolution rather than revolution. It was not until the 1960s and 1970s that the first real revolutionary changes in the industry's production technology occurred. This is not to indicate that the technology of newspaper production did not change during the eighteenth, nineteenth and twentieth centuries, but that it did so in incremental improvements that built upon core processes and techniques. When change occurred, it often was the result of the needs of newspapers in large cities to respond to social changes and the demands of readers.

The first press reached North America in 1539 when Catholic missionaries imported a press to Mexico to print materials for use in converting natives to Christianity. Nearly one hundred years later, in 1638, the first press in what is the now the United States was established in Cambridge, Massachusetts, to print religious material for the education of colonists. These presses were slow, relatively complex wooden machines based on the integrated press system of movable type introduced by Johannes Gutenberg in Germany in 1440. In this system, individual letters of type were locked into a form. Ink was placed onto the letters and paper was pressed onto the letters, transferring the ink to paper.

Throughout the seventeenth and eighteenth centuries, northern, mid-Atlantic, and southern colonial institutions imported presses primarily from England. The most popular machine was the English Common Press, which required more than a dozen separate actions by printers to produce a single impression and which could produce only about 200 impressions per hour with the most highly skilled operators. The design and process were ultimately replicated by some colonial manufacturers so that the presses no longer had to be imported.

It was not until 1822 that the system was simplified through the use of lever action, an improvement developed by R. Hoe and Co. that placed them in the forefront of press development during the nineteenth century. The installation of lever action reduced the number of steps necessary in the printing process and allowed the production of copies four times faster than with the previous system.

In 1830 Isaac Adam applied steam power to the printing industry, but the most popular steam press of the period became the Hoe Cylinder Press of 1832, which was constructed of metal and had a movable flatbed and printing cylinders. This adaptation of designs made by Friedrich Koenig in Germany and David Napier in England increased production speed to 4,000 impressions per hour.

The introduction of "hot type" made it possible to increase the speed of production and quality of reproduction even more. In the hot type system, lines of type—rather than single movable type letters, were cast from molten lead, bolted together in a form, and placed on the press.

In 1846 R. Hoe and Co. introduced a type-revolving rotary press system using a more advanced hot type system that boosted production to more than 10,000 impressions per hour. In this hot type system, single metal plates of type containing a full page were molded from hot lead and placed into the press, instead of separate lines or individual letters of type.

Both the Hoe cylinder press and type-revolving press were far more advanced than needed by most newspapers in the United States. Only papers in the largest cities had circulations high enough to warrant the investment in such equipment at the time, but the needs of papers in major East Coast cities kept press companies seeking improvements.

TABLE 3.1   Historic Advances in Newspaper Press Technology

Date	Press	Description	Power	Paper	Copies/Hour
Colonial	English Common Press	Flatbed	Hand	Sheet	200
1832	Cylinder Press	Movable Flatbed	Steam	Sheet	4,000
1846	Type Revolving Press	Horizontal Cylinder	Steam	Sheet	10,000
1871	Perfecting Rotary Press	Rotary	Steam	Web	35,000

In 1871 the web perfecting press was created, which used a continuous roll of paper rather than sheets. This development permitted printing on two sides of the paper simultaneously at great speed and made it possible to produce more than 30,000 impressions per hour. The introduction of webs was an important improvement that remains in use today because of its practicality and efficiency.

The ability to produce hot type rapidly was greatly increased by Ottmar Mergenthaler, a toolmaker who invented a keyboard-based mechanical typesetter in 1884, the linecasting Linotype™, and patented fifty improvements to the machine before his death. His best-known machine was the 1886 model, and many of the improvements he patented were integrated into that model. His invention later faced competition from another popular linecaster, the Monotype™, created by Tolbert Lanston, that indirectly set lines of type using punched tape produced on a keyboard.

The development of stereotyping, a process of making duplicate pages of a newspaper, was developed by the 1880s, allowing newspapers with large circulations to use several presses to simultaneously produce the same paper, thus reducing the time needed to produce the total pressrun. In stereotyping, individual letters or lines of type were locked into a frame and then a mold was created from the type into which liquid metal would be poured to create a solid full-page plate for printing.

Electrification, beginning with the design and construction of a power and lighting system in New York City in 1881 and 1882 by Thomas Edison, soon made it possible to begin replacing the steam engines that powered presses with electrical motors. Nevertheless, the slow process of electrification nationwide kept many printers in rural areas and small towns using hand- and steam-press systems well into the twentieth century.

In 1890, the introduction of new Hoe rotary presses increased the production speed of single presses to 48,000 impressions an hour, a critical factor in the development of large city newspaper production.

Concurrently with such advances, developments in photography were seen as a means of improving artwork, primarily drawings, reproduced through the use of woodcuts and later relief images engraved in metal. The development of workable applications of photoengraving by Frederic Ives created the means by which photographs could be rephotographed through a grid pattern to create dots of varying sizes that reproduce the original image. Stephen Hogan adapted the process for newspaper printing at the *Daily Graphic* in New York, and then helped establish and put the system into regular use at the *New York Tribune* in 1897.

Although these improvements in press design made printing simpler and more rapid, and helped increase the availability of papers to the public, none represented radical departures from previous printing technology. They were all based on the same technology of bringing paper into contact with inked type and merely provided refinements and improvements that provided more efficiency and increased the capabilities of the basic printing technique.

The development of "cold type" photocomposition in the late 1950s marked the first real twentieth-century advance in newspaper production by using techniques developed in photochemistry to replace metal type produced through hot-type methods. Now, words and photographic images were placed on film and transferred to a metal printing plate with raised printing images that would be placed on the printing press. This cold-type production was much faster and required fewer personnel and less maintenance than hot-type methods. By the 1960s, typesetters such as the Photon™ and Fotosetter™ were beginning to replace linecasting machines in newspapers throughout the country. When cold-type methods were combined with the introduction of offset printing presses, the first major revolution in newspaper production since the establishment of printing in North America occurred.

Although the offset technology was related to lithography, which had long been used in artistic activity, the creation of workable offset presses for mass printing made it possible to radically change the means, quality, and speed of reproduction. It made it possible to reduce the large numbers of composing, stereotyping, and printing personnel that had previously been required.

In offset printing, the paper never comes into contact with type or a type plate, unlike the traditional letterpress printing process of bringing paper into contact with raised type on which ink is placed. Instead, ink and water are placed on a photochemically engraved plate, the ink separates itself from the water, and settles into the engraved depressions. A rubber roller is then moved across the plate, picking up the ink. The roller is pressed against the paper, transferring the ink to the paper. The image produced by offset is much sharper than that produced by the older method. Offset also creates impressions in a shorter period of time, thus increasing the speed of production.

Offset technology was initially most suited for weeklies and small dailies, and the Opelousas (Louisiana) *Daily World* became the first daily to install an offset press. By the 1980s, improvements in the durability of offset printing plates and the capacity of presses made the technology serviceable for most newspapers throughout the nation.

The combination of phototypesetting and computers in the 1970s further increased the speed of production and reduced the need for backshop personnel to typeset material. The general availability of computerized pagination systems in the 1980s further reduced backshop personnel by reducing the need for personnel to paste galleys of type onto pages before they were processed for platemaking.

The benefits of electronic production also provided the capability to combine the technology with telecommunications advances to permit offsite printing. By the 1970s a number of newspapers began moving their printing plants away from their downtown editorial and business offices and using telephone and microwave links to transmit stories and pages for production. These opportunities were further exploited by the *Wall Street Journal*, which in 1968 combined electronic typesetting, layout, and a digital transmission system to begin sending pages by satellite from New York to a printing plant in Riverside, California, thus permitting simultaneous printing and same-day distribution on both sides of the continent. The technique has since been implemented by other newspapers in the United States and abroad to permit widespread distribution.

CHANGES IN CONTENT AND JOURNALISM STYLES

News in early American newspapers tended to be reported as announcements or was written in a literary or letter style far different from the style found in newspapers today. In addition, far more information was conveyed in the form of essays and correspondence. Opinions were regularly found in the news columns, and articles and commentaries were often filled with invective and accusations that are shocking by comparison to today's news and editorial columns. Significant amounts of space were devoted to intellectual discussions of social and political ideas and concepts. The earliest papers carried little advertising, and that which was carried tended to be unillustrated, straightforward announcements of goods that were available from shipping companies.

The primary reason for these characteristics was that papers were highly personal communication vehicles for their publishers. Often the only "staff" of the paper was the publisher, who wrote most of the material alone or solicited it from friends and then set the type and printed the paper, usually only with the assistance of a young apprentice. Newspapers were seen as devices for conveying information but also for carrying out the social and political purposes of the publisher.

This approach to newspapers continued for almost a century, and helped spawn the revolution and the development of unified government and its institutions during the creation of the United States. For the most part, newspapers were a vehicle for elites. They were published and written by members of the educated and merchant classes. The circulations of such papers were relatively low and they were primarily purchased and read by individuals similar to their publishers.

The 1830s brought the establishment of papers intended for readers who were not part of the traditional elite group of newspaper readers. These papers were designed and written for common people, and because most sold for a penny, they became known as the Penny Press. The paper that introduced this publishing formula, the *New York Sun*, was an almost immediate success, becoming the city's largest paper with more than 8,000 copies daily within its first year of operation.

Because readers of these new styles of papers were not attracted to the papers for news and discussions of interest to elites, a new style of journalism—story journalism—appeared that emphasized drama, pathos, and other elements to make news reports or features more entertaining and appealing to a wider audience. The style tended to be sensational and trivial. Reports of crime, disasters, human failings, and serialized fiction, using simple but involving language, became the norm.

The language of news reporting began to change around mid-century, however, taking on the recognizable elements of journalese, the writing style characterized by short lead paragraphs that sum up events, followed by information in descending order of importance. The style developed in response to the needs of sending short, terse news reports by telegraph and because it was easier for editors when they needed to reduce the length of a story.

The telegraph was not developed for newspapers and is not itself a newspaper technology, but its use by journalists played a role in changing the style of newspaper writing and the content of newspapers. The wire-borne communication system was developed by Samuel Morse in 1844 and its value to journalists was immediately recognized by publishers who promoted and widely used the system for newsgathering. In 1849, a ship, pony express, and telegraph relay was created to speed up trans-Atlantic communications. Messages were sent from Britain to North America on Cunard Line ships that stopped in Halifax, Nova Scotia. The messages would be carried across Nova Scotia on horseback, put on a ferry to St. John, New Brunswick, and then sent by telegraph throughout North America and vice versa. During the Civil War the telegraph became an important means of coverage. James Gordon Bennett of the *New York Herald* is noted for his early and regular use of the system. In 1866, the Atlantic cable linked London and Newfoundland, and the *Herald* became one of the first papers to regularly move news to and from Europe on the cable.

The development of telegraphy was a major impetus for the establishment of news services worldwide as newspapers began demanding news via telegraph and pooled resources to accomplish the task. A major step in that development occurred when the Associated Press was formed as a national and international news agency through the merger of the Associated Press of New York and the Associated Press of Illinois in 1900, cooperative newsgathering organizations that had first begun half a century earlier and whose work was facilitated by extensive use of the telegraph.

Such developments need to be seen in context as part of the progressive and increasing commercialization of news and newspapers that occurred during the nineteenth century. This trend altered the creation and acquisition of news and features, and the editorial section and editing of those materials, in the production of newspapers. They played a major role in transforming the small cottage industry into the large commercial industry and economic force in operation today.

In the late nineteenth and early twentieth centuries this trend included the development of a new writing and presentation style that focused on social problems, often in an emotional and sensational manner. The approach was used to help increase readership among lower- and middle-class urban readers and became characteristic of big city journalism in the period. One important journalistic contribution of the period that remains in use today was the human interest story, a style developed at the *New York Tribune* and *New York Sun* while those papers were edited by Charles A. Dana in the last half of nineteenth century. These stories gained a special slant with "The Sob Sisters," a term applied to writers who were primarily female and specialized in heartrending and sentimental stories about social problems and news events.

James Gordon Bennett, who founded the New York *Morning Herald*, also played a major role in making news more entertaining to readers. His efforts were carried on by his son, James Gordon Bennett Jr., who founded the *Evening Telegram* and continued efforts to popularize journalism by mounting expeditions worldwide that were reported in dramatic styles designed to attract and keep readers purchasing the paper during the entire expedition.

When pushed to its limits, as it was done by the *World* and the *Journal* in New York City, the new journalism style became a highly sensationalized style known as Yellow Journalism, which often involved altering, creating, or twisting facts. This offshoot style of the new journalism took its name from the circulation war between the Hearst and Pulitzer papers during which the *World* began using bright yellow ink and other colors on some items to draw more attention to itself in 1893.

During the 1890s humorous stories, illustrated with drawings, which later became what we know as comic strips, began appearing in newspapers. The first comic, "Hogan's Alley," began appearing in the *World* in 1895. Because the paper was using yellow ink, it began applying it to the comic strip, creating "The Yellow Kid" as its protaganist.

On December 21, 1913, the *New York World* introduced one of the most popular and enduring nonjournalistic newspaper features, the crossword puzzle. The first puzzle was a diamond-shaped "Word-Cross" consisting of thirty-one words.

A moderated style of sensational journalism called Jazz Journalism emerged in the 1920s, placing an emphasis on gangsters and sports, entertainment, society, and other celebrities. This style was popularized by the *Illustrated Daily News* and *Daily Graphic* in New York and the *Daily Mirror* in Boston, all of which became leading photography newspapers of the period.

A backlash to Yellow and Jazz Journalism helped promote a movement of journalistic professionalism in the 1920s. Professional workshops and university education programs were established to help raise the quality of journalists, and organizations began establishing ideals of journalistic behavior. The American Society of Newspaper Editors issued its Canons of Journalism in 1923 and the Society of Professional Journalists adopted its Code of Ethics in 1926 as part of the movement.

At the same time the concept of objectivity began to pervade American journalism. Elements of the concept had earlier emerged with the Penny Press, when publishers displaced political partisanship in hopes of attracting wider audiences and more advertisers, and with the development of news services such as the Associated Press, because such services had to provide news reports that were acceptable to all clients. During the growth of professionalism in the 1920s and 1930s, however, the concept of objectivity and its elements of fairness, balance, and impartiality became a major focus. By the middle of the twentieth century, some of its most vocal proponents argued that journalists should have no political or social views. By the 1970s, however, the view that full objectivity was impossible overcame those arguments, and a renewed emphasis was placed on the ideals of fairness and balance.

During the 1950s and 1960s, individuals and organizations involved in the counterculture established nondaily papers that supported their social and political views, which were not well represented in the mainstream press. During the 1970s, these special audience papers began evolving into weekly newspapers known today as the alternative press.

The 1970s also saw broad recognition of a style of journalism called investigative reporting that emerged from political and criminal investigations by journalists. The style involved focusing on problems and issues using extensive research not normally undertaken in day-to-day news coverage. Although some journalists had used such techniques earlier, the investigative reporting style and techniques became a journalistic specialty during the 1970s and 1980s with major newspapers often assigning reporters or teams of reporters to such work.

In the last two decades of the twentieth century, publishers began placing greater emphasis on the use of illustrations and graphic devices and the general design of their newspapers. Although limited color printing had been available to publishers for almost a century, its use had been primarily confined to advertising copy, Sunday comics, and front pages of big city newspapers. Improvements in color reproduction during the 1980s and 1990s, as well as the increased visual orientation of newspapers, led to increased use of color not only in advertising but in photographs, illustrations, and screens in both news and feature sections of newspapers. The visual orientation and expectations of readers used to color images on television and colorful magazines are playing important roles in newspaper layout and design and the ways in which newspaper managers are positioning newspapers for the future.

DEVELOPMENTS IN THE BUSINESS ASPECTS OF NEWSPAPERS

Early newspapers were dependent primarily on income from readers, but the development of significant advertising support in the early nineteenth century soon made publishers more dependent on advertising than readers for income. The increasing number of papers and the complexity of advertising in different locations led to the development of advertising agencies by the mid-nineteenth century. The advertising industry boomed in the last half of the century in response to the industrial revolution, population growth, and the concurrent growth of the newspaper industry.

The growth of advertising and large city newspapers soon made journalism a highly commercial activity. During the last part of the nineteenth and early twentieth centuries, Victor Lawson, who published the Chicago *Daily News*, and Frank Munsey, publisher of the *New York Sun*, *Herald*, and *Daily News*, as well as the Boston *Journal* and Washington *Times*, introduced many business management ideas and techniques to their newspapers and the industry.

The development of newspapers as business enterprises soon led to the concept of the newspaper group or chain. Although other publishers had previously owned a few papers, the real development of newspaper groups was led by Edward W. Scripps and Milton McRae, who in 1890 created the Scripps–McRae League, the first true newspaper chain in the U.S. The group operated primarily in Midwest and Western states and ultimately included papers such as the Cleveland *Press*, Cincinnati *Post*, St. Louis *Chronicle*, San Diego *Sun*, Kansas City *World*, and Seattle *Sun*. Although Scripps's and McRae's efforts began earlier, William Randolph Hearst is better known for his efforts at developing a newspaper group because he established the first group that brought together big city newspapers. His group started with the San Francisco *Examiner* and ultimately included papers such as the New York *Journal*, Chicago *American*, and Boston *American*. Joseph Pulitzer also began a major newspaper chain in the last half of the nineteenth century based on his flagship papers, the St. Louis *Post Dispatch* and New York *World*.

In response to the growing economic power of publishers, newspaper workers began to unionize. By the end of the nineteenth century, the most significant labor organization in the industry became the International Typographical Union, which organized printers and other workers in production jobs. It was not until 1933 that unionization of journalists began with the formation of the Newspaper Guild. Originally created by Heywood Broun and other New York journalists as a local organization, chapters were formed in other cities and a national union emerged. Today it includes not only journalists but other newspaper employees among its members.

During the first hundred years of their operation, U.S. newspapers were primarily available through subscriptions. Newspapers were delivered primarily by post until the 1760s when young boys began to be hired to deliver papers to subscribers. The development of popular papers in the nineteenth century brought with it the idea of single-copy sales through newsstands and individuals hawking papers from street corners. These sellers were not employed by the papers but purchased copies from the paper and then resold them to customers. This idea was later transferred to those who delivered to subscribers and this wholesaler–retailer relationship between newspapers and carriers still exists in the majority of newspapers. By the middle of the twentieth century, rising costs, child labor laws, and difficulties in managing sellers led many newspapers to abandon hawkers and utilize coin-operated news racks for single-copy sales.

Newspapers remained primarily owned and operated by proprietors and relatively small corporations prior to World War II and truly large newspaper groups did not develop until the last half of the twentieth century. A small group of small and mid-sized New England newspapers, created by Frank E. Gannett and nurtured by his successor Paul Miller, was built into the largest chain of daily newspapers between the 1970s and 1990s by Al Neuharth. In 1982 the company began publishing *USA Today*, a graphically innovative national paper, that serves as the flagship paper for the group. A financially smaller newspaper group, Donrey Media, developed simultaneously under the ownership of Donald Reynolds. Although the firm owned nearly one hundred papers long before Gannett, it was a private company, its holdings were far smaller and included more nondaily newspapers, and Reynolds did not seek public attention, so the existence and development of Donrey Media is not as widely known.

The development of the newspaper business in the late nineteenth and twentieth centuries also brought with it changes in the marketing of newspapers. Until the arrival of Yellow Journalism, the concept was generally unknown in the industry. With the development of big city newspaper competition, marketing was introduced primarily as a sales promotion activity. Contests, promotions, and content were created to spur sales, but few comprehensive marketing efforts were made. By the end of the twentieth century, however, newspaper marketing plans that integrated all departments of newspapers had emerged. These were designed to simultaneously promote advertising and circulation sales, to deliberately plan and create content for specific groups of readers, and to change the appearance of papers.

SUMMARY

Developments in technologies, news styles and presentation, financial support for newspapers, and attitudes and practices of owners and workers have been important forces in changing the nature of the industry throughout its 300-year history. These developments have changed the availability and content of newspapers, the audience of newspapers, the definitions of news, and the services provided by newspapers.

The newspaper industry will continue to be affected by these forces and new forces will emerge to influence its development in the twenty-first century. The history of the industry has been filled with change and evolution and one can only expect that such changes will continue as those who produce, read, and fund the industry react to social, economic, and technical developments in the years to come.

ENDNOTES

1. Among the most useful histories of individual newspapers and newspaper personalities are: Williard Bleyer, *Main Currents in the History of American Journalism* (Boston: Houghton Mifflin, 1927), Edwin Emery and Michael Emery, *The Press and America: An Interpretive History of the Mass Media*, 5th ed. (Englewood Cliffs, NJ: Prentice–Hall, 1984), Alfred McClung Lee, *The Daily Newspaper in America* (New York: Macmillan, 1937), Frank Luther Mott, *American Journalism*, rev. ed. (New York: Macmillan, 1962), and George H. Payne, *History of Journalism in the United States* (New York: Appleton–Crofts, 1920).

4

Operations of
a Newspaper

The basic functions that must be carried out in the operation of all newspapers, regardless of their size or frequency, are similar. These functions include editorial, advertising, circulation, photography and graphics, business, and production activities. In the smallest weekly newspapers all of these functions may be handled by a single individual—the proprietor. As the size and frequency of newspapers increase, the number of employees rises and specialization in and division of labor develops. Soon the time requirements of the different positions reduce the ability of employees to carry out multiple functions and a more complex organizational structure emerges.

Once more than a few employees are involved, the newspapers typically divide their operations into distinct departments or operating entities. The most common division of operations is into departments. Many companies also carry on subsidiary operations that may be centralized in a separate department or spread through existing departments.

A typical mid-sized daily newspaper, for example, would divide its operations into components as shown in the organizational chart in Figure 4.1.

In terms of employment, about half of all employees are engaged in pre-press activities and the rest in production and maintenance. Advertising and promotional employees typically represent about 10 percent of the workforce in a newspaper, circulation about 12 percent, executives and administration about 15 percent, editorial about 8–12 percent, and production and maintenance about 48 percent. Even

FIGURE 4.1   Basic Organizational Chart for a Daily Newspaper

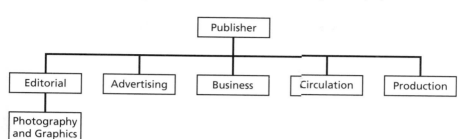

with computerization and technological improvements in production, newspapers remain labor intensive enterprises and labor costs account for about forty cents of each revenue dollar.

EDITORIAL OPERATIONS

The editorial operations of the newspaper include creating, acquiring, and preparing the nonadvertising content of the newspaper, which includes the news, sports, business, features, editorials, opinion pages, and comics portions. Newspapers carry out the editorial function by creating original content and by purchasing material from individuals and various editorial services and syndicates. Managers of each newspaper make their own decisions about the amount of material created or purchased but—as a general rule—the larger the newspaper, the larger the amount of material original to the staff of that newspaper, particularly features and non-news items.

In organizing editorial operations, daily newspaper managers typically divide the functions according to the various sections their newspaper publishes (Figure 4.2). Separate working groups of journalists are created for news coverage, sports coverage, business coverage, and special feature sections such as lifestyle, food, and health. Photographers may operate out of a separate department or from within these groups. Within these groups reporters may be assigned to specific beats, such as education or consumer affairs. Others are assigned as editorial writers and columnists and these may be assigned to separate working groups. Each group is typically headed by an editor and sometimes subeditors, depending on the size of the staffs involved. In recent years papers have begun creating teams of reporters, photographers, and design specialists to tackle specific projects.

FIGURE 4.2   EDITORIAL ORGANIZATION IN A MID-SIZED DAILY

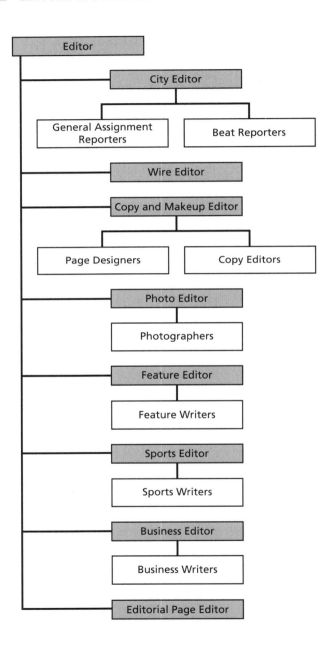

Coordination of the various groups is overseen by the editor—or a managing editor, if the editor designates the job to another—whose job it is to bring together the editorial functions of the entire paper into a cohesive product. Part of this task is accomplished by daily editorial meetings with editors and subeditors in which the placement and emphasis to be given stories, graphics and artwork to be employed, and work assignments and coordinating decisions are made.

In weekly newspapers, where staffs are typically smaller and produce smaller papers, the organization is often more fluid. In moderately small weeklies, there are sometimes only one or two editorial employees who divide all the editorial tasks between themselves. In larger weeklies, even though the editorial staffs remain small by comparison to dailies, individuals may have a primary assignment to a particular type of coverage.

Once material is created and acquired for use, it is reviewed by the appropriate editor and sent to copy editors who ensure that the material contains proper spelling and grammar, and conforms to the style and form established for the publication.

The design and layout of the pages on which material is to be printed is done by section editors and the copy desk. When questions of whether items should be in one section or another arises, these are typically decided in daily editorial conferences.

News Services and Syndicates

Although newspapers maintain significant staffs of writers, the majority of editorial content in most newspapers is not created by newspaper staffs themselves, but purchased from news services and syndicates that offer editorial materials designed to serve every editorial need. Approximately 500 services syndicate the work of thousands of artists, photographers, and writers for daily and weekly newspapers.

Syndicates developed through efforts of newspaper groups to cut their costs by sharing the expense of materials among members of the group, and soon these groups began offering materials to noncompeting papers in other markets. The first syndicates were small operations begun more than 100 years ago. Syndicates have flourished as newspapers have expanded their non-news sections, especially in the last half of the twentieth century. For the most part, materials produced and syndicated tend to have nonlocal interest, thus making them more marketable.

In their earliest days, syndicates distributed material by post, then by telegraph and telephone lines. Large news services and syndicates are increasingly distributing via satellite and through Internet connections.

Syndicates vary widely in size and scope. Some distribute hundreds of features, while most distribute only a few. Some syndicates provide general services with materials for all sections of newspapers. Others concentrate on specialty topics such as agriculture, soap operas, home decorating, auto repairs, or weather.

Most syndicates provide materials without geographical limitations, but others are willing to produce or localize materials to serve the needs of specific newspapers or readers within geographical regions of the nation or states. Some syndicates distribute only material that they originate, whereas others distribute for a variety of services that produce editorial matter.

A criticism of syndication has been that it creates a homogenization of voices and topics in newspapers nationwide, reducing distinctive regionalism and the opportunity for unique voices to be heard. There is merit in the argument because, just as national culture has been affected by the creation of national retailers such as Wal-Mart, fast food restaurants such as McDonald's, and nationwide television networks, syndicates have brought a uniformity to newspapers and similar types of information and viewpoints to the entire nation by making it possible for commentary, comics, and feature materials from the same writers to appear in hundreds of papers simultaneously.

Although there is a great deal of competition among the hundreds of existing news services and syndicates, the markets of each are dominated by a few major firms. In the news service area, the primary provider of daily news and information is the Associated Press, with significant material also coming from Reuters and Agence France-Presse. United Press International, which has been a major provider for decades, has declined markedly in its size and scope in recent years but still provides some materials for many subscribers. These news agencies are also major suppliers of news photos for newspaper use, and their resources are supplemented by major international photo services such as Gamma–Liaison and Magnum Photos.

Most newspaper groups continue to share news and other features with other papers in their groups and noncompeting papers through services such as the Hearst News Service, Newhouse News Service, New York Times News Service, and Los Angeles Times–Washington Post News Service.

Specialized news agencies such as Jewish Telegraphic Agency, Catholic News Services, Black Press Service, and Maturity News Services provide news and features that focus on issues affecting the focus of their specialization. State or local orientations are served by agencies such as Capitol News Service in California, which provides extensive coverage of state government for local newspapers, or City News Service in Chicago, which provides extensive local coverage not provided by traditional news agencies.

In the syndication area, the primary providers include companies such as Copley News Service, Creators Syndicate, King Features, Los Angeles Times Syndicate, Tribune Media Services, United Media, Universal Press Syndicate, and Washington Post Writer's Group.

Major News and Feature Services

Top Four News Providers

Two firms—Associated Press and United Press International—have long been the dominant sources of news in the United States. In the past two decades, however, Agence France-Presse and Reuters have gained significant numbers of newspaper subscribers. The firms primarily provide their services through telecommunication-based news and photo distribution networks, but are increasingly providing supplementary information and materials via on-line services.

Associated Press

The Associated Press is the major source for national and international news carried in U.S. newspapers. It was formed in 1848 by New York City newspapers to reduce the costs of news gathering and distribution by telegraph, and now serves more than 1,500 daily and 200 nondaily newspapers in the U.S., as well as about 8,500 subscribers outside of the United States. It employs approximately 3,300 individuals in 143 news bureaus in the United States and in more than 90 bureaus in more than 70 other countries.

The Associated Press is tied very closely to newspapers because it is a not-for-profit cooperative owned by the papers themselves. In addition to material from AP staff, the service also carries stories submitted by its members, which allows the service to provide access to even more news and feature stories. The service offers a variety of services including regional wires that provide greater amounts of news from specific states so subscribing papers in the region can emphasize coverage from their state and region.

United Press International

Created by the merger of Scripps's United Press and Hearst's International News Service in 1958, United Press International today has about 1,000 employees in ninety bureaus in seventy countries. Although it once was a strong rival to Associated Press, it was plagued by financial difficulties in the 1980s and 1990s and lost much of its strength as a competitor and—in some ways—made it possible for Agence France-Presse and Reuters to make inroads in the U.S. market. Today, new owners are attempting to update the firm's telecommunications network and have reoriented its services and marketing to small dailies in the United States.

Agence France-Presse

Begun in 1835 as Havas agency and reestablished as Agence France-Presse after World War II, this highly regarded agency employs 1,100 individuals worldwide. It serves about 8,000 newspapers throughout the world, including about 100 in the United States. AFP became an important news photo source in the 1980s when it established the first fully digitized photo distribution system.

Reuters

Begun as a financial reporting service in 1851, Reuters is now a worldwide information gathering agency that operates 138 bureaus in eighty-six countries with a staff of more than 14,000 employees, most of whom are engaged in its financial information operation, which remains the core of its operations. The news operations of this British firm are well regarded worldwide and have made the agency the most important foreign source for news in U.S. newspapers.

Major Providers of News Features and Other Materials

The bulk of editorial material is news features and non-news materials that are provided by a variety of feature services. The materials originally were dispatched to newspapers by postal and other package distribution systems, and materials not bound by time are still provided this way by many services. For materials with time value, feature providers use telecommunication-based distribution—like the news agencies—but they are also turning to on-line services as an additional means of distribution.

Copley News Service

Originally established to serve the needs of the newspapers owned by Copley Press, the products of their service are now used by more than 1,000 newspapers. The syndicate provides an outlet for editorial writers and cartoonists at Copley newspapers but is especially well known for its features on decorating, food, gardening, health, travel, and editorial material for packaged special advertising sections.

Creators Syndicate

This syndicate offers commentary from writers such as Mark Shields, Paul Harvey, Robert Novack, and Alexander Cockburn, as well as columns by Ann Landers, Molly Ivins, and David Horowitz. It carries the editorial cartoons of Herb Block and Mike Luckovich and comics such as *B.C.*, *Wizard of Id*, *Momma*, and *Archie*.

King Features

A division of the Hearst Corporation, this syndicate provides cartoons, comics, and editorial materials to nearly 2,000 newspapers worldwide. The company distributes comics such as *Sally Forth*, *Dennis the Menace*, *Beetle Bailey*, and *Blondie*. It distributes commentary by columnists such as Julianne Malveaux, Carl Rowan, and Jeffrey Hart and advice columns such as "Hints from Heloise," "A Question of Ethics," and "Ask Dr. Ruth."

Los Angeles Times Syndicate

The syndicate distributes the work of cartoonists Paul Conrad and Dan Wasserman, columnists such as Henry Kissinger, Jesse Jackson, Cal Thomas, and Jeane Kirkpatrick, and sports writers such as Jim Murray and Mike Downey.

In addition to material produced by staff at the *Los Angeles Times* and in other Times Mirror papers, the syndicate distributes materials from the Christian Science Monitor News Service, Gannett News Service, El País News Service, and the Gallup Poll.

It provides a wealth of editorial columns and materials covering topics ranging from real estate to health and fitness and astrology to crossword puzzles.

Tribune Media Services

A division of Tribune Publishing this full-service syndicate distributes comics, such as *Mother Goose & Grimm* and *Shoe*. Its distributes the work of editorial cartoonists, such as Mike Peters and Jeff MacNelly, and columns by writers such as Dave Barry, Jack Germond and Jules Witcover, Bob Green, Pat Buchanan, and Mike Royko. It distributes topical columns ranging from travel to religion and medicine to children, as well as television and stock listings.

The syndicate also distributes materials from Knight–Ridder/Tribune Information Services, McClatchy News Service, and News Wire.

United Media

United Media is a Scripps Howard Company and operates syndication services including United Feature Syndicate, Newspaper Enterprise Association and Scripps Howard News Service, which carries articles from their papers.

Its comics include *Peanuts, Marmaduke*, and *Dilbert*. Commentary comes from Michael Kinsey, Alan Dershowitz, William Rusher, and Ben Wattenberg. The syndicate's columns cover entertainment, food, health, lifestyles, and family finance. It also provides games and informational graphics, as well as articles from specialty magazines.

Universal Press Syndicate

This firm distributes comic strips such as *Garfield, Cathy*, and *Tank McNamara*, and the work of editorial cartoonists such as Jules Feiffer, Pat Oliphant, and Tony Auth. It provides commentary from writers, including Georgie Anne Geyer, William F. Buckley, Mary McGrory, and Keith Owens. Among its columns are "Dear Abby," "Your Horoscope" by Jeane Dixon, Erma Bombeck, and Roger Ebert.

Washington Post Writers Group

Originally a syndicate for writers at the *Washington Post*, the service primarily distributed social and political commentary. In recent years, it has broadened its services to include general features and comics.

Among its well-known commentators are William Raspberry, George F. Will, Ellen Goodman, Charles Krauthammer, and Donna Britt. The service also syndicates comics such as *Non Sequitur*.

ADVERTISING OPERATIONS

The advertising operations of newspapers involve the selling and creating of display, insert, and classified advertising. Display ads are those ads found throughout the paper that include information and, often, illustrations and photographs for various goods and services. Insert advertisements, sometimes called pre-print advertisements, are those not printed as part of the paper itself but added to the paper in bundles after the printing process. Classified advertising is that advertising usually found at the back of the paper in which products and services are listed in categories such as, "Automobiles," "Help Wanted," "Livestock," "Computers," and "Real Estate." Advertising departments of newspapers divide responsibilities for the different types of advertising among managers to provide for better service and attention to their specific needs (Figure 4.3)

Although newspapers carry advertisements for nearly every type of product and service available, they are dependent on a few categories for the bulk of their income: automobile and truck dealers, computer and electronics retailers, home furnishing and appliance retailers, clothing retailers, real estate brokers and developers, food and liquor retailers, and financial institutions. Although newspapers typically have hundreds of retail advertisers, most depend on about two dozen advertisers for most of their display advertising revenue—sometimes for as much as 80 to 90 percent of that total.

Individual newspapers attract advertising from both the national and local markets. National advertising typically comes from large national and multinational

FIGURE 4.3 Advertising Department Organization in a Mid-Sized Daily

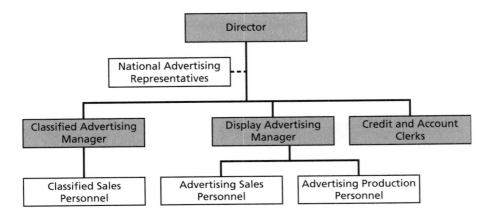

firms that have branch stores and other operations that do business in the market of those newspapers. These companies are an important source of revenue for newspapers. Individual newspapers, newspaper groups, and newspaper associations have worked closely with national advertisers in the last two decades to standardize the sizes of advertisements and to create advertising networks that make it easier for advertisers to reach newspapers and their markets nationwide. Although national advertising is important, the average newspaper gains—as noted in Chapter 3— about five to six times as much money from local advertising. Gaining local advertising requires that the newspapers maintain extensive sales forces and that they be able to design and create the advertisements themselves.

Newspapers have been the number one medium for advertising but newspapers' share of advertising expenditures is declining. It is estimated that television's share will shortly surpass that of newspapers for the first time.[1] Although the share is diminishing, actual spending has shown regular growth, as discussed in Chapter 1, and that growth is expected to continue. One can expect, however, that it will continue to be affected by expansion and contraction in the economy and by structure changes in the number of newspapers.

Ad Sales and Production

When advertising comes from national or regional sources, newspapers typically work with the advertising agencies representing firms that wish to advertise in a paper's geographic market. These agencies prepare the advertisement and ship it to the paper, which then only has to process the advertisement for printing. With local advertising, however, two-thirds or more of the advertising clients typically do not employ advertising agencies, so newspaper sales personnel work directly with the retailer in selling and then creating advertisements. Advertising sales personnel typically work on a commission basis, but usually have a small base salary or "draw."

When ads are sold and designed by sales personnel, they are then produced by an ad production staff that acquires and creates appropriate artwork and photographs and combines them with type to create a display advertisement. These ads are then reviewed and approved by the sales personnel and customers before they are published. For classified advertisements, sales personnel type ads directly into computers after talking with customers in sales offices or by telephone. The computers automatically typeset the material for use in the paper, as well as provide accounting and other records of the transaction.

About 100 newspaper representatives nationwide help newspapers sell advertising to national and regional advertisers. The companies include independent firms with whom newspapers contract for services, firms operated by newspaper groups to serve the papers they own, and firms operated by state and regional newspaper associations. Because newspapers want as much advertising a possible, it is not unusual for a newspaper to be represented by more than one firm at a time.

Because of the great differences in newspaper formats, national and regional advertisers have been faced with difficulties in preparing ads for simultaneous publication in multiple newspapers. To help alleviate the problem, more than a dozen newspapers and advertising associations and organizations cooperated in creating the Standard Advertising Unit System. The system, introduced in the 1980s, creates standard advertising widths and lengths applicable to newspapers of different column formats, and papers set rates based on those standard sizes. The system has been used to make it easier for advertisers to prepare advertising, plan budgets, and order space from newspapers nationwide.

Advertising, Circulation, and the Desirability of Newspapers

Because of the dual product nature of newspapers, the willingness of advertisers to advertise and the prices they are willing to pay are related to the success of newspapers in gaining circulation. Because advertisers make choices based on the number of readers newspapers have in a specific geographic market and their demographics, figures on newspaper circulation are critical. Such figures are problematic, however, because there are many methods used to report circulation. Papers may use a production-based figure showing the pressrun or actual number printed. Other newspapers may use a distribution-based figure based on copies delivered to homes, newsstands, news racks, and other points of distribution. Other papers may report paid circulation or paid circulation adjusted for returns and discounts, and still others may use an audience-based figure reporting household penetration—the percentage of households in the market that subscribe to the paper, readers per copy, or circulation per 1,000 population. Penetration measures are becoming the most requested audience data by major advertisers.

All of these methods are appropriate for some circumstances, but each has its own problems, and comparisons between papers using different ways are not possible. As a result, to make comparisons possible and to ensure the accuracy of circulation data, advertisers and newspapers have created organizations that verify circulation according to accepted standards. [2]

The largest and most highly regarded of these firms is the Audit Bureau of Circulations (ABC), which is used by most daily newspapers. ABC audits the circulation of newspapers to achieve a comparable net paid circulation figure, accounting for returns and discounts.

Because of the costs of those audits and the fact that they focus on paid circulation, some small daily, weekly, and alternative newspapers use other firms that verify circulation in other, less costly ways, or by other methods. Two major firms providing alternative circulation audits are Verified Audit Circulation (VAC) and Business Publications Audit of Circulation (BPA). Because many of the weekly papers are free distribution products, their circulation is often verified using standards that measure circulation based on copies of papers actually distributed.

Although newspapers face a variety of competitors for advertising dollars, research continues to show that audiences use newspapers first and most, and that newspapers are most influential when readers are searching for jobs, and buying food, automobiles, and houses. Newspapers also tend to generate audiences that are most attractive to major apparel, home furnishing, consumer electronics, and sporting goods retailers, as well as to financial institutions, travel services, and professional services. These factors, as well as the competitive advantages of format and durability, continue to make newspapers the number one advertising medium.[3] Newspapers are viewed as having strong value by local advertisers and have significant competitive advantages they can use in competition with other media.[4]

Classified ads are the prevalent way that readers seek information about automobile sales and many other desired items. A recent study shows that classifieds remain the most popular method for seeking jobs, with five out of six individuals looking for employment reading the Sunday classifieds. The Newspaper Association of America study also found that on-line job-hunting is increasing.[5] Because newspapers are so strongly tied to employment searches and many already have, or are developing, on-line abilities, they should be able to maintain their hold on that submarket of advertising if they begin using on-line employment listings as a subsidiary operation.

The potential for competition from other providers of on-line classified employment and real estate listings has recently led some newspapers to begin rejecting advertisements from services providing competing listings.

Advertising Pricing

The price charged for advertising is primarily influenced by circulation, the demographics of readers, what others are charging for similar ads, production services required, and the general condition of the local economy. Newspapers generally charge different rates for different categories of advertising and provide discounts on bulk purchases of advertising space and for republishing the same ad materials. Although the size of an ad is a factor in price, the other factors play more of a role in price differences overall. The prices charged for pre-print/insert advertising are influenced by those factors, but they are also strongly affected by the availability of other delivery services, such as weekly papers or shoppers, which provide total market coverage, or the presence of advertising mail services.

Newspaper advertising managers have traditionally ignored economics when setting advertising rates, and tend to rely on intuition and what others in the industry are doing.[6] Part of the reason that demand has not been so important in setting ad rates is that most papers set them annually and publish them in rate cards that are provided to advertisers. Newspapers have been able to maintain this practice because of the lack of markets in which direct competition exists with other papers, and because newspaper advertising personnel often sell display (retail) ads at prices below those listed in the rate cards. The prices are usually maintained at rate card levels for national advertisers but, even then, research has shown that price does not play a important role in whether or not national advertisers purchase newspaper ads.[7] The price of advertising in weekly newspapers also seems to follow similar patterns, with the distance between a weekly and a competing daily, weekly, or shopper or broadcast stations not affecting its advertising prices.[8]

Getting Ads to Newspapers

Because newspapers are widely dispersed throughout the nation, the actual process of getting an advertisement from a national or regional advertiser to one or to all newspapers is important. The time and money required for distribution are important factors. Because timeliness is a factor in much advertising, advertisers as well as newspapers wish to reduce the time between an ad leaving the advertiser's office and when it appears in the paper. Newspapers and advertisers also wish to reduce the costs for preparing the ad for printing.

To help achieve these goals, newspapers are moving rapidly to have advertising agencies deliver advertisements in digital form on floppy disks or storage cartridges rather than in the traditional hard copy. Digital advertisements improve the reproduction quality of ads and reduce the work required at newspapers because they can be downloaded directly into the newspaper's pagination system.

Methods to improve delivery have already appeared. AD/SAT, a private firm, is now sending material directly to newspapers via satellite, and the Associated Press has developed and begun operating a satellite distribution service called AdSend that uses digital technology. Some other advertisers and ad agencies are experimenting with the development of web sites that newspapers can access to get completed advertisements and artwork.

With the development of digital standards and an integrated services digital network (ISDN) most ads will ultimately be delivered to the newspaper by telephone or satellite, decreasing the lead time needed for an ad to reach newspapers nationwide. This change will have significant implications regarding employment, because it will allow reduction in the size of advertising composing staffs.

To help speed this process, the Newspaper Association of America formed a task force on the topic of digital advertising in 1994 to try to establish standards that newspapers, advertisers, and technology providers can agree upon. The group is concerned not merely with issues of how advertisements should be formatted and transmitted, but how improvements can be made in an entire range of operations from the creation to reproduction of ads.

CIRCULATION OPERATIONS

Circulation departments are responsible for selling and delivering the newspaper product to readers. Although seemingly simple, this is one of the most complex operations of the newspaper and is heavily labor intensive. The duties of circulation departments include a wide variety of marketing activities, including advertising, sales promotion, and telemarketing, designed to sell subscriptions and boost single-copy sales. In addition, circulation departments must organize and operate distribution systems that provide timely and proper delivery to homes and businesses. Finally, circulation departments have the duty of collecting payments from readers. The structure of circulation departments reflects the complexity of their operations (Figure 4.4).

Distribution Systems

Three major types of distribution systems are used by newspapers. The primary system used for delivery of daily newspapers is independent distributorships. This type of distribution arrangement was found in about three-fourths of papers. Under this system, independent distributors purchase copies from the newspapers at wholesale prices and sell to subscribers or single-copy buyers at retail prices on assigned subscription routes or in assigned single-copy sales locations.

Contract distributors or agents, who are paid a set fee for delivering each subscription or servicing retail outlets, are used in about 15 percent of papers. About 10 percent of papers use employees who receive hourly wages or salaries for distribution. The use of employees for servicing subscribers has been declining in daily

FIGURE 4.4   Circulation Department Organization in a Mid-Sized Daily

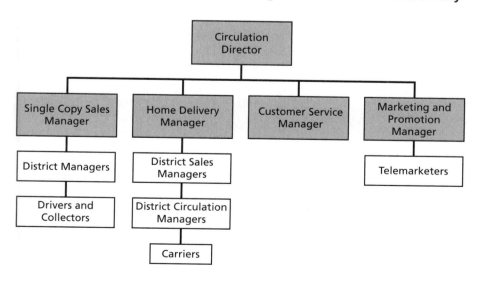

newspapers because there is rarely sufficient work to keep them busy for a full workday and the costs of salaries and benefits are very high.

Circulation Pricing

Circulation policies and pricing have traditionally not been a great concern of publishers, most of whom have maintained distribution and collection systems established long before their employment and most of whom have set circulation prices based on industry averages rather than economic factors.[9] Because of the lack of attention to pricing, the amount that circulation contributes to revenues has declined over time and now accounts for only about 15 percent of income in some papers. Rising production, labor, and circulation costs, and changes in advertisers' purchasing habits in recent years are leading some publishers to reconsider their practices and prices.

Economic studies have revealed that publishers in markets with one daily newspaper need not be overly fearful of the consequences of reasonable circulation rate increases because demand for daily newspapers by media consumers is generally inelastic over time—that is, when the price for a paper changes, it is not accompanied by a significant change in consumer demand for the paper. Studies have concluded that circulation price increases are not harmful and that newspapers are currently underpriced and are losing potential revenue.[10]

Newspapers that operate as monopolies have the ability to increase circulation prices without significant fear of competition because barriers to entry into newspaper markets are prohibitive. If a new competitor should seek to enter the daily newspaper market, the existing paper enjoys economies of scale—cost savings for each copy printed created by spreading production costs across the larger number of papers printed—that the new paper would not enjoy. The existing paper can use these economies and circulation price discounting to compete vigorously with the new entry.

Daily newspapers operating in monopoly situations have the opportunity of selecting the optimal circulation size and price per copy or subscription to maximize revenues and minimize expenses. This can be done with less concern about the behavior of competitors, which normally affects economic decisions in other, more competitive industries. This engineering of profit is easily done in monopoly newspaper markets because there is no need to achieve the highest possible circulation. In such situations, papers can reduce circulation by raising prices or can cease circulation in unprofitable geographical areas or where the demographics of readers are not as desirable to advertisers. Cathleen Black, former chair of the Newspaper Association of America, recently reported that this strategy has been responsible for many changes in newspaper circulation: "While audited numbers continue to show circulation declines at many daily newspapers, much of it is due to internal business decisions newspapers are making in adjusting to changing market fundamentals."[11]

This was done by cutting fringe distribution and becoming more aggressive in circulation pricing.

The effects of competition on prices is clearly seen in markets where competition is low and adjacent markets where it is high. In south Florida, for example, the *Miami Herald* charged 35 cents for single copies in Dade County, but only 25 cents in Broward County, where the Ft. Lauderdale *Sun-Sentinel* was available for 25 cents. When the *Sun-Sentinel* raised its price to 35 cents cover increased costs, the *Herald* immediately followed suit for its Broward County edition. A similar differential in prices is seen in southern California, where the *Los Angeles Times* is available for 35 cents in Los Angeles County but for 25 cents in Orange County, where it faces stiff competition from the *Orange County Register*, which sells at 25 cents.

In markets in which two or more daily newspapers compete, the newspaper with the largest circulation and highest market penetration receives a disproportionate amount of advertising revenue, even when the circulation differences are small.[12] Thus, competitive papers must continually seek to increase circulation lest they fall prey to the circulation spiral phenomenon, caused by the newspaper with the largest circulation share getting a disproportionate share of the advertising.[13] Because secondary paper(s) have fewer financial resources, they then cannot provide content that is as attractive to readers, resulting in a decline in circulation, which in turn causes a decline in advertising, putting the paper into a downward spiral of circulation and advertising losses until it ceases publishing. Because of the impact of circulation on advertising, many of the second newspapers competing in multi-newspaper markets such as Boston, Chicago, Denver, Los Angeles, and New York are experiencing difficulties.

More than 99 percent of all newspaper markets are noncompetitive in the sense that they have no head-to-head local daily newspaper competitor, however. Publishers in these markets need not be as greatly concerned about circulation levels as their counterparts in competitive markets. Such publishers need only ensure that the market penetration of their paper is strong and not vulnerable to a new daily newspaper entering the market or so low as to induce significant use of substitute media by advertisers. The only other important concern regarding circulation for these publishers is the engineering of profit by choosing any reasonable price and circulation quantity combination to yield optimal results.

The practice of cutting circulation has increased in the past two decades with papers halting circulation to areas where readers don't interest advertisers—such as inner cities or districts with lower incomes or other unwanted demographics—or where distribution costs are higher. Although these practices may serve the interests of the economic role of newspapers, they are harmful to newspapers' social roles of conveying information and providing the communication links necessary for a healthy society.

A few circulation studies related to chain-owned papers have been undertaken in recent years and have concluded that papers owned by newspaper groups tend to charge more for monthly subscriptions than independent papers. These results should not be surprising, because managers of chain-owned newspapers emphasize financial performance more than those at independent papers and place greater emphasis on pricing behavior.[14]

The average industry retail price for daily newspapers is 25 cents and the average Sunday retail price is 50 cents. These prices have been moved upward in recent years, with about 10 percent of all papers now charging 35 cents daily and 16 percent charging one dollar for Sunday papers.[15] Over time, the prices for Sunday newspapers have risen more quickly than the prices for daily newspapers (Figure 4.5).

Gannett is an industry leader in moving prices upward. Allen Neuharth, former chairman of the board of Gannett, continues to urge newspaper managers to raise circulation prices, noting the relative inelasticity of demand on circulation.[16] Monopoly markets are able to absorb such rate increases, so subscription prices typically increase when a market changes from competition to monopoly through cessation of publication or merger. Nevertheless, newspapers in the average monopoly newspaper market have had lower subscription rates than papers in the average competing market, although their single-copy prices are not significantly different.[17] The lower prices in monopoly markets appear to be the result of fear of increasing prices, whereas the higher prices in competing markets seem to be the result of the need to cover costs.

FIGURE 4.5 Average (Mode) Single-Copy Price

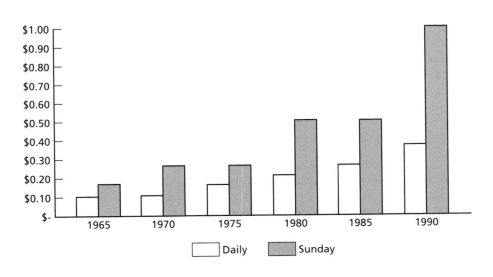

One difficulty with setting circulation prices comes from the fact that the most common delivery system relies on independent distributors. Because these are independent businessmen and women who purchase papers for resale, newspapers do not set the sales price but can print a suggested retail price for subscriptions. Some newspapers have encountered difficulties by discouraging distributors from setting prices different from the suggested retail price, because some of their actions, designed to maintain the suggested price, have violated provisions of antitrust laws involving price-fixing, leaving them vulnerable to prosecution and litigation.

The price markup from variable costs—the actual costs to produce each additional copy— to average retail price for a single copy of a newspaper is about 100 to 130 percent. The average price markup from wholesale to retail price for single copies and subscriptions is about 40 percent.

Collection Types

Collection is the term used for getting payment from subscribers. The primary means used by papers has been for their independent distributors or agents to collect payments from subscribers and then forward payment to the paper after taking their percentage or fee from the amount collected.

In greater numbers of papers, however, pay-by-mail collection is now being used. Today, about one-third of papers have bills delivered or mailed to subscribers, and payments are then mailed back directly to the paper. The paper then calculates and makes the payments that are owed to distribution personnel. Newspaper managers prefer this system because it reduces the number of individuals that must handle and record payments and does not require that delivery personnel find a time when subscribers are at home in order to collect.

In order to avoid collection issues, some newspaper managers have been promoting paid-in-advance subscriptions or credit card payments for subscriptions, but those practices have not been significantly embraced by subscribers.

The Problem of "Churn"

Although newspaper circulation has been relatively stable in broad terms, individual newspapers daily face the problem of turnover in newspaper readers. This turnover, or *churn* is caused by different subscribers simultaneously placing orders to start or stop subscriptions. Circulation departments thus devote a significant amount of their marketing efforts to reduce circulation churn and increase circulation.

Churn is a measure of the percentage of subscribers that are replaced each year to maintain the same level of subscribed circulation. The churn rate increases as the circulation size of the newspaper increases (Table 4.1). This occurs because newspapers with less circulation tend to be the most significant source of local information and advertising in smaller markets and thus cannot be easily replaced by other media. Also, smaller publications tend to reflect their readers more closely and thus generate greater loyalty from them.

One of the major reasons given by subscribers who start and then stop a subscription is the lack of time to read the paper or the whole paper. When they feel they are not getting their money's worth and don't take the time to read the paper, they will not renew their subscriptions for the next period. One reason smaller newspapers tend to have less churn may be the result of their size and scope. Smaller newspapers tend to have fewer pages than those with larger circulations, thus reducing the time needed to read the paper, and smaller papers often have a strong local emphasis that may more closely match the interests of readers and thus keep them interested in reading.

The greatest amount of churn occurs among new subscribers rather than long-term subscribers. This is especially true among subscribers gained through special marketing campaigns in fringe areas or those who probably would not have purchased a trial subscription if they were not offered very large discounts. When the discount is no longer available, many of these subscribers are not likely to renew.

The problem has been growing in recent years as newspapers have more aggressively moved into marketing to potential subscribers, a move necessary to maintain and increase circulation levels. By the early 1990s the growth of churn led the industry to study the problem of how to overcome it and retain existing subscribers. It issued a report showing that the elements most likely to help reduce churn are developing a complaint resolution system to deal with customer problems rapidly and reducing available discounts because they produce unstable circulation.[18]

PHOTOGRAPHY AND GRAPHICS OPERATIONS

Photography and graphics are important functions needed for the production of all parts of the newspaper, in the editorial as well as advertising sections, in news sections as well as all other sections.

TABLE 4.1 Average Churn Rates for Different Circulation Groups

Below 25,000	30 percent
25,000 to 50,000	42 percent
50,000 to 100,000	60 percent
100,000 to 200,000	71 percent
200,000 to 400,000	66 percent
Above 400,000	68 percent

In most papers photography functions are served by a photography division of the editorial department This office serves news and feature needs through *photojournalism* and provides photo services needed for ads by the advertising department. In larger papers, advertising departments may have a permanent photographer or photo staff, and some feature sections may have photographers permanently assigned to their operations, who may or may not work under the supervision of a newsroom photo division. In smaller papers these services tend to be centralized, but in larger papers some graphic artists are increasingly being located in major feature section offices.

Photographers are daily given assignments of planned events for which they are to provide photo coverage or other photo assignments needed by the various departments. Although the photo editor will hold some staff time in reserve for unexpected breaking stories, all photographers regularly have their assignments adjusted and altered to meet the constantly changing needs and priorities of the news operation. As a result, photographers have traditionally had and continue to use the most advanced communication systems available to link them to the newsroom from the field.

Although traditional chemical-based photography remains the mainstay of newspaper operations, the development of digital electronic cameras is now allowing photographers to send photos directly from the field via satellite or digital networks, reducing their need to constantly return to the darkroom to process film. Even though most newspapers still use traditional photography to capture images, fewer and fewer are actually making prints from the negatives. Most now use digital equipment to scan the negatives and produce computerized images that can be selected and edited directly in the computer as part of the pagination process.

The visual appearance of newspapers has received significant attention during the past two decades and newspapers spend a great deal of staff time creating a visual style for their publications. Some pursue this style as part of the layout process done by editors and copy desks, but many are now setting up separate graphics divisions associated with copy desks. In addition to providing page design services, these graphics divisions are called on to create informational graphics, including charts, graphs, maps, and illustrations that help illustrate various elements of stories.

BUSINESS OPERATIONS

Business operations include those administrative and general business operations not delegated to specific departments. In most newspapers, the business offices handle accounting, billing, insurance for the company and its employees, payroll, personnel matters, and general promotional activities. As the size of the newspaper increases, however, these duties may be broken out into separate departments, especially human relations departments and promotion departments. It is also more likely that, as the size of a paper increases, its advertising and circulation departments will handle their own billing and collection activities.

When newspapers are parts of groups, some business activities may be centralized into the group headquarters or into regional or division headquarters for cost savings purposes, especially if the individual newspapers are small.

PRODUCTION OPERATIONS

Production operations of the newspaper include all those activities occurring after content materials have left the editorial and advertising departments, including composition, camera work and platemaking, printing, and inserting and bundling (Figure 4.6). Production departments are also often responsible for building and grounds maintenance. Depending on the type of production technology used in a paper, it may begin with taking material set by editorial and advertising departments and laying it out on paste-up boards as pages. In papers where pagination systems are in place, this part of the production process is done electronically by graphics and layout persons in the editorial department.

Once this initial step has been taken, images of the pages must be made and transferred onto the presses for use in printing. A variety of methods are used. Among the most common is chemical engraving of a metal plate that is then placed on the press. Although this process is an improvement over previous methods, it remains time consuming and costly. Because of advances in laser and ink-jet printing, there is hope that those or related technologies can be adapted for cost-efficient newspaper application to create a method that skips the intermediate step and allows images to go directly to printers in the future.

Newspapers are increasingly using flexible and integrated press systems that allow them to print color on any page in the paper and to print not only in folios of four pages but to include two-page sheets where needed. Much of the impetus for these improvements has come from advertiser requests for improved color capabilities and the desire to be able to incrementally increase the number of pages in various sections.

After papers are printed they are combined with previously printed materials, including insert advertising and sections not subject to the immediacy deadlines of news sections, and bundled for delivery. In years past, these post-press activities were labor-intensive, using large numbers of unskilled employees, and were quite time-consuming. As costs of labor have risen, newspapers have increasingly adopted a wide variety of mechanized and computer-controlled inserting, sorting, and bundling equipment to perform these tasks. The types of equipment found in particular papers vary widely, but because mechanization offers not only cost savings but increased speed in the production process, the amount and capabilities of the equipment increase with the circulation size of papers.

FIGURE 4.6   Organization of the Production Department in a Mid-Sized Daily

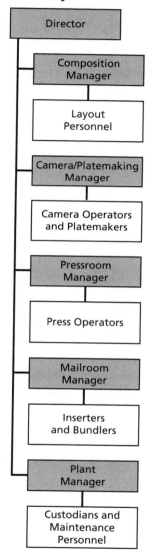

A continuing issue in the production of newspapers is the use of newsprint. The costliest item for newspapers, newsprint accounts for as much as one-third of all operating costs for many papers. For many years newspapers have worked to reduce the waste of newsprint in the production process, but the consumption of newsprint has continued to rise as newspapers have increased their pages to provide more and more features and sections designed to appeal to readers. Between 1970 and 1994, newsprint consumption in the United States increased 30 percent, while the number of newspapers decreased about 12 percent and total circulation decreased 5 percent.

Beginning in 1995 the issue of newsprint prices became particularly important because the price of newsprint increased tremendously, immediately putting a lot of pressure on the 1995 budgets of publishers. The problem was particularly distressing to them because they had been enjoying declining prices (in real terms) for nearly two decades. In 1980, for example, newsprint was available at an average price of $440 per metric ton. By 1994, the price (adjusted for inflation) was only $241 (see Figure 4.7). The sudden price rise in 1995, a 30 percent jump by midyear, came as the recession that affected advertising demand in the first half of the 1990s ended, creating an immediate demand for larger newspapers. Newsprint producers, meanwhile, had been reducing production throughout the time because of lack of demand. The intersecting of those forces as well environmental requirements for recycled newsprint resulted in the price increase.

SUBSIDIARY OPERATIONS

Although the primary business of newspapers is producing newspapers, many operate subsidiary operations that including total market coverage free circulation

FIGURE 4.7   Newsprint List Prices (per metric ton)

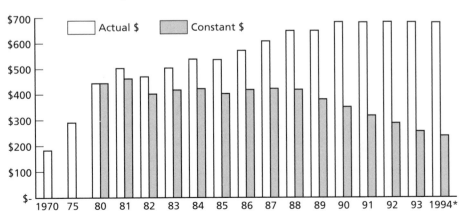

*Based on NAA data showing end of the year list prices, converted to 30-pound weight basis.

papers, specialized advertising publications for homes and autos, audio-text services, on-line services, general advertising services, and public printing services.

The amount and extent of these operations are usually dictated by the time available to use existing printing equipment, other types of media already present in a market, and the size of the community. In smaller communities, the newspaper may use the printing press only a few hours daily and have the only available printing press, so it may be able to do a significant amount of work from job printing. In a large metropolitan area, the newspaper will typically need to use its presses for a much larger portion of every day, and its press capabilities may make it unable or undesirable for it to undertake a significant amount of small job printing. Weekly newspapers nationwide that own presses, especially those in smaller communities, count on job printing for a significant amount of their revenue. In some cases, it is the job printing that makes it possible to keep the newspaper publishing.

Subsidiary operations using electronic media, such as fax newspapers, telephone audio services, and on-line information services, have developed rapidly in the past two decades as newspapers prepare for changes in media use that are occurring and will have greater effect in the twenty-first century. The nature and extent of these operations will be discussed in future chapters.

ENDNOTES

1. Tony Case, "A Rocky Road Predicted for Newspaper Ads," *Editor & Publisher* (September 23, 1995), 128: 27.

2. Charles O. Bennett, *Facts Without Opinion* (Chicago: Audit Bureau of Circulations, 1965).

3. Newspaper Association of America, *Why Newspapers? They Add Value for Advertisers* (New York: Newspaper Association of America, 1994).

4. Glen T. Cameron, Glen T. Nowak, and Dean M. Krugman, "The Competitive Position of Newspapers in the Local Retail Market," *Newspaper Research Journal* 14 (Summer/Fall 1993): 70–81.

5. Dorothy Giobbe, "Study: Classified Ads Remain Most Popular Source for Finding a Job," *Editor & Publisher* (August 5, 1995), 128: 20.

6. Robert G. Picard, "Rate-Setting and Competition in Newspaper Advertising," *Newspaper Research Journal* 3 (April 1982):23–33.

7. John C. Busterna, "The Cross-Elasticity of Demand for National Newspaper Advertising," *Journalism Quarterly* 64 (Summer–Autumn 1987), 346–351.

8. William B. Blankenburg, "Determinants of Pricing of Advertising in Weeklies," *Journalism Quarterly* 57 (Winter 1980): 663–666.

9 Edmund Landau and John Scott Davenport, "Price Anomalies of the Mass Media," *Journalism Quarterly* 36 (Summer 1959):291-294.

10. Regina Lewis, "Relation Between Newspaper Subscription Price and Circulation, 1971–1992," *Journal of Media Economics* 8 (1995):25–41 ; Robert G. Picard, "The Effect of Price Increases on Newspaper Circulation: A Case Study of Inelasticity of Demand," *Newspaper Research Journal* 12 (Summer 1991): 65–75; Robert G. Picard, "Pricing

Behavior of Newspapers," in Picard, Winter, McCombs, and Lacy, Eds., 1988; Robert W. Field, "Circulation Price Inelasticity in the Daily Newspaper Industry" (M.A. Thesis, Norman: University of Oklahoma, 1978); Jeff Clark, "Circulation Increase Despite Higher Subscription Rates," *Editor & Publisher* (February 4, 1976): 32; Gerald Grotta, "Daily Newspaper Circulation Price Inelastic for 1970–75," *Journalism Quarterly* 54 (Summer 1977):379–382 .

11. "Lower Circulation Lifts Readership, NAA Chief Asserts," *Editor & Publisher* (May 20, 1995), p.11.

12. John G. Udell, *The Economics of the American Daily Newspaper* (New York: Hastings House, 1978).

13. Lars Furhoff, "Some Reflections on Newspaper Concentration," *Scandinavian Economic History Review* 21 (1973):1–27 and Karl Erik Gustafsson, "The Circulation Spiral and the Theory of Household Coverage," *Scandinavian Economic History Review* 28 (1978):1–14 .

14. William Blankenburg, "Newspaper Ownership and Control of Circulation to Increase Profits," *Journalism Quarterly* 59 (Autumn 1982):390–398 ; F. Dennis Hale, "An In-Depth Look at Chain Ownership," *Editor & Publisher* (April 28, 1984): 30ff.; Robert G. Picard, "Pricing Behavior of Newspapers," pp. 55–69 in Picard, Winter, McCombs, and Lacy, Eds.,1988; Press Concetration and monopoly: New Perspectives on Newspaper Ownership and Operation John Soloski, "Economics and Management: The Real Influence of Newspaper Groups," *Newspaper Research Journal* 1 (November 1979):19–28.

15. Newspaper Association of America, *Facts about Newspapers* (Reston, VA: Newspaper Association of America, 1994).

16. "Neuharth Urges Higher Newspaper Prices," *Editor & Publisher* (October 26, 1985): 20.

17. Gerald Grotta, "Consolidation of Newspapers: What Happens to the Consumer," *Journalism Quarterly* 48 (Summer 1971):245–250 and Robert G. Picard, "Pricing in Competing and Monopoly Newspapers, 1972–1982," *LSU School of Journalism Research Bulletin* (1986).

18. Newspaper Association of America, *NAA Subscriber Churn Management Handbook* (Reston, VA: Newspaper Association of America, 1995).

5

A Day in the Life of a Newspaper

The daily newspaper industry is unique among manufacturers in that it creates a new product every day, 365 days a year. Although the format of the newspaper, whether it is a broadsheet or a tabloid, stays the same—and many sections and features are constant—the actual editorial and advertising content and layout of the newspaper, sections, and features change daily.

Newspaper editors monitor events within their communities and advertising managers stay on top of market trends and advertising demand. No one can predict tomorrow's headlines or the amount and type of classified and display advertising that will appear in next Tuesday's edition.

Newspapers work under deadline pressure and are subject to the vagaries of the day's events, not only within their circulation areas, but across the country and around the world. A breaking news story—such as an earthquake, airplane crash, or civil unrest—can change the entire news plan for a day. The sudden merger of two rival supermarket chains or the closing of a major department store can have a major impact on the amount of advertising space sold and the normal operations of an advertising department.

Because news can happen at any time most newspapers have editorial staffers working almost around the clock or on call for major news events. Because circulation sales efforts, especially telemarketing, must take place when potential subscribers are at home, sales personnel often work in the evenings. Because retail advertising sales visits target businessmen and women, they normally must take place during conventional business hours. The ways that newspapers structure their work days must take into account all of these factors.

The primary factor in the production cycle for newspapers is whether the paper is a morning or evening paper. Morning papers typically close their editorial operating cycle about 11 p.m. and evening papers typically close their editorial operating cycle about 11 a.m. The needs of morning and evening distribution create significantly different operating cycles for each type of paper (Figure 5.1). The most immediately visible difference is that morning papers tend to need employees and managers in their facilities twenty four hours a day, whereas afternoon papers are able to have a four to eight hour downtime period for most employees and managers overnight.

FIGURE 5.1 Production Cycles of Morning and Evening Newspapers

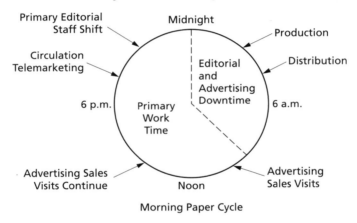

Morning Paper Cycle

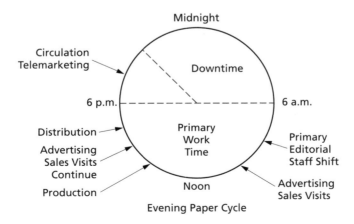

Evening Paper Cycle

Most reporters and editors working for morning papers will typically depart before midnight, but it is not unusual for a few reporters to be at their desks after midnight at an afternoon newspaper because they are completing stories about meetings of governmental bodies—such as city councils or school boards—that meet at night, or writing stories about the night's police or fire activities for the next day's paper. Because of the differences in cycles, afternoon newspapers have some advantages over morning counterparts in covering city councils, school boards, and other evening events with more depth, especially in smaller towns and suburbs where elected officials typically work at other jobs during the day and schedule governmental meetings at night.

Although the content of the newspaper changes daily, the most important local, state, national, and international news are traditionally published or highlighted on the front page to gain reader interest and promote single-copy sales. Although the days of children hawking newspapers on street corners are over, editors still display the most prominent articles with big, bold headlines above the fold to boost sales in circulation racks.

Depending on the size of the newspaper, the rest of the day's news and features is parceled out in sections. In mid- to large-size newspapers, one section usually contains the front page and state, national, and local news. The second section often contains metropolitan or local news, editorial pages, and obituaries; a third section will contain human interest articles, columns, social events, and comic pages; a fourth section will contain sports, giving a complete account of local prep, high school, and college sports, as well as professional athletics. Larger papers may have additional sections for business and entertainment news, and almost every paper has a weekly food section to help support supermarket advertising. Special advertising supplements, as well as special sections focusing on specific news events, such as fires, floods, or visits by the president, may occur throughout the year.

Preparation of the various elements of a newspaper goes on constantly. Work on special sections is usually assigned weeks and months in advance and is accomplished along with daily activities, during lulls in the preparation of materials for the next day's paper. Sunday papers, which often have significant sections devoted to nonbreaking news—such as travel sections, special entertainment and book sections, and enlarged opinion sections—will have those sections produced during the week, often with Thursday or Friday deadlines. Work in various departments, including advertising sales, business activities, circulation, editorial, and production takes place simultaneously, with all the efforts converging to meet the final deadlines. In order to even the flow of work and make it possible to adjust for unexpected events, different functions and preparation of different newspaper sections have different deadlines throughout the day. Advertising production, feature sections, business, and other materials that don't require writing and editing late in the cycle are prepared earlier.

The publication time, the size of the paper, the size of the community, production and printing equipment used, and a variety of other technical and financial factors influence the exact time events take place in the cycles of specific papers, but the events in the daily cycle are comparable for most papers. To illustrate the sequence, this chapter will follow a day in the life of a morning newspaper.

A MORNING PAPER'S DAILY CYCLE

The cycle of newspaper production is continuous and most newspaper facilities are never completely empty or closed as different activities must take place throughout the day and night. A number of major time periods of activity exist and, for a morning paper, the cycle includes work that can be divided into morning, mid-morning, early afternoon, early evening, mid-evening, midnight, and early morning activities.

Although completing the next day's edition is the primary goal every day, personnel from all the paper's departments simultaneously carry out work that is necessary to produce editions for the day-after-tomorrow, next week, next month, and even as much as three months ahead.

Morning

The earliest staff to arrive are typically editorial employees, who begin arriving after dawn, bleary-eyed, to read through material provided by news services to determine what has occurred throughout the world overnight and to begin checking police and other emergency agencies for overnight activities. These initial morning news reviews and contacts, usually completed between 6 a.m. and 8 a.m., are made to catch up on events and to plan activities that will be needed during the day to follow up on the important ones.

Because newspapers have traditionally placed a heavy emphasis on crime and emergency coverage, reporters may call or visit police departments as much as half a dozen times during a twenty-four-hour period. Like the initial morning contacts with police departments, reporters also use the time to contact fire departments, hospitals, the coroner's office, the district attorney's office, and other relevant agencies such as the Coast Guard, Border Patrol, FBI, and state police for information on events that have occurred since the last contact.

The newsroom really comes to life between 8 a.m. and 10 a.m. as more reporters and editors arrive. Editors begin creating a news budget—a list of stories to be prepared by staff reporters as well as stories available from news services that may be used in the next issue. Reporters begin checking their beats for more tips and stories and general assignment reporters are given assignments by editors.

Most newspapers assign reporters to cover specific topics or beats such as cities, county government, courts, education, business, police, politics, religion, or science/health. Newspapers also tailor beats to meet the demands of news coverage and the needs of subscribers. The *Detroit Free Press* and *Detroit News*, for example, cover the automobile industry in detail. The *Los Angeles Times* has beats covering the entertainment industries. Papers located adjacent to major military bases may have a military affairs beat. Newspapers in areas with large immigrant populations may have immigration beats, and metropolitan newspapers with large inner cities may have specialists on minority affairs. The Orange County *Register*, in suburban Southern California, won notoriety for assigning a reporter to cover shopping malls.

When a journalist finds a story on his or her beat, the reporter writes a short note to his or her editor summarizing the story and identifying it with a key word or short slug line. These one-paragraph summaries or budget notes are placed on a master news budget list that is tracked by editors throughout the day.

Newspapers keep some reporters for general assignment, that is, to cover stories not related to specific beats or to be shifted to assist a particular beat if an unusual number of stories or stories requiring extensive work arise on a particular day. These reporters take their assignments directly from editors but are also encouraged to suggest news and feature stories on which they might work.

Mid-Morning

As traditional office hours begin, business, advertising, and circulation offices begin operations and continue throughout the usual eight-hour work day. Classified advertising sales representatives begin answering telephone calls from customers wishing to place classified advertisements for employment, used cars, personals, and other categories. After a brief meeting—which can be either informal or formal depending on the size of the paper and the preferences of the advertising director—to coordinate activities, announce upcoming special sections, issues, or promotions, and to discuss problems, salespersons for display advertising begin contacting customers to whom they have been assigned, as well as soliciting new business in their territories. At the same time, clerks in the circulation department accept orders and update subscription and distribution lists. Accountants and clerks in the business offices order supplies, send and pay bills, and prepare the payroll.

By mid-morning reporters begin leaving the newsroom to conduct interviews, gather materials, and cover news events taking place during the day. Editors meet to discuss what the next issue of the paper will look like.

This meeting often takes place around 11 a.m., with senior editors and section editors conferring about events that are shaping the day and which stories they believe should appear in the next paper. The editor and managing editor usually sit behind their desks or at the head of a conference table and listen as the business editor, city editor, features editor, photo editor, and wire editor present their individual news budgets and pitch stories for inclusion on the front page. There is much give and take at these meetings as decisions are made about the placement of stories and the amount of space that will be devoted to them. Also present is an air of uncertainty. Suggestions, sidebar stories, and new angles or different approaches to stories are raised and discussed. Everyone knows that the thrust of a story can change within minutes: A hostage situation can end peacefully or in a hail of bullets; a winning team can smother its opponent or be crushed in an upset; a surprise announcement from the White House can preempt space for a local story. A small wire story about an increase in interest rates in Japan may turn into a big local story if it has a major effect on a local manufacturer.

The meeting ends with a general plan for the next issue in place, and the bulk of that plan will normally be seen in the following day's paper, subject to sudden changes for breaking news or the success or failure of journalists in producing the assigned and expected stories.

Early Afternoon

The editorial department begins moving into a deadline pace by early afternoon. Pressure mounts first on those producing the feature, food, entertainment, and other sections that are less constrained by time and will be the first to go into production. Line editors review story drafts with reporters, request additions or revisions, and then pass on the completed stories to the copy desk where they are edited, given a headline, and laid out on the page.

By afternoon the classified advertising section for the following day is also passed on to production, and any new advertisements obtained later during the day will not be included until subsequent issues.

Mid-Afternoon

By mid-afternoon the newsroom begins buzzing with activity as reporters return from assignments, begin banging out their stories on word processors, grab phones to find more information, and pace beside their desks searching for the right word or phrase. Unexpected stories that have developed suddenly during the day are thrust on reporters, who must rapidly develop information and find time in their schedules to write the story. Although some anticipated stories fizzle or must be postponed, most stories included in the news budget are developing or being completed by mid-afternoon.

Advertising sales personnel begin returning to write sales reports and to begin preparing advertising copy for future issues.

Concurrently, a basic plan for the paper to be printed two days later is completed. This plan includes the number of pages scheduled by the publisher or general manager, and is passed on to the advertising department, which creates page dummies indicating the positions of all scheduled advertising.

Production personnel then complete creation of specific ads and begin laying them out on the pages in preparation for the next day's activities. This process continues throughout the afternoon and evening as schedules and the time needed to produce the following day's paper permit.

Early Evening

About 5 p.m., senior editors meet again to finalize the news budget. The wire editor outlines the top international, national, and state stories available from news services. The city editor pitches the best local stories. The photo editor presents proofs of the day's best shots. The managing editor and editor then weigh each story in terms of its impact and art. At newspapers with art directors, potential layouts, graphics, and story packages with photographs and illustrations are discussed.

Soon four to eight stories are selected for the front page, for the cover of the local or metro section, and for other sections that have yet to be completed. As the evening progresses, each section will be completed and sent to production in ascending order of importance, with the front page being delivered last.

Because many of the newspaper's customers and potential customers are away from home during the day, circulation offices often stay open in the evening to accept orders, to handle customer complaints, and to solicit subscribers with telemarketing.

Late Evening

Throughout the evening materials and layouts for the remaining sections of the paper are completed in the newsroom and sent to production, with a few pages withheld for breaking news and sports (because of night games). Although production personnel can rapidly remake a page for a late-breaking story, the bulk of the sections and pages must be completed and ready for placement on presses at least an hour before printing time.

Beginning in the late evening hours and lasting long after midnight, janitorial personnel begin moving throughout various newspaper departments, timing their appearance to coincide with the end of the work day in those offices so that their activities do not interfere with ongoing work.

Midnight

Press operators typically begin rolling the presses at midnight and, depending on the circulation and capacity of the presses, will finish their printing by 4 a.m. As papers come off the press line, they are bundled and placed in trucks for delivery to homes and news racks. If the paper delivers to a large geographic area, trucks will begin departing shortly after midnight, as soon as they are filled. If the paper is delivered to a smaller area, they may not depart until later in the morning hours.

Very Early Morning

Trucks deliver bundles of papers to news racks or delivery points where they are picked up by circulation personnel who make home deliveries.

Nationwide, circulation managers strive to have the paper in driveways and on doorsteps before 6:30 a.m., in time for subscribers to peruse the papers at breakfast and before they go to work. Prompt and punctual as letter carriers used to be, delivery personnel must be prepared to deliver newspapers in rain, snow, sleet, and other inclement weather.

WEEKLY NEWSPAPERS

Weekly newspapers have an entire week in which to produce their editions but operate with much smaller staffs than their daily counterparts. As a result, employees at weeklies must be able to carry out a wide variety of functions, often simultaneously. An average weekly may divide duties among the publisher, ad salesperson, editor, and office manager. The publisher may handle not only business responsibilities but sometimes even promotional, advertising sales, and circulation duties. At extremely small papers, he or she may additionally handle the editor's duties.

The staff works toward the printing deadline, usually the afternoon prior to the day of distribution. The ad salesperson will usually do his or her own creation and pasteup of advertisements. The editor will not only write stories and edit those from syndicates and stringers (part-time correspondents), but punch them into the computer or typesetting equipment and handle layout and pasteup of editorial material as well. Because most weeklies contract for printing, the production process generally ceases at layout, either in electronic form or in the form of pasteup sheets. These layouts are then taken to a printing company for final production.

Unlike dailies, which must operate every day, weekly papers have opportunities to close on Saturdays and Sundays, except when events require weekend editorial coverage, so staffs at weeklies typically work on a five-day workweek cycle (Figure 5.2).

Day 1

Distribution of the paper is the first task on the day following printing. Staff members, ranging from the publisher to reporters, may take part in the process. Ad salespersons may carry papers with them while on sales calls, dropping them at distribution points. If the paper delivers to homes, it may use part-time carriers to accomplish that task.

The second task of the day is the planning and setting up of the next edition. This usually takes place in an informal staff meeting involving the publisher, ad salespersons, and editor to discuss anything that is out of the ordinary in terms of the next edition. Then the process of selling advertisements and covering the community begins.

FIGURE 5.2   Production Cycle of a Weekly Newspaper

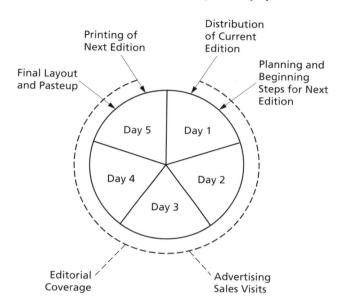

Days 2–4

In the middle days of the production cycle, advertising salespersons and reporters gather material and write and edit ads and stories to be included. As some pages fill up with ads and materials, the staff may prepare them ahead of time to reduce the workload on production day, which tends to be very hectic.

Day 5

On production day, many of the traditional functions of advertising sales and news coverage are scaled back to accommodate the deadlines for getting the paper to the press. Final layout decisions are made and pagination by computer or paste-up on layout boards is completed. The materials are then checked by the editor and ad salespersons and any corrections are made before they are taken to the printer.

SUMMARY

In both daily and weekly newspapers there are no clear starts and stops to the production cycle because personnel are constantly working ahead on future issues. As a result, the production of a newspaper is a never-ending cycle. For daily newspapers, producing an edition is the word equivalent of producing a novel every twenty-four hours. Accompanying those words are intensive graphic and layout activities that must take be done.

Changing content, unanticipated developments in advertising and circulation, inevitable problems in the production cycle, and deadlines keep the constancy of the process from becoming boring or monotonous. The process, however, can be stressful and wearisome for some newspaper staffers who are unable to find ways to cope with the confusion, crises, pressures, and excitement of the production cycle.

6

Technology and Labor Issues

Because producing a newspaper is a labor-intensive activity, issues of technology and labor have always been important in the industry. For most of its history, the newspaper industry has been primarily concerned about issues of technology and labor in the pressroom, because that portion of newspaper operations has required the bulk of technological investment and traditionally required the greatest portion of the employee workforce. In the past two decades, technological developments have been increasingly affecting journalistic operations of newspapers and portend significant changes in the distribution operations of newspapers in years to come.

LABOR IN NEWSPAPERS

Labor is a resource, like land, equipment, supplies, and capital, that newspaper managers must acquire and manage. Newspaper companies are labor-intensive and the types of personnel they use in their different operations vary widely. The qualities and specializations of managers are not at all like the qualities and abilities sought in journalists. The abilities and personalities of advertising sales personnel differ widely from those of production personnel. The talents and qualities sought in design and layout personnel are dissimilar from those of circulation personnel.

In order to fill these different needs, newspapers seek employees in an economic marketplace in which employers compete as buyers of labor with the sellers of labor, that is, individual workers or collective groups of workers, as well as with other potential buyers of labor. These relationships are unfamiliar to many because newspapers have traditionally been thought of as only producers and sellers of newspaper products rather than also as buyers of goods and services, and labor.

Workers selling their labor to newspapers do so with a variety of needs and wants. First, they wish to sell their labor at the highest price possible, thus achieving high wages. This primary goal of workers is no different than the goal of the newspaper to sell its advertising and circulation at a price that will bring it the highest possible profit. Secondly, employees wish to gain the highest possible benefits, fair and equal treatment from those who manage their labor, safe and pleasant working conditions, and psychological satisfaction about the work they perform and the firm for which they work. Thirdly, employees want job security and reasonable guarantees of the continuation of their employment.

When individuals are hired by a firm they negotiate the price of their labor (their salary or wages), the benefits they receive, and the terms of their employment. Most employers that hire more than a few workers are not willing to engage in full individual negotiations with every potential worker, because doing so would be incredibly time-consuming. Instead, companies set up organized wage scales and standardized benefits, and establish companywide personnel policies. By doing so, however, they limit the operation of the economic market in the rivalry of buyer and seller.

When employees feel that this relationship produces unfair economic results, that they are unfairly treated on the job, or that their jobs are in jeopardy, they sometimes respond by establishing employee representatives or councils to convey their concerns and feelings about issues to management. In other cases, they join established unions or create unions to engage in collective bargaining over the wages, hours, benefits, work requirements and working conditions, and company policies. These responses help counterbalance the limitations on the marketplace created by the standards and policies set by the employer.

As noted in Chapter 2, a variety of unions exist in the newspaper industry and represent different types of workers. The strongest unions tend to be those representing printers and other backshop workers who have a significant ability to stop production of the newspaper if disputes arise, and those representing employees who transport papers because they have the ability to stop distribution of the newspaper if conflicts between management and labor develop.

When newspapers are unionized or efforts are being made to unionize a newspaper, a variety of state and federal labor laws govern the relationships between the paper and its employees and put specific requirements on the collective bargaining process and contract enforcement. When dealing with unions, newspapers face recognition issues, that is, issues involving the acceptance of a particular union and its local as the bargaining unit for employees. They face issues of membership in the bargaining unit, including what personnel or types of jobs are included, as well as issues of job security and union rights, such as the ability of a bargaining unit to carry out business at the job site by using equipment and facilities, to have dues payments taken from paychecks, and so on. In addition, they must deal with structured and standardized methods of employee discipline and specific grievance procedures that protect employee rights and ensure equity and fairness.

Because of laws and regulations regarding union–newspaper relationships, because newspapers typically give up managerial options in contract negotiations, and because collective bargaining restores some economic power to employees, many newspapers try to avoid the development of unions at their papers. This is possible in the United States because unions organize workers at and negotiate with individual newspapers rather than all newspapers simultaneously or with newspaper groups, as is done in other nations. As a result, some newspapers try to keep unions out by adequately meeting the traditional concerns of employees—good wages and benefits, job security, perceptions of fairness in employee relations, psychological rewards—in ways that ameliorate a need and desire to unionize.

Where unions exist in papers, some newspaper managers have attempted to end the presence of unions or reduce their influence. This has been done in some papers by meeting the primary need of employees in ways that reduce the benefits of union membership and representation. At other times, managers have aggressively attacked unions in hopes of breaking the power they provide to employees or to change terms of contracts to which both had previously agreed. The results of such actions are not always beneficial to newspapers. In 1990 and 1991, for example, the Tribune Co. engaged in a highly confrontational anti-union campaign at the New York *Daily News* that precipitated a lengthy strike. The company lost more than $300 million because of advertising and circulation losses due to the strike and it ultimately gave the paper away to get out from under the mounting financial problems and its inability to come to terms with workers. In 1995 and 1996, efforts by Gannett and Knight-Ridder to convert employees into independent contractors in the circulation department of the Detroit Newspaper Agency, which serves Gannett's *Detroit News* and Knight-Ridder's *Detroit Free Press*, led to an impasse and a highly emotional strike that led to more than $150 million losses that still had a significant effect on the financial performance of both companies after one year.

Technology also has a significant influence on the relationships between newspapers and their employees. From the seventeenth to early nineteenth centuries, newspapers were relatively small operations run primarily by publisher-editor-printers who did most of the work with a small staff of assistants, often family members. As the mass production and consumption of newspapers increased in the latter half of the nineteenth century, the rapid developments in printing technology and capacity—discussed in Chapter 3—forced newspapers to hire large workforces of printers and printing-related employees. By the beginning of the twentieth century printers and other production personnel at most large newspapers were being unionized at a rapid rate, and those unions began spreading their representation to include production personnel at mid-sized papers across the country during the first half of the century.

The industry requirement for a large number of production personnel and the influence of production unions remained significant until the introduction of photo-composition and offset printing after midcentury. These developments permitted most newspapers to reduce the number of employees in their backshop operations by one-third to one-half and transferred many of the typesetting and layout functions to newsrooms and advertising offices, which had not traditionally been unionized, except in major metropolitan papers.

The shift to these new technologies resulted in unions working to protect their members' interests through collective bargaining.[1] Nevertheless, the introduction of new technology was not accompanied by significant labor disputes as in some European nations; the decline in production positions and the transfer of functions occurred relatively smoothly in the United States because newspapers and unions often worked together to reasonably meet the needs of employees displaced by the technology through early retirement incentives, contract buyouts, and retraining. Today, newspaper unions are active primarily in the northeast and northwest and almost absent from newspapers in the south.

The computerization of newspapers in the 1980s and 1990s has had a significant impact on journalistic practices and employment and is beginning to have an impact on the delivery of news and information to readers. Continuing developments in these areas are pivotal in redefining the roles and functions of newspapers and increasingly significant in the marketing of newspaper products.

COMPUTER TECHNOLOGY CHANGES NEWSPAPERS

In 1963, John Diebold, a young management consultant, presented the annual convention of the American Society of Newspaper Editors with a forecast of a computerized future that seemed light years away.[2] Diebold told editors they would write, edit, dummy pages, and store copy in computers. He said production systems would be automated and that they would have the ability to update stories right up to press time. He predicted news managers would create supplemental and specialized editions to generate advertising revenue and sell information from electronic libraries.[3]

To understand why Diebold's remarks about a high-tech news operation awed executives, one must recall what newspapers were like at the time. Reporters banged out stories on manual typewriters. Editors revised stories with pencils and marked copy with proofreaders' symbols. Newspaper libraries held bulging files of yellowing clips—some cross-referenced—in manila envelopes. Photographers developed prints on proof sheets with chemicals. And clattering wire service teleprinters spat out copy at the Model T rate of a little more than one word per second.

Diebold's predictions came true. The information age has dawned on American newspapers. The changes have been so remarkable that some forget the interim steps of short-lived investments by newspapers in punch tape typesetting technology and optical scanners that read copy typed on paper forms using special typefaces and scanable codes. Those technologies began disappearing rapidly after the first newsroom computer terminals for creating and editing copy were introduced at the *Detroit News* in 1970. Reporters and editors began relying on computers for writing and revising. Videodisplay terminals linked to a mainframe computer eliminated the need to cut and paste stories and doomed the typewriter to oblivion. A simple word-processing program enabled writers to move paragraphs, delete words and sentences, and correct spelling errors at the push of a button. The increasing switch to the computer in newspapers and other businesses has taken its toll on traditional business machine manufacturers. For example, the Smith–Corona Corporation, one of the nation's largest typewriter manufacturers, declared bankruptcy in 1995. The computer became an artist's tool as well, as design programs enabled artists to produce stunning color illustrations and detailed graphics under deadline pressure. The development of flat-bed photo scanners and photography software programs, such as "Photoshop," freed photographers from the darkroom. Negatives can now be scanned in the computer and edited and cropped electronically to ensure the right quality of texture and composition. Pagination or computerized page layout has streamlined the process from page design to production and can be accomplished with off-the-shelf technology and software in smaller papers and sophisticated, specialized systems in larger papers.[4] And newspapers are now replacing outdated videodisplay terminals at work stations with personal computers linked to a network that allows access to the Internet and computer databases across the country. The more powerful personal computers have the added advantage of allowing reporters to build their own databases by using spreadsheets and other software file-management systems. Computers have not only changed the process by which news is written, edited, and produced on paper, but also the way in which information is analyzed, collected and stored. Computers have opened the door to a myriad of information sources previously unavailable to reporters and slashed the time it takes to process that information. Newspaper libraries have gone electronic, storing articles in databases that can be retrieved by a simple keyword search. In addition, computers have helped the accounting, advertising, business, and circulation departments streamline operations, eliminating hundreds of jobs in some cases, such as those of typesetters who used to lay out classified ads. The computer revolution may have as profound an effect on print as the invention of movable type. Newspapers are moving toward a paperless future.

As Diebold said in a 1988 address to the American Society of Newspaper Editors:

> Technology is the driving force in all of this and it is a very important driving force that is still going on. When I spoke to the ASNE in 1963 there were no personal computers; they had not been invented. It was more than a decade later before they were invented. At that time, people were think-

ing about one computer per company. As the 1960s went on, it became one to a division. In the 1970s it was one to a department. In the 1980s it is one to a person, and we have a number of clients who have 10,000 to 20,000 personal computers in a single organization.[5]

This change is bringing additional costs to newspapers as they convert from the use of workstations linked to mainframe computers to individual personal computers linked by networks. The shift is requiring continuing investments in computer and network hardware and software, as well as regular upgrades to provide improved functions and flexibility. Funds for regular replacement and upgrading of technology for newsroom and preproduction use are becoming a regular budget item in editorial operating budgets rather than an occasional capital budget item as they had been in the past.

That computerization is spreading outside of the workplace as well. About one in every five American households, some 23 million homes, have personal computers, and that market is expected to grow at a 24 percent compounded annual rate from 1996 through 1998, according to Forrester Research, Inc.[6]

Bill Gates, the leader of Microsoft, envisions a future in which American households will be linked by high-speed fiber-optic cables that will connect citizens to banks, offices, government agencies, schools, stores, and entertainment and information sources, such as motion pictures and newspapers. James Flanigan, a *Los Angeles Times* business columnist, reports that by 1997–98 film and videotape will be digitized: "reduced to electronic blips that can be distributed instantly throughout the world and directly to theaters or homes through fiber-optic lines."[7]

Small wonder the delivery of on-line newspapers has become a priority among publishers. No one wants to be left behind on the information superhighway. In 1993, 300 newspaper executives attended the Interactive Newspapers conference in San Francisco. A year later, more than 600 executives flew to Tampa for the same conference.[8] "What's happening," said Dan Miller, of Kelsey Publishing Group in New Jersey, "is that the language of journalism is being taken over by the nerds in Silicon Valley."[9] Dow Jones has started a personal version of the *Wall Street Journal* that delivers stories, columns, news updates, stocks, sports, and weather to home computers by 3 a.m. EST for $12.95 per month. There are presently 496 on-line newspapers and 508 on-line magazines. One of the most prominent is Knight–Ridder's San Jose *Mercury News* in California, which is available through America Online. The Mercury Center electronic newspaper allows readers to send letters to the editor, chat with newspaper reporters, conduct library searches, read classified advertising, and find supplemental information to news stories for a small fee. It's been a success with readers. But Bill Mitchell, director of electronic publishing at the *Mercury News* told *Quill* magazine that the service has one major pitfall—a lack of advertising: "I don't think we'll declare victory yet....Ultimately, for us to make money, we need to use advertising effectively."[10] Another excellent example of newspaper use of the technology is McClatchy Newspapers' nando.net which was originally established by the Raleigh *News and Observer*.

David Easterly, president of Cox Newspapers, said that, while newspapers earn 80 percent of their income from advertisers and 20 percent from subscribers, the reverse may be true with electronic services. However, electronic services can include information, such as bowling scores and country club golf results, that newspapers may not publish because of the cost of newsprint.[11]

The dilemma for media executives is how to turn a profit through electronic delivery of the news. Some publishers remain haunted by memories of Knight–Ridder's electronic teletext service, Viewtron, which was introduced in the mid-1980s. Viewtron cost $50 million and closed after three years, a colossal flop that attracted a mere 50,000 subscribers.[12] Near the end of 1995, Knight–Ridder, perhaps sobered by the lesson of Viewtron, pulled the plug on its flat-panel newspaper project, which cost about $2 million annually. Another flat panel, Apple's pocket-size Newton message pad, also has flopped with consumers. But the Media Lab of the Massachusetts Institute of Technology continues to experiment with a flat-panel newspaper. Sponsors of the MIT project include: American Broadcasting Corporation, Hearst Corporation, Gannett, Thomson Newspapers, IBM, Lotus, Bell, and even Knight–Ridder.[13]

Heralded at the Knight–Ridder Information Design Lab in Boulder, Colorado, the flat panel was viewed as the prototype newspaper of the future—a paperless newspaper about 9 by 12 inches, 3/4 of an inch thick, and weighing a little more than two pounds. The impetus behind the prototype was to put out a newspaper on a portable display panel that would receive information in the home through cable, satellite, or telephone outlets. News accounts lauded the flat panel as a computer that looks like a newspaper in shape and size, but resembles the stone tablets of the Ten Commandments.[14] The panel could be taken anywhere—the office, coffee shop, park, beach—and be read standing, sitting, reclining, or lying down. Roger Fidler, head of the Knight–Ridder Information Design Lab, predicted that the panel would replace ink and paper by the year 2025.[15]

If successful, the flat-panel newspaper would eliminate the need for printing presses, delivery trucks, and carriers. Many jobs would be eliminated, and the threat of a union closing down a newspaper through a strike would almost disappear. Organized labor, as in other automated industries, would lose the ability to stop production or distribution. The cost of newsprint and maintaining presses would no longer plague publishers, and the news would be delivered electronically as soon as it was edited.

Another advantage the flat panel would have over print and on-line newspapers is greater depth. With the portable flat panel, which has the same power as a laptop computer, a "person could read a six-paragraph story on page one and then access a fuller story and a vast array of related information such as analysis, opinion and maps, videos, and still photographs."[16] Advertisers could take advantage of multimedia: automobile ads could feature video commercials of cars. Record stores could play snippets of songs and department stores could show their entire line of stock for an item such as shoes. A flat panel could also be tailored to individual needs: if a reader just wanted the sports and business sections, that's all that would be delivered to his or her home.

Effects on the News and Advertising Work

Use of computerized technologies has created a new labor problem for newspapers in the newsroom. Both unionized and nonunionized journalists are increasingly requesting additional compensation for their new typesetting and pagination functions and the increasing technical training and skills they possess. In addition, they are demanding additional compensation when materials prepared for the newspaper are used in other electronic formats that bring additional revenue to newspapers.

The changes are also having an effect on the well-being of employees and the conditions in which they work. Newsrooms, for example, were traditionally rather shabbily furnished and journalists spent most of their time outside the facility. Computerized technology and the shifting of production functions to the newsroom is requiring journalists to spend more time working at computer terminals in the office and increasing the number of people that never leave their desks during the workday.

Movement of computer equipment to desktops and the new functions are forcing newspapers to address a variety of environmental and employee comfort issues previously ignored. The new technology and functions have required a level of cleanliness in the newsroom that was not previously required in order to ensure that equipment is not damaged by dirt, food, or beverages. In many papers, new air-conditioning units were required to provide cooling and air cleaning for computers. Productivity issues have required renovations including new lighting, desks designed for computers, and chairs designed to provide comfort during increasingly long periods of deskwork.

In advertising departments, similar changes in working conditions have resulted in order to accommodate computerization. The general working conditions in advertising offices in the past had typically been better than newsrooms because customers tended to visit the advertising offices and because many advertising staff members already spent the majority of their time in the office. Nevertheless, the introduction of computer technology also required changes in air-conditioning and seating arrangements to make it possible for the advertising departments to carry out the computerized production, layout, and business functions that the technology brought to their operations.

Health Effects

An important result of the introduction of computer technology has been unanticipated health effects on employees, which have forced newspapers to adjust the relationship between workers and the technology. A major health problem caused by computerization is the rise of repetitive stress injuries (RSI). Complaints and workers compensation claims involving RSI have increased dramatically since computers replaced typewriters in newsrooms in the late 1970s and early 1980s. It is now common to see reporters, editors, advertising employees, and others wearing braces, splints, and other prosthetic devices to alleviate pain while word processing on computer keyboards. Although these injuries should not be exaggerated—they are clearly not as violent as attacks on journalists and carriers, do not produce the visible effects of injuries caused by accidents involving company machinery or vehicles, and are not as well understood as ailments caused by exposure to hazardous chemicals—computer-related injuries have become a significant concern to newspaper industry managers because of the costs of workers' compensation and of specialized equipment required to reduce such injuries and to assist workers who have been affected.

The most common ailments related to keyboard typing are carpal tunnel syndrome and tendinitis as well as sore joints and muscle stiffness. Researchers attribute the rise in complaints to the speed and ease of word-processing on a computer keyboard. The computer allows an operator to strike the keys continuously without breaking to hit the carriage return, change paper, fix stuck keys, or use liquid paper to correct mistakes. The repetitive action of word processing over a long period of time can cause tendons to swell and pinch the nerve that runs from the arm to the hand through the carpal tunnel, a small opening in the wrist. Reporters also have experienced painful tendinitis, a condition similar to tennis elbow.

Although many newspaper managers initially denied or downplayed the association between computers and employee medical complaints, by the 1990s research studies and the increasingly widespread number of workers receiving treatment forced the industry to recognize and confront the problem.

A University of California study of reporters and editors at the *San Francisco Chronicle*, for example, found that more than half reported some degree of pain during their work. The university researchers found that 44 of the 150 editorial workers in their year-long study met the criteria for "potential cumulative trauma disorders"—musculoskeletal injuries caused by the performance of highly repetitive tasks, such as striking letters on a keyboard.[17] A National Institute of Occupational Safety and Health study of 1,000 *Los Angeles Times* employees found that 41 percent of the workers reported that they had been injured. Investigators found objective evidence of injuries in more than half those cases.[18] The *Times*, which had computerized jobs in the early 1980s, asked NIOSH to conduct a study after more than 200 employees—mostly editors and reporters—filed workers' compensation claims for repetitive stress injury.[19]

RSI has become the most dreaded ailment in the news business as well as other industries where workers, such as meat packers and supermarket checkout clerks, perform the same repetitive motions throughout the day. The number of workers diagnosed with disorders caused by repeated trauma on the job increased from

22,600 in 1982 to 332,100 in 1995, according to the Bureau of Labor Statistics. Carpal tunnel syndrome has cut short the careers of many veteran journalists. It is ironic that RSI often strikes the best and most experienced editorial employees, because problems arise with productivity; the more one works on a computer terminal, the more likely a repetitive stress injury will occur. Reporters who bang out two to three stories per day or write several drafts of their stories are more likely to experience RSI than those who are less active. The syndrome can become a minor nuisance treated with over-the-counter medication or a major health problem that causes people to lose their ability to drive, lift a newspaper, and perform fine movements with their hands.

Cheryl Downey, who developed carpal tunnel syndrome in 1990 while working as a reporter at the *Orange County Register*, exemplifies the extent to which RSI can affect employees. "I had shooting pains in the palms of my hands at work," she said. "Within two weeks, I had a serious case. I couldn't lift things. I had trouble writing. The pain was unbearable." Downey received anti-inflammatory drugs and cortisone injections. When they failed, she had surgery on both wrists. She returned to work after several months and has experienced occasional flare-ups. "I've changed my work habits," Downey said. "I take breaks. I do exercises. I wear braces when I write."

Alarmed by the rise in injuries, newspaper managers have taken steps to reduce their occurrence. Many newspapers have conducted workshops on how to avoid RSI. They counsel reporters to take breaks, stretch, maintain good posture, and watch their hand position on the keyboard. To encourage reporters to stop keystroking and walk around, *Newsday* has mostly dismantled its office terminal message system. At the *Los Angeles Times,* terminals automatically remind reporters to take a break every fifty minutes, and an "RSI Room" has been stocked with exercise equipment and a refrigerator full of ice packs.[20] To avoid workers' compensation cases, newspapers ask staff members to notify their supervisors at the first sign of pain. In addition, many newspapers are refurbishing their offices with special desks designed for computers and seating arrangements designed for computer users.

The computer industry has responded to RSI by designing a new generation of ergonomic keyboards. These keyboards, which are often split down the middle, allow workers to position their hands in a more comfortable and less stressful manner. Physiologists believe the old-fashioned notion that hands should be in a palm-down attitude for typing may be incorrect—the more beneficial way may be to angle the palms inward.[21] Some inventors have even come up with vertical keyboards, so that the hands face each other, and molded glide-rules that provide support for the hands. Some reporters have experimented with voice-activated computers that eliminate the need for keystrokes. Journalists of the future may very well dictate a story that will be displayed in front of them on the computer screen. While Apple and Microsoft have developed user-friendly, ergonomic keyboards to meet the challenge of RSI, computer manufacturers have steadfastly refused to take the blame for RSI and have fought every attempt for compensation in the courts. The computer industry denies that its keyboards cause RSI.

The courts in jury and judge trials across the country have unanimously backed the industry's contention that there is no scientific evidence to prove that keyboards themselves cause RSI and that keyboard manufacturers should be held responsible. Six attempts by injured workers in six different court jurisdictions have failed. In a multimillion-dollar suit against Apple Computer, a San Francisco Superior Court judge, in August 1995, found no evidence of a specific causal link between keyboard or mouse use and RSI. In April 1995, Larry Lewis, a *Philadelphia Inquirer* reporter, lost a federal court case against IBM and Atex. The jury found that neither production defects nor design flaws in keyboards manufactured by the two companies caused Lewis's carpal tunnel syndrome.[22] Lewis, a reporter for thirty years, failed to convince jurors of any product defect. Cases against IBM and Compaq Computer have also failed. These court cases, combined with Congressional pressure, have prompted the Occupational Safety and Health Administration to abandon plans to issue tough regulations aimed at protecting workers from RSI. In June 1995, OSHA backed down after intense opposition from Republicans in Congress and business groups.[23]

That manufacturers have escaped blame for RSI and the federal government has not issued work standards has put more pressure and responsibility directly on the newspaper industry. Editors and reporters have been highly successful in obtaining workers' compensation for their injuries. Newspapers and other employers have to pay for the medical costs of injured workers and their workers' compensation awards, so the burden of coping with RSI has fallen on newspapers and other heavily computerized businesses.

Additional health concerns are also arising over computerized technology. Newspaper employees report that prolonged use of the video display terminals is causing eyestrain, headaches, and fatigue. These problems are being addressed in some newspapers by required work breaks. A new concern has also arisen because electromagnetic fields emanating from computer terminals have caused some scientists to fear employees may be subjected to harmful doses of radiation. Studies of that issue are currently under way.

The introduction of computerized technology to newspapers and the industry's increasing reliance on and heavy use of computers has had both benefits and costs. Although the benefits were realized immediately, the costs are increasing over time and the industry is wrestling with means to control the economic costs and the effects of the new technology on its employees.

Computer Assisted Reporting

Another important and unanticipated benefit of the introduction of computers to the newsroom has been the capacity it introduced for information-gathering and reporting techniques. The computer has streamlined journalistic research and opened up avenues of inquiry that were previously unavailable to reporters. Scrutinizing government documents, searching records for elusive information, and other tasks that may have taken months, even years, can now be done quickly and efficiently by computer. A new generation of journalists demonstrated the efficacy of computer-assisted reporting in the last half of the 1980s and first half of the 1990s. Elliot Jaspin, one of the pioneers in the field, used computer tapes in 1985 to search through the records of 30,000 loans of the Rhode Island Housing and Mortgage Finance Company. Then a reporter with the Providence *Journal*, Jaspin found evidence of political favoritism at the agency, whose mission was to finance mortgages for low-income home buyers. One loan went to the governor's daughter.[24] That same year, two Alaskan reporters, Rich Mauer and Larry Makinson of the Anchorage *Daily News*, analyzed political contributions from lobbyists, oil companies, and labor unions by putting together a database on a Macintosh that generated a series of charts, graphs, and stories about influence peddling in Juneau.[25] Jaspin, who now works for Cox Newspapers, went on to found the National Institute for Computer Assisted Reporting at the University of Missouri School of Journalism. Mauer used his Mac to build databases on alcohol-fueled suicides and accidental deaths among young Native Alaskans, and the *Daily News* won a 1989 Pulitzer Prize for a series on alcohol abuse that was spawned by the computer research. The rise of computer-assisted reporting can be traced to the development of affordable personal computers in the mid-1980s. But journalism first entered the computer age in 1967 when a *Detroit Free Press* reporter used a computer to study survey data of African Americans living in neighborhoods hit by an urban riot that year. The *Detroit Free Press* won a Pulitzer Prize for its analysis of the Detroit riot, coverage that was aided by computer research.[26] The success of computer assisted reporting has prompted newspapers and universities across the country to train reporters and students in database skills and tapping into electronic information.

Yet the number of reporters skilled in such areas and the number of newspapers committed to computer research remains surprisingly low. At least two dozen newspapers out of more than 1,200 in the United States have a staff member who specializes in working with computer data.[27] Investigative Reporters and Editors, a professional organization, estimates that the number of news organizations using computer tapes, tape cartridges, CD-ROMs and other technology as part of their information-gathering is in the hundreds.[28] This palls in comparison to the number of them that use computers for word processing. That so few news organizations engage in computer research seems appalling, especially since the technology has been available to them for a decade, and the method has proven itself by helping to produce Pulitzer Prize-winning stories. The small number of reporters across the country specializing in computer research reflects the trend among modern-day editors to report the sensational and the trivial at the expense of investigative reporting and in-depth work.

The Woodward and Bernstein era has passed. Computer-assisted reporting takes time, investigations often go on for months, and sometimes they fail to produce anything. Fifty short features can be written in the time it takes to produce an investigative story. News managers in this era of fluff and reader-friendly stories consider investigative reporting a poor investment, one that is not cost-effective and fails to meet the bottom line. Two 1994 surveys of computer use in journalism by the University of Miami and the Columbia University Graduate School of Journalism found that newspapers have been slow to embrace computer technology.[29] Bruce Garrison, a Miami journalism professor, surveyed 208 Sunday newspapers with circulations of 20,000 or more, and found that about half had created or planned to create a computer reporting team; only 14.4 percent were using specialized statistical software such as SPSS or SAS, and only 7 percent used software that kept track of names, numbers, appointments, and to-do lists. Steve Ross, a Columbia University professor, and Don Middleberg, of Middleberg & Associates, surveyed 6,000 writers, reporters, and editors and found that only 16 percent used on-line services daily. One-third said they used e-mail, databases, and bulletin board services at least weekly. The low numbers may reflect the lack of personal computers in the newsroom. Newspapers need to catch up to other industries where e-mail and the use of on-line services are common.

The need for more computer training is apparent throughout the industry and will be necessary as news organizations move from mainframe computers and videodisplay terminals to PC networks. Besides the institute at the University of Missouri, the Graduate School of Journalism at Columbia University, the University of Minnesota, University of North Carolina, Syracuse University, and Indiana University offer courses and programs in computer-assisted reporting. But some critics charge that universities also have been slow to respond to the promise of the technological future. J. T. ("Tom") Johnson, a San Francisco State University journalism professor, said surveys show that less than 15 percent of all journalism schools have integrated computer research in their programs. "It appears a large majority of journalism students—indeed the great mass of all students in most universities—are not being adequately prepared to cope with...information-retrieval and analysis," Johnson said. "Our students, therefore, are being defrauded, bilked out of the skills vital to their intellectual and professional due."[30] Johnson found journalism schools, perhaps picking up on trends within the industry, have been quicker to train students in word processing, page design, and pagination than computer-assisted reporting. As with graphic design, computer-assisted reporting is an area in which the universities can offer needed training to those entering the profession. With just more than two dozen reporters specializing in the field, opportunities will abound for journalists proficient in analyzing data.

Universities and newspapers need only follow the lead of the largest news organization in the world, the Associated Press, which committed itself to computer-assisted reporting in 1995. The AP established a database lab at its New York headquarters in the fall of 1995, and plans to equip bureaus in every state with a workstation for computer-assisted reporting. AP reporters already use telephone databases on computer disks to match phone numbers and addresses anywhere in the country; on-line government services to check court dockets and federal agency reports, commercial services to check clips, to find lawsuits and tax liens, or to read a public company's proxy statement, and the Internet to find experts and sources in discussion groups.[31]

Computer-assisted reporting has three main aspects: the analysis of government databases, the creation and analysis of in-house databases, and accessing information from the Internet and commercial on-line services. When *St. Petersburg Times* reporters wanted to find out which restaurants were ranked filthiest in their circulation area, the newspaper had the Florida Department of Business and Professional Regulations copy all of its information about inspections onto computer tapes.[32] In a six-month investigation, reporters examined hundreds of files about restaurants and the state's restaurant inspection system to produce a report that turned some readers' stomachs. The *St. Louis Post Dispatch* compared voter registration lists with death certificates and found two dozen people who had kept on voting from the grave and 270 of the dead still registered to vote.[33] The Indianapolis *News* reviewed more than 50,000 records from a database purchased from the Justice Information System of Indianapolis/Marion County, and produced a series that showed the probation system had broken down and that thousands of people were victimized by probationers who committed crimes while under probation department supervision.[34]

The *Miami Herald's* Pulitzer Prize-winning coverage of Hurricane Andrew depended on computers to build databases. Writing in *Quill,* Stephen K. Doig, associate editor for research, explained how the newspaper ran a graphic showing the climatology of Florida hurricanes by making a database of the paths, dates, and damage of all fifty-seven hurricanes to hit Florida this century.[35] To determine whether human error played a role in the damage from the storm, Doig built a database of nearly 60,000 damage reports. Using a mainframe computer and a powerful statistical-analysis language called SAS, Doig merged damage reports against the county's property-tax roll and found that the newer a house, the more likely it would be significantly damaged. Reporters followed up on this information by checking building code regulations and discovered how they had been weakened over the years. After reporters found that many collapsed structures were not built to code, the newspaper purchased the county's entire building and zoning database—thirty-five reels of magnetic tape holding more than 7 million records. Doig said the tapes revealed that inspectors often had to make more than fifty inspections a day, a workload far too high to monitor construction effectively. To measure the construction industry's political influence, the *Herald* hired a service to keypunch more than $8 million of local campaign contributions since 1982. Doig said the paper uncovered that one out of every four campaign dollars came from the building industry. "A few years ago, we simply could not have reported with such depth and precision," Doig told *Quill* readers.

Although it takes sophistication and training to build in-house databases, reporters and editors can retrieve information at the push of a few computer keys by purchasing an on-line data service and accessing information from the Internet. Commercial database services provide bibliographies and abstracts, articles and transcripts, books and directories, government documents, public records and information about individuals as well as visual images.[36] Services, such as Prentice–Hall On-line, will list court records, bankruptcies, real estate holdings, and environmental information. They have helped reporters and private investigators track people's addresses, business connections, and criminal records. Searches that once took weeks to complete by legwork can now be done in a matter of minutes.

By plugging into the Vu/Text database, which contains stories from newspapers across the country, Mike Berens of the *Columbus Dispatch* was able to discover a serial killer who murdered prostitutes at truck stops. From newspaper articles about truck-stop killings, Berens put together a profile of a killer, previously unknown to police, who preyed on prostitutes for six years. He was able to show law enforcement officials a common pattern to a series of homicides that had occurred in several states.[37] Using on-line databases, even the newspaper's own computerized library files, a reporter can come up with the pattern of rapes within a geographic area or even freeway deaths within a given state. The on-line databases can be used for all types of reporting and research: political reporters can assemble news articles and scholarly books and papers on voting patterns, medical writers can look up the latest research on a specific disease, and entertainment reporters can find background information and articles written about the stars. Bulletin board services on the Internet, America Online, Compuserve, and others have opened a world of sources for reporters. From anthropology to zoology, almost any research area has a chat room where reporters can question experts. Profnet puts journalists in touch with university experts in a variety of fields. The Internet allows journalists to glean information from libraries around the world and talk to sources all over the planet. Newspapers have interviewed scientists at the South Pole via the Internet. Whereas investigative reporters used to spend days wading through files at the county courthouse and hall of administration, the Dayton *Daily News* cut research time by more than half by connecting its newsroom electronically to county databases, enabling reporters to examine property tax records and court actions. The challenge for journalists is to take advantage of the technology. The challenge for news organizations is to buy the equipment and provide the training to take advantage of the technology, and the challenge for editors is to go beyond hack reporting and allow reporters to use the technology to flush out the hidden stories.

SUMMARY

Electronic technology and its applications have been useful and provide promising developments in the newspaper industry. But the real challenge for the news industry, which always has been on top of gathering information and conveying information, is how to limit the costs of using the technology and how to link it to the developing information superhighway and still earn a profit. In the area of information distribution, the problem is not how to bridge the gap from newsprint to a paperless future, but how to earn a favorable rate of return. The rate at which newspapers wed themselves to a fiber-optic future may be determined more by the rate of return than the speed of technological progress. One should remember that despite predictions, television failed to destroy radio and that home video failed to destroy motion picture theaters. The lesson is that new technology does not always supersede the old and that mere technological capability does not mean that it is desirable to both producers and consumer. Although new electronic technology is clearly having an impact on newspapers, it will not displace traditional newspapers unless and until it becomes the most attractive alternative to publishers and readers in both format and financial terms. To paraphrase Marshall McLuhan, the medium is the money.

ENDNOTES

1. J. N. Dertouzous and T. H. Quinn, *Bargaining Responses to the Technology Revolution: The Case of the Newspaper Industry* (Santa Monica, CA: Rand Corp., 1985).

2. American Society of Newspaper Editors, "Newspapers and the Future," *Proceedings of the 1988 Convention of the American Society of Newspaper Editors*, 239. Reston, v2.: American Society of Newspaper Editors, 1988.

3. "Newspapers and the Future," 239.

4. David M. Cole, "Pagination, Page by Page," *Presstime*, February 1995, 27–32.

5. "Newspapers and the Future," 240.

6. Ellen Hume, *Tabloids, Talk Radio, and the Future of News—Technology's Impact on Journalism* (Washington, DC: Annenberg Washington Program in Communication Policy Studies, Northwestern University, 1995), 200.

7. James Flanigan, "Pixar Makes a Great Story, but the Big Picture Belongs to Computers," *Los Angeles Times*, 3 December 1995, D-1.

8. "Silicon Valley Nerds Herald Newspapers of Tomorrow," *South China Morning Post*, March 1994, Media Supplement.

9. Ibid.

10. Jack D. Lail, "Newspaper On-line," *Quill* (January/February 1994), 40.

11. Lail, 40.

12. Lail, 41.

13. Chris Cobb, "A No-Paper Paper in a Future Near You," *Ottawa Citizen,* 9 April 1994, B1.

14. Cobb, B1.

15. Amy Balen and William Glaberson, "A Tablet Moses Just Couldn't Have Dreamed Of," *Business Times,* 8 February 1994, 13.

16. Cobb, B1.

17. "Computer Users Suffer Ailments, UC Study Finds," *San Francisco Chronicle,* 21 November 1992, A2.

18. Bob Baker, "NIOSH Study Backs Claims of Stress Injury," *Los Angeles Times,* 29 October 1992, D1.

19. Baker, D1.

20. Jerry Adler, "Typing Without Keys," *Newsweek (*Dec. 7, 1992), 59:63.

21. Adler, 63.

22. "Jury finds for Atex, IBM," *National Law Journal (*May 8, 1995), 19:B2.

23. Cindy Skrycki, "OSHA Abandons Rules Effort on Repetitive Injury; Opposition by GOP, Business Cited," *Washington Post,* 13 June 1995, D1.

24. Steve Weinberg, *The Reporter's Handbook, An Investigator's Guide to Documents and Techniques* New York: St. Martin's Press, 1996), 48.

25. Richard Mauer, "I was a Mac Agitator," *Quill (*September 1993), 81:24.

26. J.T. Johnson, "The Unconscious Fraud of Journalism Education; Failure of Journalism Schools to Teach Database Skills," *Quill (*June 1992), 80:31.

27. George Landau, "Computer Journalism Takes Off," *Columbia Journalism Review (*May 1992), 30:61.

28. Steve Weinberg, 49.

29. J.T. Johnson, "Newspapers Slow to Embrace Advances in Computer World," *Quill (*September 1995), 83:83:20.

30. Weinberg, 49.

31. Jerry Walker, "Computer Helps AP Reporters Get News," *Jack O'Dwyer's Newsletter,* 4 October, 1995, 4.

32. "How We Did It," *St. Petersburg Times,* 22 October 1995, 7A.

33. Landau, 61.

34. "50,000 Records Analyzed for Series," *Indianapolis Star,* 24 September 1995, A11.

35. Stephen K. Doig, "The Big One," *Quill (*September 1993), 26.

36. Nora Paul, *"Computer Assisted Research,"* St. Petersburg, FL: Poynter Institute, 2.

37. Weinberg, 16.

7

Contemporary Editorial Issues and Problems

Editorial philosophies have evolved throughout the history of U.S. newspapers, with changes occurring in response to economic and demographic changes that altered the situations in which papers operated. Today, rapid economic, technological, and social changes are changing American society and newspaper editors are struggling to find an editorial philosophy that will help them meet the new challenges.

The pragmatic, personal political philosophies of printer–editors such as Benjamin Franklin in the late eighteenth century gave way to the social orientation of publisher–editors such as Henry Grady in the nineteenth century, and moved toward the anything-goes philosophy of foul-mouthed, cigar-chomping city editors of big city papers in the late nineteenth and early twentieth century that inspired the movie *Front Page*. Even tough gut-instinct editors who rose to prominence in the post-Vietnam, Watergate era, like Ben Bradlee of the *Washington Post* and Abe Rosenthal of the *New York Times*, seem out of place in the staid, carpeted newsrooms found in newspapers as the twenty-first century approaches.

In the 1980s and 1990s, the newspaper industry became seriously concerned with signficant changes in readers' and advertisers' behavior, new information sources and technologies, and the effect that these changes will have on the economic future of the industry. Those concerns led editors and publishers to begin seeking new ideas to address those issues and looking for leadership in how to respond with changes in editorial philosophy.

The contemporary editor—who is normally a graduate from a university journalism school—is being given extensive training by his or her newspaper company and industry associations in company strategy, market research, editing by design, customer service, financial management, and employee relations. Many also seek advanced degrees in business and management. As a result, content and employment decisions based on business and management concerns, rather than journalistic factors, are increasingly driving the industry.

The role of the editor and the newspaper itself dominates the issues and problems with which the industry is wrestling today. The professionalism that produced an aggressive press that brought down a presidency and published the Pentagon Papers has faded during the last decade in many papers as their editors and managers began turning away from traditional news definitions and philosophies and embracing marketing concepts for news. Critics argue that Walter Lippmann's image of a press illuminating social problems like a lighthouse in the dark has been engulfed in a fog of celebrity-oriented sell-papers-at-all-costs journalism that has become the fashion at many newspapers.

The spotlight shines on Madonna, Michael Jackson, and Pamela Anderson rather than on public affairs and issues that demand debate or public discourse in U.S. democracy. As ownership of newspapers has become more corporate, a corporate persona has taken over the industry and filtered down to the reporters, some of whom now complain they are pawns pandering to popular taste, chasing the latest sensational tidbit from television, rather than independent news gatherers. In a 1995 report on *Tabloids, Talk Radio, and the Future of News: Technology's Impact on Journalism,* Ellen Hume, an Annenberg Senior Fellow at Northwestern University, noted that "it grows more difficult every day to describe the differences between news and sheer entertainment or propaganda."[1]

These changes are producing significant problems because many papers are missing stories, overlooking important trends and social issues, and downplaying important stories that can't be conveyed and illustrated in ways that sell newspapers.

The modern-day editor is unlikely to lead like a Bradlee or a Rosenthal but more likely to manage like an MBA—"immersed in readership surveys, marketing plans, memos on management training, and budget planning goals."[2] Just like a publisher, the modern-day editor views the reader as a customer and works with advertising and circulation department heads to increase market share. In some papers, the traditional walls that have provided a buffer between editorial and other sections of the newspaper are being deliberately breached.

It is difficult to conceive of many executive editors who have undergone corporate training standing in a newsroom, telling other editors to forget what readers will think and to use their own news judgment in deciding what to cover, or telling reporters to damn the economic consequences of their reporting. We must recognize that some corporate training has professionalized the newsroom.

Nevertheless, the changes emphasizing perceived reader wants and perspectives have brought significant changes to newsrooms. It is unlikely that a Bradlee or a Rosenthal would invite readers to e-mail, fax, or phone in personal messages to the family of Nicole Brown Simpson as the *Orange County Register* did in a front-page box—headlined in bold-faced caps, "Send A Message To The Browns"—just after the verdict in the O.J. Simpson trial.

The corporate culture of contemporary news organizations has not only generated a new type of editor (the market-oriented MBA) but has also imposed a new editorial philosophy that has dramatically changed the way news is presented, edited, and gathered. It can be summed up in two phrases: reader-friendly and reader-directed. Declining national circulation and the inability of newspapers to increase penetration has created a fear among editors and publishers that newspapers will become passé in a computer age in which news can be broadcast instantaneously around the world and information can be conveyed immediately on-line. As a result, great efforts are being made to ensure that material in newspapers is prepared for easy use and understanding by readers and that it matches the interests and wants of readers.

The rationale for adopting a marketing approach to the news was well stated in a 1991 American Society of Newspaper Editors report on marginal or potential readers (individuals who enjoy reading newspapers but do so only occasionally) and at-risk readers (occasional readers who are lukewarm toward newspapers).[3] The two groups, which have poor newspaper reading habits, make up one-fourth of the adult population in the United States. Both groups are young and share common lifestyle characteristics of people under thirty-five, including having fewer ties to the communities in which they reside than loyal newspaper readers, who read newspapers almost every day and who number more than half of all adults in the United States.

The study argued that, to attract new readers, newspapers should have a feature section written for children and write more about families and raising kids, health and shopping, home remodeling and decorating, as well as giving listings of where to go and what to do during leisure time. These changes would appeal to the at-risk readers who say they have little interest in public affairs and feel overwhelmed by the world. At-risk readers have short attention spans and are not interested in government, the report found, but would be excited about a chart on where to recycle Christmas trees. These potential readers like off-beat topics, frivolous news, and, in the words of one editor involved in the study, "calendars, shortcuts and bargains." There were significant differences, however, in the news judgment of the second group of readers, the marginal readers, who described themselves as serious and career-oriented. These potential readers want more depth, explanation, and detail in stories than newspapers now offer, according to the study. The American Society of Newspaper Editors found it was easier to attract at-risk readers than marginal readers because the latter were not sold on the value of reading daily newspapers as a way to gain knowledge and were turned off by the superficiality of the news.

The decision by many newspapers to shift editorial direction toward attracting at-risk readers has led to appeals to the lowest common denominator, to "dumbing down" the news, and moving newspaper content toward what is found in magazines and television morning shows.

In their attempts to capture readers, newspapers have employed a variety of strategies to prove themselves reader-friendly and reader-directed:

- The use of color presses and changes in newspaper layout and design, including large pictures, colorful maps, lists and graphics, bold headlines, short stories, and stories that do not jump.
- A shift from reporting on government and reliance on traditional reporting beats to covering topics—often nonnews topics—that are hoped to be of interest to readers and working on stories suggested by focus groups.
- Appealing to young readers with sections aimed at children and teenagers.
- Allowing readers to participate in the newspaper by writing articles and directly speaking to editors and reporters, and once again publishing fiction and creative writing from readers in feature pages.
- Using the newspaper as an information service, i.e., providing information in formats and listings that were previously only available from specialized sources.

Leading this revolution have been national newspaper groups such as Gannett, Knight–Ridder, and Freedom Communications. Gannett has actively led the changes through development of its flagship paper, *USA Today*, and its "News 2000" program. Knight–Ridder has been influential through its experiments with *The News* in Boca Raton, Florida, and Freedom Communications has contributed industry leadership with alterations to the *Orange County Register*. Because the industry has felt such strong anxiety over its future, and other directions and voices were unclear, editors and publishers across the country have watched their efforts carefully and many have chosen to follow their leads. The following sections will explore the development, influence, and implications of these strategies in the newspaper business.

THE DESIGN-DRIVEN NEWSPAPER

For more than a decade, *USA Today* has promoted itself as the newspaper of the future and the nation's newspaper. Distributed in every state, and found at almost every major airport and hotel, the Gannett newspaper strives to be the nation's voice. Yet its influence among business leaders and policy-makers hardly matches that of the gray *Wall Street Journal* and the sober *New York Times*. But *USA Today* has been highly influential among a large number of newspaper editors and publishers and it reigns supreme among newspaper designers. Since it was launched in

1982, *USA Today* has sparked a series of editorial innovations and design changes in newspapers beyond the Gannett chain. Pick up almost any newspaper today and you'll see the shadow of *USA Today* across the front page and interior sections.[4] The *Orange County Register* has a city-by-city county scan of one- or two-paragraph items in its metro section that closely resembles *USA Today's* news nuggets of the fifty states. The 11,000-circulation weekly *Ellsworth American* in Ellsworth, Maine, uses a similar feature, "Around the County," to briefly report developments in cities such as Bucksport, Penobscot, and Sedgewick.

The *Tallahassee* (Florida) *Democrat* uses the left column of its front page to generate interest in about a half-dozen stories and features on inside pages. This "Briefing" column includes photos and précis of the highlighted stories, as well as an index and phone numbers that readers can use to contact the paper. The *Los Angeles Times* runs a front-page column of news nuggets—one-paragraph items of trendy, trivial, gossipy briefs—in its Orange County edition. Opposite coverage of the Pope's October 1995 visit to the United States was a tidbit for *Times* readers about the acquisition of three new burros for the farm at the Orange County fairgrounds and a reminder that Knott's Berry Farm's annual Halloween Haunt began at 7 p.m. The *Los Angeles Times* conducted two years of market research, twenty-four focus groups, and nearly 900 in-depth interviews before redesigning to a "faster format" in October 1989.[5]

USA Today ushered in a revolution in newspaper design that stresses style over substance. The look and intrinsic feel of a page counts more to the editors than the depth of the news. Editors want short stories—quick reads.[6] Packaging news stories with charts, graphs, maps, and photographs has become the mainstay of the *USA Today* school of design and its approach has been copied from coast to coast. The style was created after a great deal of research on what would please and attract readers who do not traditionally read newspapers. University of Washington journalism professor Doug Underwood has described the *USA Today* emphasis on blurbs instead of in-depth reporting as "the cult of colorful tidbits."[7]

When design changes that mandated short stories and stories that do not jump were implemented at the *Orange County Register* in the early 1990s, Terry Wimmer, the affable night city editor, kept a toy chainsaw at his desk as a reminder to reporters to write tightly and cut their copy rather than have it chopped by him or another editor. At a 1994 conference of the Newspaper Association of America in San Francisco, publishers were presented with a prototype of the front page of the future, based on suggestions from focus groups, that looked more like a menu of the paper and a listing of calendar items and nuggets of information than a showcase of the top news stories of the day.[8] The prototype resembled *USA Today* and it prompted one researcher, Anthony Casele, president of American Opinion Research, to warn that newspapers thoughtlessly emulating *USA Today* were starting to look the same. The American Society of Newspaper Design has expressed alarm that newspapers across the country have adopted the same format: a standard modular layout with a three-or four-column graphic or photograph anchoring the page over a centerpiece story.

The changes have brought some welcomed changes, such as the development of informational graphics to help illustrate complicated stories and features. In a recent story about cutbacks in the use of medical evacuation helicopters, the Newark, New Jersey, *Star-Ledger* recently included informational graphics depicting the layout and equipment on a Sikorsky S-76B air ambulance, a graphic of the heliocopter in flight, a depiction of how injured persons are loaded on the aircraft, and a map of New Jersey indicating where the heliocopters are based and where they transport patients.

Another useful change has been in the presentation of weather page information, which has brought new readability and emphasis to weather pages at papers nationwide. Gannett's *San Bernardino Sun*, for example, publishes a full-color weather page that includes state and national maps, a five-day forecast, air quality and pollen index graphs, a thirty-day rain outlook chart, weather tables, including major cities in the United States and around the world, and maritime weather forecasts.

The Houston, Texas, *Chronicle*, regularly publishes a "Getting Around Houston" map and table that reports construction sites and road closures on the freeways and main arteries around the city. This feature is a great help to motorists as they begin their daily commutes in and around the metropolis.

The developing trend toward uniformity of page layout has been under way for a decade. American newspapers in 1984 adopted a standard six-column, thirteen-inch-wide page designed to facilitate the placement of advertising.[9] During the past ten years, the ratio of hard news to features has decreased and newspapers have increased local news in the belief that people want "fast food" news, rather than international and national news.

Newspapers such as the *San Francisco Chronicle, Houston Post, Atlanta Constitution, Denver Post, Miami Herald, Chicago Tribune, Los Angeles Times, Baltimore Sun* and *Philadelphia Inquirer*, which have traditionally been noted for their serious approach to news, have all—to varying degrees—pursued elements of the modern design-driven, reader-directed philosophy.

THE READER AS EDITOR

The pursuit of reader interests is radically changing the definition of news and the means by which newspaper content is selected. Media critic Edwin Diamond says the trend has affected even the *New York Times*. The "Gray Lady of 43rd Street" has abandoned its mission as paper of record for hard-hitting stories about news developments throughout the world, he says. Instead, the *Times,* especially its Sunday Styles section, has become softer, lighter, brighter, and friendlier, a newspaper—in Arthur Ochs Sulzberger Jr.'s words—that should be read for the fun of it.[10] The changes that Sulzberger initiated follow the trend toward soft news at the *Times* that began in 1976 when it introduced three new weekly sections, Weekend, Living, and Home. These three sections were implemented to draw suburban readers who had abandoned the *Times,* and were promoted with the marketing slogan, "the new *New York Times*—It's a lot more than the news."[11] Diamond's views are echoed by others.

"What we used to think of as the mainstream, the respectable press," says *Washington Post* media critic Howard Kurtz, "has been just awash in tabloid type stories for the last two or three years. You know the litany—the Bobbitt case, Michael Jackson, Heidi Fleiss and so forth. And I think while that's sort of a cheap, quick, attractive fix for editors...over the long haul, it erodes our credibility because it makes us look like we're playing the same kind of game as some of our low-rent cousins." ["Many Causes of News Decline," Live Report, hosted by Lou Waters, Cable News Network, April 7, 1995, 4:48 pm EST.] As a result, even in some of the most respected newsrooms, critics argue that some of the traditional standards of verification, objectivity, and relevance have become more elusive by the day as more gossip, trivia, and non-news features are used to fill the pages.

The costs of reader-driven news are both economic and social. The *Los Angeles Times*, for example, devoted huge financial resources to play the O.J. Simpson story on page one more than 300 times. The paper published more than 1,500 Simpson stories, averaging three stories per day during the trial.[12] Simultaneously, it stopped publication of its weekly *CitiTimes* edition that had been born in the aftermath of the 1992 Los Angeles riots and covered predominantly minority sections of the city. *CitiTimes*, as an experiment to provide coverage of Black, Latino and Asian communities that had been overlooked by reporters and editors, was dropped for budget reasons because the edition apparently failed to meet the bottom line in a market-driven newspaper world.

In Northern California, the editors of the *West County Times* wanted to make sure readers got their share of happy news, a desire found in their audience research and in much of the nation. The 32,000 circulation daily designed a "Good News" logo to appear with every uplifting story in their publication.[13] The logo—a smiling dog with the *Times* in its mouth—signals a feature or a hard-news story with a positive spin, such as a profile of a woman living in a drug-infested neighborhood who vows to attend college.

The strategy to boost circulation by giving the readers whatever they request in audience studies has prompted Gannett to introduce a program, called "News 2000," that aims at finding ways to package the news for new readers, especially baby boomers. "Gannett has taken its cue from the *Orange County Register,* which shook up newspaper traditionalists with its switch to reader-friendly beats and its New Age approach to newsroom management, and from Knight–Ridder's experimental newspaper in Boca Raton, Florida, which demonstrated that even a company that has built its reputation on the winning of Pulitzer Prizes and the slogan that quality pays sees the future in reader-driven news formulas."[14] The *Boca Raton News* was redesigned to appeal to twenty five- to forty three-year-olds. At the 106th annual convention of the California Newspaper Publishers Association in Beverly Hills in 1994, Wayne Ezell, editor and vice president of the *Boca Raton News,* spoke about his paper's heavy reliance on focus groups. Editors talked to thirty focus groups before revamping the paper for Knight–Ridder's "25/43 Project."[15] Both Gannett and Knight–Ridder have sought to increase advertising revenue by publishing a product that suits the fancy of targeted age groups. Some observers see this as a sign that there is a growing number of publishers and editors who no longer trust their own instincts and that of their journalists to determine what is newsworthy.

The *Cleveland Plain Dealer* recently told its readers that it had adopted this approach in an article with the headline: "PD ATTUNED TO READERS' DIVERSE INTERESTS." "Readers are still paying for the news judgment of the reporters, editors and photographers who work here," said Gary Clark, managing editor, but now that judgment takes into account the interests of an increasingly diverse group of readers.[16] The changes for that paper include increased coverage of high school sports, women's sports, recreation, teenagers, and community news. Editors who attended focus groups with women developed "Everywoman," a Tuesday section containing time-saving tips, listings of events, and parenting information along with in-depth feature stories.

The *Times* in Munster, Indiana, prides itself on the "maestro concept," a system designed to focus stories on answering readers' questions.[17] Developed by Leland "Buck" Ryan, the maestro concept allows an editor to act like a referee in strategy sessions with reporters, photographers, and designers, so stories can be planned and packaged in a neat design with the reader in mind. The underlying philosophy is to move away from source-generated stories and explore what is relevant to readers' lives in a more readable and visually attractive manner.

As citizens have questioned the relevance of big government, newspapers have questioned the relevance of covering government news. In response, some papers have radically altered their organizational structure to accommodate the new interests they perceive in their readers. *The State,* South Carolina's largest newspaper, for example, reorganized its newsroom in 1993 to move away from institutional coverage, such as city hall, and report more about people as an anthropologist would.[18] The metro, state, and feature staffs were rearranged into quality circles that cover community roots, leisure, city life, and other topics. In line with Southern culture, a kinship beat was developed by the staff.

Nowhere was the move to de-emphasize government coverage, and cover topics instead of beats, implemented at a greater cost than in Orange County, California, where the hometown paper, the *Orange County Register,* and its main competitor, the *Los Angeles Times,* missed the biggest county story of the era, a

1995 bankruptcy that left taxpayers with almost a $2 billion loss. The irony was that both papers were handed the story but failed to vigorously pursue it.

The editorial philosophy behind the *Register* and the *Times* in Orange County, to an extent, is to avoid covering routine, so-called boring government news. The two papers will spare no expense going head-to-head on sensational, breaking stories. And both papers offer a full plate of lists, nuggets, and features. The media in Orange County failed to live up to the mandates of good journalism, said Fred Smoller, a media critic and professor of political science at Chapman University in Orange. "This is one more wake-up call that the media better get back to basics, they better start covering government—and the political process—the way the framers of the Constitution intended."[19]

A style of New Age editorial philosophy permeates some papers, with journalists and other employees receiving sensitivity training, briefings on audience research, and working in teams to change newspapers' relations with different customers.

APPEALING TO YOUNG READERS

The modern editor's willingness to lower standards to attract new readers and to boost circulation by crossing the boundaries of language and taste is best illustrated in the special sections for children and youth that have sprung up in the 1990s. Although newspapers have never had strong readership among teens, the fear of losing readership among people under thirty has prompted market-oriented editors to abandon tradition and publish new sections for young people that contain more entertainment features than news. The rationalization behind the shift to light news and fluffy features are studies, such as a 1990 survey by the Times Mirror Center for The People and The Press, that show a marked decline in readership among young people and general lack of interest in public affairs stories.[20] The Times Mirror Center found that 40 percent of respondents under age thirty said they read a newspaper every day, compared to 53 percent of the thirty- to forty-nine year-olds and 65 percent of those over age fifty. "If we don't attract the younger readers and all the old readers die, we're out of business," said noted publisher William Dean Singleton.[21]

The correct response to attact readers is for newspapers to increase coverage of teens and teen activities, and publish features on youth fashion and products they wish to buy, publish unusual news and tidbits to give them something to talk about, according to research by the Poynter Institute for Media Studies, commissioned by the American Society of Newspaper Editors and funded by a *New York Times* subsidiary. The study, "Truths to Tell: Youth and Newspaper Reading," also recommended that newspapers turn one of their staff into a celebrity to help promote the paper and its youth orientation and that they publish series that "celebrate" youth.[22]

Such advice has moved many publishers and editors to target teenagers. Editors intent on boosting circulation and appealing to Generation X have eschewed proper English to include street talk, slang and other affectations of a post-literate society in the pages of their newspapers. The underlying assumption is that anyone under eighteen can't or won't read conventional newspapers and that people in that age group lack the capacity to use or understand proper English. Mimicking MTV, editors have created youth sections with splashy graphics and illustrations that appeal to an audience weaned on television rather than newspapers. The *Syracuse Herald-Journal* in New York addresses kids as: "Hey you. Yea, you" or "You Knuckleheads" and "Yo, buttheads."[23] The *New York Daily News* has a section called "Yo."

The *Sacramento Bee* features an entertainment section geared toward youth that tells kids which restaurants have the best video games.[24] It also has pages written by and for teenagers. The *Orange County Register* has a teen panel that reviews movies, so kids can tell their peers what movies are cool. When the Syracuse paper introduced its youth pages, editors at more than one hundred other newspapers requested copies. The trend toward separate youth sections has mushroomed across the United States. Gannett distributes a "Kids Today" weekly. The *Seattle Times, Chicago Tribune, Fort Worth Star-Telegram* and *Atlanta Journal-Constitution* have reached out into the kid market.[25] The *Tribune*'s KidNews editor, Steve Cvengros, said the weekly section appeals to the video generation with lots of MTV-like graphics and short stories (350 words maximum).[26] The parent company of *Parade Magazine,* the nation's largest Sunday circulation insert, started *React,* an insert aimed at teenagers, in the fall of 1995.

Even Walt Disney has gotten into the act. In the spring of 1995, the entertainment company launched *Big Time Magazine*, a newspaper-insert tabloid targeted at readers ages seven to fifteen, in several leading newspapers, including the *Los Angeles Times, New York Times,* and *Chicago Tribune.* Disney officials said *Big Time* can be considered a cross between an entertainment weekly magazine for kids and *Parade Magazine.* "Our timing has been delicious," *Big Time* publisher Dorian Adams told the *Los Angeles Business Journal.* "There's a need out there. Editorially, there is nothing in newspapers for kids."[27]

Although some newspapers continue to distribute copies in schools through the Newspaper in Education program (which will be discussed later), so teachers can talk about the function of newspapers in a democratic society and instruct students about current events, the special kid and youth sections bypass public affairs in favor of entertainment, preparing students for television, tabloid-style news. One does not have to be unusually cynical to understand that after a steady dose of "Yo," they will be able to graduate to *USA Today.* Young Americans, aged eighteen to thirty, know less and care less about news and public affairs than any other generation of Americans in the past fifty years, according to "The Age of Indifference," a study by the Times Mirror Center for People and the Press.[28] None of the major efforts by newspaper firms to reach out to the teen market appear to be trying to ameliorate that problem.

READERS AS WRITERS

Is Yasir Arafat scary? Maybe to some of his political opponents and those who recall his days as head of a terrorist organization. But should the Palestine Liberation Organization chairman be the subject of a Halloween joke for a reader contest in a major newspaper that has foreign correspondents in the Middle East? The *Los Angeles Times,* which has initiated strict policies against stereotyping Arabs and other minorities, poked fun at Arafat's stubble in an October 2, 1995, promotion for its third annual Scariest Halloween Story Ever Told contest. "How scary are you?" the *Times* asked readers. "After signing the peace agreement at the White House, Arafat asked to make an appointment with Clinton's barber...Think you can come up with a scarier story?"[29]

Such promotions as the Halloween contest on the front page of the feature section have become common for newspapers. Reader-friendly newspapers want readers to write their own stories—fact or fiction. It doesn't matter. The point is to generate reader interest by having readers tell their stories in print for a pittance of what reporters are paid. The *Herald Times* of Bloomington, Indiana, in conjunction with New Directions for News, an industry think tank, has started a fiction column that allows readers to compose episodes of a story ranging from science fiction to spiritual fantasy.[30] Editors call this interactive journalism and it is intended to get readers connected to their newspapers. The readers are encouraged to write about personal problems, their life experiences, and their feelings. "Welcome to Back Fence," says an editor's note in the Sunday *Orange County Register.* "You're invited to share what's on your mind and reach over our Back Fence to help other readers....We invite you to talk to your "neighbors" in Back Fence or enlist their help with your own problems." In "Back Fence" on October 29, 1995, readers heard from the "scarred and desperate" hirsute woman and from "Devastated," whose husband wants a divorce after ten years, so he can see a woman twenty-two years his junior. At best this section copies Ann Landers; at worst, it allows readers to play amateur psychologist and offer advice that could be harmful.

A June 27, 1991, *Christian Science Monitor* survey of newspapers across the country found a variety of interactive practices:

- The *Concord Monitor* in New Hampshire created a board of community people who regularly contribute articles and suggestions.
- The *Sioux Falls Argus Leader* in South Dakota asked readers to identify the city's ten worst intersections and write stories about them.
- The *Merced Sun-Star* in California conducted a reader call-in at night with editors and the circulation manager answering questions.[31]

Many newspapers have copied CNN phone-in polls, asking readers to respond to questions, such as "Should the United States pull out of the United Nations?" Such polls are far from random or scientific, yet newspapers publish them as a gauge of public opinion. The practice is fraught with danger because phone-in polls can be manipulated by special interest groups, which could have members make repeated phone calls to the poll line to artificially influence public opinion. A poll on gun control, for example, could be manipulated by groups in favor of or opposed to banning handguns. Some papers use call-ins and e-mail systems to get readers' reactions to news events, social developments, and news coverage, a more immediate and verbal form of "letters to the editor."

Jay Rosen, a journalism professor at New York University and director of the Project on Public Life and the Press, has advocated a turn toward "public journalism." Rosen promotes consulting with readers and nonreaders before writing stories to get a taste of what the community wants before covering a story. Instead of solely relying on official sources, reporters cast a wide net before embarking on a project, talking to various people in the community, both ordinary folks and leaders. The concept has gained a wide range of supporters and detractors within the newspaper industry.

The *Dayton Daily News* in Ohio has taken Rosen's advice to heart. In preparing a package on the twentieth anniversary of the tornadoes that destroyed the town of Xenia, the newspaper staff sat down with a dozen Xenia residents and discussed how the community responded to the disaster. Public journalism allows for a partnership between a newspaper and the community it serves. The danger, however, is that the newspaper will become an advocate for the chamber of commerce or other partisan points of view. A newspaper must be careful about the type of people serving on its advisory board; the readers should represent a cross-section of the community. Also, both sides of a story, even a reader-generated story, must be covered.

NEWS AS INFORMATION

The information age has forever changed the newspaper industry. News executives no longer look upon themselves as newspaper managers, putting out a product on paper every day. Rather, they have become purveyors of information services and information products in both print and electronic form. Data collected by reporters can be used for news stories, charts, graphs and lists, computer bulletin boards, and electronic data retrieval systems, such as Lexis-Nexis and the Internet. Already, there are 496 on-line newspapers and 508 on-line magazines.[32] A reporter can see his story in print, on Lexis-Nexis and in an on-line newspaper. No longer does a reporter write for one medium. Work takes on a print and electronic form and can be published in a multitude of ways. Gannett's business and product development department features a *USA Today* library database service, a 900-number fax service, an overnight sports wire, a variety of dial-up, on-line information services, and Sky Radio, a live news, sports and weather service for airline passengers.[33]

Peter Francese, president and founder of American Demographics, has suggested that newspapers can meet the information needs of aging baby boomers by publishing guides to help people find what they want in a hurry.[34] Local market guides, restaurant guides, health care guides, travel guides, investment guides, best school guides, night club guides, coffee bar guides—the list is endless and newspapers have the know-how and employees to publish them. Stories can be repackaged and sold as supplements as some newspapers have done. Reprints of photographs can be offered for sale to the public. Whereas a newspaper has a short life, i.e., it is published one day and thrown into the garbage the next, the information in the newspaper, collected and edited by professional news gatherers, can be recycled in a multitude of ways forever.

Dow Jones, which publishes the *Wall Street Journal,* considers itself more in the information business than the news business. As early as 1988, 50 percent of its income came from forty electronic services.[35] The reason has to do with the rise of personal computers. John Diebold told the American Society of Newspaper Editors in 1988 that whereas there were no personal computers in the early 1960s, by the end of the 1980s some companies had up to 20,000 personal computers for workers to receive information services.[36] The strength of a news organization, compared to a telephone company or broadcasting company, is that it has the capacity, with its staff of editors and reporters, to collect and process vast quantities of information, not merely deliver it over a wire. This has contributed to the changed definition of news and the function of newspapers in this century. Newspapers already have copied magazines, publishing lists of the ten best pizza places in a city, and the best vacation spots in Hawaii. If reader-directed newspapers find through focus groups that readers are more interested in shopping malls than city halls, might editors focus more coverage on fashion than on politics? If covering a city council meeting generates one story, and covering fashion generates a story, a spring fashion guide, a list of the ten best places to shop, and a bulletin board item that tells readers where to buy bathing suits, which beat will market-driven editors pursue? Already, newspapers provide telephone call-in lines where readers can listen to songs by the latest rock stars. Instead of recording speeches by the president and the pope, newspapers titillate readers with entertainment tidbits. The challenge of the information age is to provide news that won't get buried in a plethora of information. As John Dewey said: "Society not only continues to exist by transmission, by communication, but it may fairly be said to exist in transmission, in communication. There is more than a verbal tie between the words common, community, and communication. Men live in a community in virtue of the things they have in common; and communication is the way in which they come to possess things in common."[37]

CRITICS

The influence of market-driven, reader-directed journalism is not without critics in the industry and it is not being embraced by all editors and publishers. There has been a backlash among journalists and publishers committed to conscience and the values of public affairs reporting. They contend that, by mimicking the tabloid press and television, newspapers are in danger of losing their relevance and the respect they have held in the community.

A 1994 survey by the Foundation for American Communications showed that content is critical for retaining readers and that readers expect newspapers to provide them with the local news that's ignored by television.[38] In her study of the tabloid press, Ellen Hume warned that newspapers copying the tabloids may be losing their most important consumer group—"people who want news as opposed to those simply looking for entertaining background noise."[39] A social contract exists between the freedom of the press guaranteed by the First Amendment and the responsibility of the press in a free society. To abandon either part of the contract—freedom or responsibility—would be irresponsible. Said Bill Kovach, curator of the Nieman Fellowship at Harvard University: "I think the notion of giving people what they want in order to have an ever-expanding market of consumers in order to capitalize your profit— well, I don't believe that's the reason the press is protected by the constitution. At some point managers of the press have to remember that there is a responsibility attached to the protection we have. Constantly thinking in commercial terms is ignoring that responsibility."[40]

Doug Underwood concludes his book *When MBAs Rule the Newsroom,* with the admonishment that newspapers face a clear choice: "They can continue to go down the path of trying to match television as an entertainment and visual medium — where they will finish far behind. Or they can provide the depth and context and perspective that society can't find in other media. If marketing and pleasing the public become the primary reason for their existence, newspapers risk the loss of their identity and the abandonment of any claim to the public conscience."[41]

Whenever news organizations have introduced changes that trivialize news coverage, journalists committed to the standards of the profession have objected and rebelled. One of the chief complaints of editors advocating the new direction in news has been the reluctance of staff members to go along and to be enthusiastic about writing stories that don't jump. That's why changes have been implemented from the top down—with little discussion—in the form of management directives. As Tonnie Katz, editor of the *Orange County Register,* was fond of saying, "the train is leaving the station, you can get on or get off."

Some editors and reporters have followed that advice and quit in disgust. Others quietly work on novels and on freelance magazine assignments. They consider the newspaper a day job. Geneva Overholser, the distinguished editor of the *Des Moines Register,* resigned from her position in February, 1995, blaming in part "pressure for profit at the expense of news quality." Under Overholser the newspaper won a Pulitzer Prize for a series about the life of an Iowa rape victim. She is now the ombudsman for the *Washington Post.*[42]

James P. Gannon left journalism in 1994 after thirty three years as a reporter, columnist, Washington bureau chief, and editor. "There is a struggle underway for the soul of journalism—and many respected veterans of our business believe the struggle is being lost," Gannon wrote in *Editor & Publisher.* "I think we seriously underestimate our readers. I believe they are more interested in hard news and helpful information than many editors think they are. I think they care more about everyday problems of ordinary people than about the bizarre problems of celebrities. And I think they look to newspapers for this kind of helpful, serious news that they don't get on television, and they are disappointed when they find a second-day version of TV titillation in the newspaper."[43]

Editors who have given up on public service journalism could learn a lesson from Donald L. Barlett and James B. Steele's series in the *Philadelphia Inquirer* on "America, What Went Wrong." The nine-part series, published in 1991, took a hard look at the greed of the Reagan era and how, during the decade of the 1980s, public policy was changed to help the privileged at the expense of the middle class and the poor. The reporters spent two years working on the series and collected more than 100,000 pages of documents. The response to "America, What Went Wrong" was overwhelming. The newspaper received 20,000 letters, notes, telephone calls, and requests for reprints. People jammed the lobby of the *Inquirer* for extra copies. When the series was later published as a book, it sold more than 500,000 copies. And this was for a series filled with facts, figures, and economic analysis—reportage that took a hard look at politics and government, topics that were supposed to turn off readers.[44]

Barlett and Steele credit Gene Roberts, the legendary editor of the *Inquirer,* now managing editor of the *New York Times,* with inspiring enterprise and investigative reporting that personalized stories to make them germane to readers. The *Inquirer* won seventeen Pulitzer Prizes during Roberts' eighteen-year tenure, and the newspaper's circulation jumped from 444,489 to 522,020.

Roberts has grave concerns about the future of the industry. In a 1995 address, he lashed out at corporations that are more concerned about the flow of profits to their coffers than the flow of information to the public. He warned:

> If newspapers and journalism die, it is not likely to be death by computer. A more likely prognosis is suicide. The big threat to journalism comes from within our profession, not from the outside. We threaten our existence with the mindless rushes toward the latest journalistic trend and fad. We sabotage our newspapers by giving them a corporate look and feel, rather than letting them be as individualistic as the communities they serve…We strangle our newsrooms with meager budgets that drain away the vitality we need to attract and hold readers.[45]

Editors have a choice according to Roberts. They can follow the fads or produce a quality product. Weather maps, briefs, charts, graphs, and color won't capture readers as much as news that provides depth and understanding of events that affect their lives. Modern-day editors have sold their souls for good standing in the corporation. They have compromised their principles for profit. The irony may be that, by selling out for short-term gain, they have undermined the future of their newspapers. The operation of cosmetically changing the newspaper may be a success, but readership will die.

EFFECTS OF THE NEW EDITORIAL PHILOSOPHY AND APPROACHES

Given the industry's strong embrace of the elements in the new approaches to the content and marketing of newspapers, one would assume that it has produced significant improvements in the operations and conditions of the industry. However, there is little evidence that the changes are achieving their stated goals. The trends in newspaper circulation and advertising have *not* been altered. Although nonreaders have generally applauded the look and feel of the changes, newspaper circulation has not flourished among that group. Existing readers have generally reacted negatively to design changes but then have reluctantly accepted them, yet their opinion of the general change in the editorial tone and type of news is much more harsh.

From the newspaper side, the changes have produced important results as well. Existing newspaper staffs have been unable to absorb the new tasks and duties associated with changes in technology and changes in editorial philosophy. When journalists began taking on additional typesetting and layout duties created by the installation of computers and pagination, their ranks did not significantly increase. They began spending more time in newsrooms, and the time they devoted to stories declined. The changes required to meet the needs of reader-directed and market-driven journalism are even more labor-intensive and require specialized skills. Because existing staffs did not have the time to complete them along with their normal assignments and often lacked the specialized knowledge and skills needed, newspapers have spread some of those duties among the existing staff and hired additional personnel with graphics and informatics skills to handle the new editorial approaches. In addition, it has been discovered that design-oriented makeup and journalism force editors to increase the number of pages in newspapers or to significantly cut the amount of news and information conveyed.

Although the results of these changes have been highly touted, their effectiveness is questionable. It is estimated that Gannett has invested more than $1.5 billion dollars in startup and operating costs in *USA Today*. The paper and its owner have yet to announce that it has produced an annual profit. Although the gap between expenses and revenue is closing and the paper is expected to produce its first annual operating profit shortly, it is doubtful that Gannett will ever recoup its total investment. Major contributors to its problems have been the difficulty the paper has had in attracting a steady group of regular readers. Its primary readers today are individuals traveling away from home who read the paper when they cannot get their local newspaper and want to keep up on world and national developments quickly as they travel about on business or pleasure. The quick, easy-reading format of the paper serves their interest with a brief, entertaining scan of events. The highly visual approach and truncated presentation of news and information in an entertaining style have not successfully turned large numbers of nonreaders into readers.

The nature of the readership of *USA Today* has translated into an advertising problem. Because *USA Today* is a national paper that cannot tap local retail advertising, which is the backbone of most newspapers' finances, the paper is dependent primarily upon national advertisers. From the paper's introduction, however, those advertisers have been wary of *USA Today*'s transitory audience. In its first years many advertisers approached the paper more like a magazine than a newspaper, using magazine-styled ads and funds designated for magazine advertising if they selected the paper. The disquiet the paper created continues, but it has been successful in promoting itself as a national paper and getting advertisers to shift it into the category for newspaper advertising. Nevertheless, *USA Today* has problems attracting the range of advertisers normally found in newspapers, and its primary advertisers are large national companies associated with the travel industry or wishing to reach travelers. This continues to limit the revenue and income potential of the paper and is keeping it from becoming an important financial success story.

Knight–Ridder has also encountered difficulties in improving readership and advertising at the *Boca Raton News*. The company has significantly reduced its experimental approach of heavy national and international news, extensive use of color, maps and infographics, and stand-alone sections. The paper has reemphasized local coverage, reduced the number of pages it publishes, the number of sections it publishes, and its editorial staff.[46] Although studies revealed that the approach was appreciated by potential readers in the twenty five- to forty three year-old age group, it did not translate into significantly improved circulation and was costly to maintain because of its reliance on new personnel, color printing, and heavy newsprint usage without additional revenue.

SUMMARY

If these industry leaders in the new editorial approaches to newspapers have not enjoyed wide success, and proponents are moderating the extent to which they have embraced them and the benefits they project from the approaches, one must question why the industry still embraces the formulas they established. The answers appear to lie in three factors. First, few alternative visions of the future and the options facing newspapers are being offered. Second, the new approaches have clearly improved the general appearance of newspapers and their readability and have brought benefits that are keeping advertisers interested in the medium. Third, although the approaches have not translated into significant numbers of new readers, it is argued that it is impossible to know whether they have stemmed a potential decline in existing readers. This argument is debatable, however, because most research has indicated that newspaper readership is habitual and tends to cease only with the death of readers.

Probably the most serious effect of the new editorial philosophy and the accompanying changes has been the reduction of emphasis on the central function of newspapers—providing news and information in quantities not available elsewhere. Individually, the changes of the 1980s and 1990s are not, in and of themselves, problematic unless they are taken to extremes. Unfortunately, some papers have done exactly that in response to industry fears rhetoric. The real damage from the changes results from the combined effects of the new approaches in reducing the content wanted and needed by politically, socially, and economically active members of the community that have made up the core of newspaper readers for three centuries. In the effort to attract those who have not traditionally read papers, and to hold on to readers gained in the twentieth century who selected newspapers for features, sports, and light information, newspapers are becoming more like magazines and television and, thus, are making themselves less attractive to those individuals who have sustained papers throughout history.

It is easy to suspect that some industry leaders have not rejected and abandoned the formulas of the new approaches because they have invested so much time, money, and ego that it is difficult to recognize or admit the lack of success. However, it must also be recognized that the feelings of uncertainty and fear in the industry, combined with the lack of alternative approaches to the changes and problems of the industry, have left many clutching these ideas as flotation devices in an unpredictable sea. The security felt from the idea that the industry has found a course to a successful future, and the arguments that the contemporary approaches provide for use with advertisers and investors, are clearly playing a role in their continued promotion and use by editors and publishers around the nation.

ENDNOTES

1 Ellen Hume, *Tabloids, Talk Radio, and the Future of News: Technology's Impact on Journalism* (Washington, DC: Annenberg Washington Program in Communication Policy Studies, Northwestern University, 1995), 20.

2. Doug Underwood, *When MBAs Rule the Newsroom* (New York: Columbia University Press, 1993), *xii.*

3. American Society of Newspaper Editors, *Marginal and At-Risk Readers—Findings of Two New ASNE Studies. Proceedings of the American Society of Newspaper Editors,* (Reston, Va.: American Society of Newspaper Editors, 1991), 69–86.

4. John K. Hartman, *The USA Today Way: A Candid Look at the National Newspaper's First Decade,* (Bowling Green, OH: John K. Hartman, 1993).

5. Ira Teinowitz, "Newspapers Rethink Their Eroding Position; 'Endangered as a Mass Medium,' Papers Fight Back," *Advertising Age,* August 12, 1991, S-1.

6. David Remnick, "Last of the Red Hots," *New Yorker,* September 18, 1995, 76–84.

7. Underwood, 95.

8. Tim Jones, "Newspapers Struggle to Read between the Lines; Publishers Seek Right Definition of 'Content' as Circulation Slides," *Chicago Tribune,* May 1, 1994, B3.

9. Leo Bogart, "The State of the Industry," *The Future of News* (Washington, DC: Woodrow Wilson Center Press, 1992), 96.

10. Chris Welles, "Is the Gray Lady Slipping?" *Business Week*, March 7, 1994, 19.

11. James Devitt, "The Daily Newspaper," *The Future of News* (Washingto, DC: Woodrow Wilson Center Press, 1992), 138.

12. David Shaw, "The Story That Hijacked America," *Los Angeles Times,* October 9, 1995, S1–12.

13. "California Paper Promotes Good News," *Editor & Publisher*, February 11, 1995, 15.

14. M. L. Stein, "Re-Establishing Relevance for Readers; Panelists Examine Concepts Aimed at Stopping Erosion of Readership," *Editor & Publisher,* March 5, 1994, 16.

15. Ibid, 16.

16. Karen Sandstrom, "PD Attuned to Readers' Diverse Interests," *Cleveland Plain Dealer*, June 5, 1994, S30.

17. Ibid., 16.

18 Scott Johnson, "Newsroom Circles," *Quill, (*March 1993), 83:28.

19. Susan Paterno, "The Way to Do It," *American Journalism Review, (*March 1995), 17:29.

20. *The American Media: Who Reads, Who Watches, Who Listens, Who Cares* (Los Angeles, CA: Times Mirror Center for The People and The Press, 1990), 7.

21. Howard Kurtz, "For Nation's Newspapers, the News Isn't Good," *Messages 2: The Washington Post Media Companion* (Boston: Allyn & Bacon, 1993), 48.

22. Shirley Brice Heath and Sara DeWitt, *Truths to Tell: Youth and Newspaper Reading. A Special Report for the American Society of Newspaper Editors Literacy Committee* (St. Petersburg, FL.: Poynter Institute for Media Studies, 1995).

23. Eleanor Randolph, "Extra! Extra! Who Cares?; Newspapers Face the Incredible Shrinking Reader," *Washington Post,* April 1, 1990, C1

24. Dan Fost, "Newspapers Enter the Age of Information," *American Demographics,* September, 1990, 11: 14.

25. Jeffrey Scott, "The Next Generation Newspapers Pursue the Young with Special Features, Sections," *Atlantic Journal and Constitution,* February 2, 1993, C1.

26. Ibid., C1.

27. Greg Spring, "Disney Eyes Launch of Kid-Themed Newspaper," *Los Angeles Business Journal (*April 17, 1995), 16:8.

28. *The Age of Indifference* (Los Angeles: Times Mirror Center for The People and the Press, 1990), 11.

29. "How Scary Are You?" *Los Angeles Times*, October 2, 1995, View Section, 1.

30 Hanna Liebman, "A New Breakfast Serial. Think That You Can't Believe What the Papers Say? Newspapers Publish Fiction to Increase Readership," *Media Week,* October 11, 1993, 12.

31. Richard Louv, "Extra, Extra! Tell Me All about It!" *Christian Science Monitor*, June 27, 1991, 19.

32. Stephen Lynch, "O.J. Response Means Online Media Guilty," *Orange County Register,* October 23, 1995, B24.

33 L. Carol Christopher, "Closing the Gap," *Quill* (January/February 1994), 82:27.

34. Peter Francese, "Newspapers and the Future," *Proceedings of the 1988 Convention of the American Society of Newspaper Editors"* (Reston, Va: American Society of Newspaper Editors, 1988) 239.

35. Ibid., 242.

36. Ibid., 240.

37. John Dewey, *Democracy and Education* (New York: Macmillan), 1915, 14.

38. "Survey: Newspapers Need Better Content," *Legal Intelligencer,* April 26, 1994, 11.

39. Hume, 31.

40. Randolph, C1.

41. Underwood, 180.

42. Richard Cunningham, "Ombudsman Gives High Marks to *Washington Post*," *Quill* September, 1995, 83:17.

43. James P. Gannon, "Warning: Entertainment Values Threaten Journalism's Health," *Editor & Publisher,* Aug. 27, 1994, 48.

44. Donald L. Barlett and James B. Steele, *America, What Went Wrong?* (Kansas City: Andrews and McMeel, 1992).

45. Gene Roberts, "Suicide Hangs over Our Heads," *Quill* (November/December 1995), 84:63.

46. "Rebecca Ross Albers, "Back to Boca," *Presstime* (April 1995), 27-30.

8

Contemporary Business/ Management Issues and Problems

As noted in the last chapter, newspaper managers today face a variety of challenges that are forcing them to reconsider the ways in which they select content and present materials to readers. These issues have arisen because of changes in audiences, technology, and economics. They are also forcing publishers and editors to confront business and management problems and issues involving the ethnic and racial changes in their audiences, changing patterns of media use, rising illiteracy, and the need to develop interest in newspapers.

In addition, newspaper managers are attempting to understand the real potential for electronic delivery of newspapers and other information products and to offer a variety of telecommunications-based services. They are also confronting problems caused by the rise of advertorials within the pages of the newspaper and wrestling with economic changes that have altered the levels of profitability at which they operate.

PROMOTING DIVERSITY TO MEET THE NEEDS OF A CHANGING POPULATION

The demographic makeup of the population in the United States is rapidly shifting. The population is becoming less dominated by Caucasians of European origin, creating a need for the newspaper industry to broaden its appeal and its circulation base. In order to flourish in the emerging multicultural society, newspapers have to expand their reporting about ethnic and racial minorities and to ensure that they are sensitive to the needs and wishes of those groups.

The social structure in which about one-fourth of the population are minorities is rapidly changing as the nation's population has begun absorbing a wave of immigrants from Asia and Latin America. In the 1980s, for example, more than 7.4 million immigrants came to the United States but less than 10 percent came from Europe. Individuals from Latin America and the Caribbean accounted for 47 percent and 38 percent came from Asia. Mexico alone accounted for 23 percent of the immigrants. Five hundred thousand immigrants came from the Central American nations, and China, Korea, the Philippines, and Vietnam each accounted for more than 300,000 immigrants during the 1980s. The Bureau of the Census estimates that Hispanics, who made up 9 percent of the population in 1990, will be 22.5 percent of the population by the middle of the twenty-first century. Asians, who represented 3 percent of the population in 1990, will account for 8.3 percent by mid-century. Blacks will rise from 12.3 percent of the population in 1990 to 15.7 percent. The overall effect of immigration and a low birthrate for non-Hispanic Caucasians will be a reduction for that group from 84 percent in 1990 to 73 percent by 2050. Minority groups that today account for about one-fourth of the population will account for about 44 percent by mid-century.[1]

Just as New York was the port of call for European immigrants at the beginning of the century, Los Angeles, Miami, and New York are the ports of call for Asians and Latino immigrants at the end of the century. States including California, Florida, and Texas are already experiencing dramatic population shifts. In Southern California, for example, non-Hispanic Caucasians will be a minority by the year 2025.[2]

"The media must be able to see the large body of unserved and disenfranchised potential customers out there in the growing minority communities," says Ted Pease, former editor of the *Freedom Forum Media Studies Journal.* "Making the news product fill those consumers' needs is not just good economic sense, but the key to economic survival in an increasingly multicultural U.S. melting pot."[3]

Newspapers, which have traditionally treated minorities with indifference and sometimes intolerance, are finding they must broaden their coverage to include news and features about minorities within their communities. Many editors want their coverage to go beyond the stereotypes of blacks as gang members, Hispanics as illegal immigrants, and Asians as the model minority. Many want to cover events in the lives of people of color that go beyond the three mainstays of traditional minority coverage: crime, food, and festivals. But they find it difficult to achieve those aims because they and their staffs often do not understand the minority communities, and because the number of minority journalists and editors is so low.

In 1968 the Kerner Commission, which investigated the racial violence that spread across American cities in the late 1960s, found that "the press acts and talks about Negroes as if Negroes do not read newspapers or watch television, give birth, marry, die, or go to PTA meetings."[4] The situation has not improved a great deal since that time. As the *New York Times* introduced new sections in the mid-1970s to lure suburban readers, editors admitted that the paper covered Boston better than the Bronx. In 1978, Otis Chandler, then publisher of the *Los Angeles Times,* said in print and broadcast interviews that the *Times'* marketing strategy was directed at whites and that the paper, in effect, redlined low-income minorities because they did not have the purchasing power advertisers demanded.[5] After racial strife struck Los Angeles in 1992 in the wake of the Rodney King verdicts, the *Times* initiated two weekly news sections—*CitiTimes* and *Nuestro Tiempo*—to cover the large black and Hispanic neighborhoods of Los Angeles, respectively. The *Times* stopped publishing the two sections in 1995, however, in an effort to cut operating costs. It is a small wonder that many minorities and observers believe the press has made only token efforts to increase coverage of their communities.

Some progress has been made in broadening and improving the content of minority coverage and the number of minority journalists. Newspapers such as the Akron *Beacon Journal, Chicago Sun-Times,* New Orleans *Times-Picayune,* and *Indianapolis Star* have produced heralded in-depth series and reports about race relations in America. *USA Today* instituted a policy of publishing photographs of minorities illustrating everyday life, such as swimming at the beach during a hot spell, purchasing a home computer, or attending a Thanksgiving Day football game.

The late Robert Maynard, publisher of the Oakland (California) *Tribune,* stressed multicultural coverage of the San Francisco Bay area and, with his wife, Nancy Hicks Maynard, helped found the Institute for Journalism Education (now known as the Robert Maynard Institute for Journalism Education) to promote multicultural reporting and help develop minority journalists. The Freedom Forum pumped $4 million in grants into multicultural education programs in the newspaper industry between 1975 and 1985.[6] Major news companies, including Knight–Ridder, Times Mirror, Washington Post, Gannett, and New York Times, supported the first national Unity Conference in Atlanta in 1994 that brought together the National Association of Black Journalists, the National Association of Hispanic Journalists, the Asian American Journalists Association, and the Native American Journalists Association to discuss solutions to common problems and educate journalists who are not members of those groups. More than 5,000 journalists attended the five-day conference that addressed multiculturalism in the media.

Progress has been made in increasing nonwhite hiring in newspapers. As indicated in previous chapters, employment of minorities is increasing. The American Society of Newspaper Editors (ASNE) in 1972 reported that people of color comprised 1.5 percent of the editorial workforce, that in 1983 the number had risen to 5.6 percent, and that in 1993 people of color represented 9.8 percent.[7] Although the 9.8 percent for 1993 looks promising, it needs to be pointed out that in 1993 half of all daily newspapers in the United States still had no journalists of color on their staffs and that newspapers are experiencing problems retaining minority journalists when they are hired.

The ASNE has committed itself to a goal of minority employment equal to the percentage of minorities in the national population by the year 2000. The Newspaper Association of America established a Diversity Department to help promote minority recruitment and retention in the industry by providing training, advice, and access to resources. To boost the effort, it recently produced a significant minority recruitment kit to help publishers and editors improve their ability to attract minorities to all newspaper departments.[8] To improve the pool of qualified minority applicants, the Association for Education in Journalism and Mass Communication, which represents schools of journalism nationwide, pledged to recruit minority students and faculty, to teach the contributions made by minorities and women in journalism, and to prepare students to report about multicultural issues as part of its accreditation requirements. Although such efforts are useful, they are producing slow results and it is unlikely that newspapers will reach the goal of minority employment equal to population representation by the year 2000.

The industry hopes that the training, hiring and retention of minority journalists will help to reverse the problematic trends in reporting and covering minorities. Supporters argue that it is not only the correct moral choice but the correct business choice given the changing demographics of the United States.

DEVELOPING LITERACY AND PROMOTING NEWSPAPER READING

The newspaper industry has increasingly begun playing a significant role in the development of literacy and promotion of newspaper reading, both as public service activities and as means of maintaining and increasing its customer base. Participation of newspapers and newspaper industry associations in literacy campaigns blossomed in the 1980s in response to a growing public awareness of the problem of illiteracy that by mid-decade affected 60 million Americans.[9] Part of the response by newspapers has been renewed emphasis on promoting and developing newspaper reading among school children.

Efforts to support and take part in literacy campaigns became a major focus of individual publishers, newspaper groups, and associations when it became known that about one-third of all adult Americans are unable to read. By the 1990s that number included about 27 million functionally illiterate and an additional 65 million who are unable to read or comprehend what they have read. Despite the emphasis on literacy during the previous decade, a 1993 study by the U.S. Department of Education found that the situation had not improved significantly and that half the population has a great deal of difficulty reading a newspaper.[10] Functional illiteracy and general illiteracy are the result of a variety of factors including rapid large-scale immigration of non-English speaking persons, social problems related to poverty, poor schooling, poor attitudes toward and lack of reading in many homes, as well as the increasing demands of the complex and specialized language required in a technologically advanced society.

Literacy involves the ability of people to read, to receive messages, and to communicate in writing. It requires not only the ability to read and write, but the willingness to do so and a level of comfort in doing so. Those who are unable to meet those benchmarks fall into the categories of functional illiteracy, which involves the ability to read only at a basic survival level, or illiteracy, that is, the inability to read at all.

In promoting literacy, newspapers have helped establish, support, and promote efforts to develop reading and writing ability among adults and children. They have assisted the organization and teaching of writing in community centers and worked to help get children reading in their earliest years by seeking partnerships with television programs, stations, and schools.

One major thrust has been the revival of interest in the Newspaper in Education program, an effort in which newspapers are provided for classroom use and teachers are taught how to use daily papers to supplement traditional coursework. The effort developed from individual newspapers' activities early in the twentieth century and was formalized in 1961 when the American Newspaper Publishers Association Foundation began sponsoring and expanding the program.

Today about half of the daily newspapers in the nation, representing nearly 90 percent of newspaper circulation, participate in the program. The number of papers participating jumped by one-third during the 1980s not only to help support literacy efforts, but also because the industry became aware of low newspaper readership among young adults raised after the introduction of television. The Newspapers in Education program became a primary strategy of the industry to try to help develop the newspaper reading habit as a means of ensuring future circulation for the newspaper industry.[11]

Research about the effects of the program have found that it does not produce significant results in terms of circulation increases, but that it is important in increasing reading among minority youth, especially black youths from homes in which reading is infrequent or absent, that it is useful in increasing reading skills overall, and that students who use newspapers in classrooms read at a higher level than those who do not.[12]

ELECTRONIC DELIVERY INITIATIVES AND PROSPECTS

The ability to deliver newspapers through teletext services or computer terminals developed with the emergence of cable television and data transfer through telecommunications lines. This ability was and is particularly attractive to newspapers because it provides the potential to end the highly expensive printing and distribution aspects of newspaper production and to concentrate instead on information and advertising aspects that could be delivered via telecommunications. It is every publisher's dream to do away with the operating costs of printing plants, such as the *Los Angeles Times'* $230 million press building, which covers nearly one million square feet and turns 430 tons of newsprint and 700 gallons of ink into 600,000 newspapers every day. In addition to the printing costs are those for fueling hundreds of trucks that travel thousands of miles daily to deliver a product that is thrown away the next day. It is manufacturing, distribution, and newsprint costs, rather than the salaries of editorial and advertising salespeople, that account for the majority of the expenses of a newspaper.[13]

Experiments with electronic services in the 1980s, however, revealed a resistance by traditional readers to such services, in part because of problems in formatting and displaying information and advertising in electronic form. The main problem with such on-line delivery, however, is that it dramatically changes the ways in which the information is received, processed, and comprehended by readers. This requires significant changes in reading activity, a particularly difficult problem because newspaper reading is a habitual ritual of daily life and such change is uncomfortable for most people.

In addition, electronic delivery requires additional equipment investments by most readers, increasing the cost of newspaper reading for them. Electronic delivery suffers from portability problems as well, in that adequate technology has not yet been developed that permits ease of reading away from home. Although the situation is changing, as of the mid-1990s only 12 percent of U.S. households had a personal computer with a modem, the basic requirement for accessing on-line information. Usable portable electronic displays are not yet available. This presents a problem because many readers, such as business executives and financial analysts, would have to arrange to get the paper delivered both at home and at work, and travelers and commuters by bus, train, and airplane would need the hard copy version of the newspaper.

The development of newer technology that has begun to integrate on-line delivery with existing equipment has reawakened interest in electronic delivery, but because newspaper readers tend to be older and less familiar or comfortable with modern technology, newspapers will not be able to switch completely from printed to on-line delivery for at least one or two more generations—well into the second half of the twenty-first century. The quality of display terminals, which for the most part have glare problems, will have to be improved to reduce eyestrain and enable readers to look at a newspaper over a prolonged period. Software programs will have to be developed that enable readers to scan through the on-line newspaper to find articles they are interested in without bypassing the advertising that pays for the product.

Over time, however, as new readers and existing readers become more comfortable with electronic technology and information display, they will be willing to substitute on-line delivery, allowing newspapers to produce and distribute fewer printed editions. While this can be expected to produce some cost savings, it will also reduce economies of scale in printing and distribution and may force newspapers to provide different prices for electronic and printed editions.

Although the future of electronic delivery is uncertain, newspaper firms are moving aggressively to position themselves to participate in the benefits and changes that will occur if the public is willing to accept electronic delivery. Many newspapers have created a new position comparable to a deputy managing editor, that of media specialist, that in effect puts a high-level editorial person in charge of developing electronic newspapers, World Wide Web pages, and on-line information services. Several hundred newspapers have moved to make back issues available on-line, a relatively easy process because electronic production and library capabilities are widely used in the industry. About 100 newspapers are now offering on-line access that includes the current day's paper. Newspapers have also archived their libraries on CD-Roms that are distributed with a time delay of one to three months at a lower cost than real-time on-line delivery services.

In 1995 eight major newspaper companies (Advance Publications, Cox, Gannett, Hearst, Knight–Ridder, Times Mirror, Tribune, and Washington Post) joined forces to create the New Century Network, an Internet-based service that will provide on-line newspaper delivery and information-sharing among a network of newspapers. The initial goal of the network is to place seventy-five newspapers on-line. The system would allow users to view their local or preferred paper and then have access through that paper to the work of other papers in the network and, potentially, wire services as well. Dow Jones Business Information services makes available same-day access to the *Wall Street Journal*, *Los Angeles Times*, *Financial Times* and *New York Times*, and has a business library that includes more than 47 million documents from more than 3,400 sources.

Efforts to discover the most desirable method to reach audiences on-line is causing some papers to shuffle the delivery of their services. For example, TimesLink—the largest newspaper-based on-line service, operated by the *Los Angeles Times*—in 1996 moved its services from Prodigy to the World Wide Web in hopes of reaching a wider audience and increasing control and profit over the venture. TimesLink served 21,000 subscribers in 1995 and its managers believe that the move to the web from the proprietary service will increase access and subscribers.[14]

The move from proprietary services to the web is increasing, with about half of the papers available on-line providing access through the World Wide Web. Part of the rationale comes from newspaper companies wanting to ensure their position as identifiable publishers. "They don't want to be just information providers—providers of information to larger, third-party services in which their content ends up being buried. They want to be publishers," according to James D. Dougherty, an advertising and publishing analyst for Dean Witter Reynolds.[15]

Despite the growth of on-line delivery and services, newspapers are having a difficult time convincing large numbers of advertisers that it is an appropriate means of advertising delivery. Advertisers remain concerned about the stability of on-line audiences and the actual exposure that on-line ads provide to audiences. It will take time before on-line delivery generates substantial profits or makes money at all. Edward J. Atorino, senior vice president for Dillon Read & Co., characterizes newspaper on-line ventures as research and development. "Whether or not it's a business we'll know in the next five or so years... But just in case, you've got to establish yourself to be in this business. You don't want to miss what could be the next opportunity."[16]

Newspapers hope to create on-line networks that go beyond the news and provide ticket services, home shopping, travel guides, worldwide weather reports, stock quotes, food booklets, sports packages (including biographies and statistics on players and background information on major sporting events), entertainment guides, restaurant reviews, and listings of community activities.

Because of anxiousness about the state of the industry, many newspapers and newspaper companies began rushing into the new fields of electronic information delivery during the late 1980s and early 1990s convinced that it would rapidly displace traditional newspapers. Many companies and executives that were highly optimistic in their views about the potential have now moderated those views and expect a much longer transition period, although they plan to continue looking for ways to use the material in electronic forms.

Perhaps the most visible sign of the pace of the movement to electronic delivery was Knight–Ridder's shutdown of its developmental laboratory designed to produce portable technology on which electronic newspapers and other publications can be read—a major development needed before newspapers can start shifting away from printing. CEO Anthony Ridder explained the 1995 pullback, saying the technology was "just too far in the future. I think we need to focus more on the here and now."[17]

OTHER TELECOMMUNICATIONS-BASED INFORMATION SERVICES

Because once-a-day publication gives radio and television advantages over daily newspapers in terms of providing up-to-date news and information, and because classified advertising is a major contributor to newspaper revenues and could be moved to electronic media, newspaper executives have explored and begun to offer additional services to protect their financial interests and to benefit from the growth of telecommunications fields.

A major form of information delivery that developed in the 1980s is audiotext, information services that consumers can call using their telephones. Such services are offered both without charge and for a fee. Such services offer up-to-the-hour sports scores, stock quotes, classified advertisements, legal advice, medical information, dating services, travel guides, and other information, including packaged stories on particular subjects. For a fee, readers may call and order all the stories that have been written in the past three years about a specific subject. This enables businesses to track trends and gather information about markets within the newspaper's circulation area. Subscribers have used such services to look up articles about AIDS treatment or to find a nursing home for ailing parents. The stories are easily gleaned from the newspaper's electronic library and sold at a profit. In addition, astrological reports from the newspaper and up-to-date concert information, including sample songs, are available by phone.

The St. Paul, Minnesota, *Pioneer Press* operates "Personal Line," a voice mail dating service that prints ads in the paper three times a week listing individuals who are seeking dates or partners and allows interested parties to respond using a voice mail system. Such services grew out of a combination of voice mail technology and 900-number customer-paid services. By 1995, about 3,200 daily, weekly, and alternative publications were offering various voice services.

Although newspapers are rushing to provide these services, they do so for different reasons. A recent survey found significant differences in the reasons daily and weekly publishers begin offering such services. Daily newspapers tend to use them as experiments in hopes of maintaining their position as information providers, whereas weeklies view them primarily as a means of generating revenues.[18]

Audiotext services tend to be offered primarily in major metropolitan areas where sufficient population exists to use multiple services, but even in those large areas, audiotext has not produced great financial successes for participating newspapers. The development of these services has, however, positioned their newspapers as broader providers of information and advertising in anticipation of the growth of information and advertising products from telecommunications companies and independent producers.

Another form of information and advertising delivery gaining the interest of publishers has been specialized information fax services, typically prepared daily. Customers subscribe to these services to receive information not available in a timely manner from newspapers, such as closing stock prices, or specialized tracking of specific stocks or news topics. A customer, for example, could receive weekly all stories produced by the newspaper and received from wire services about Angola. About 100 newspapers, mainly dailies in the largest U.S. cities, were offering some type of fax services by 1994. The *New York Times*, for example, has, since 1990, offered a daily worldwide fax service of major news events, which has become a popular service for individuals who live abroad, for cruise ships, and for foreign hotels with English-speaking customers. In 1995, the *Times* expanded its service to offer an edition on the World Wide Web.

ADVERTORIAL MATERIALS

A business issue faced by many newspapers is whether and how to offer advertorial materials to audiences. The quest for profit has opened new vistas for special sections and advertisements, called advertorials, which blend ad copy with quasi-editorial material. Like their sister infomercials on television, the advertorials wrap themselves in the veneer of legitimate news by imitating the type face, font, and style of editorial copy. These special sections, filled with promotional copy and display advertising, are designed to fit in with other sections of the newspaper. Their resemblance to news should come as no surprise because the editorial staff of some newspapers writes advertorial copy. Reporters punch out bright stories for chamber of commerce-style progress editions, education supplements, and sports wrap-ups. Some weekly sections consist of corporate press releases, touting the achievements of industries that may very well be polluters, and advice from realtors who tell readers why they should purchase homes and be the kings and queens of their castle—even if the investments are risky or the housing market is about to decline. In a survey of thirty-seven major newspapers, Leo Bogart, formerly executive vice president and general manager of the Newspaper Advertising Bureau, recently found that 30 percent of the newspapers failed to label special sections as advertising matter and that 16 percent use the ad designation only on selected pages, not on the front page.[19] In a 1995 study, more than 25 percent of the respondents misidentified an R. J. Reynolds Tobacco editorial advertisement on cigarettes and science as a staff editorial item in the newspaper rather than as paid advertising. The authors note that advertorials masquerade successfully as editorials and that "recent innovations in advertising and creative adaptations of certain advertising formats continue to blur the distinction between commercial (i.e., advertising) and editorial speech."[20]

These developments present problems because many journalists and some publishers are concerned about advertisers masking their message in fake news stories. They believe that, to maintain editorial integrity, a clear separation between news and advertising should be upheld. Such critics argue that even if advertorials contain a disclaimer at the top or bottom of the page, they give the appearance of editorial legitimacy, the stamp of authenticity, to what can often be considered promotional public relations or propaganda and that they place the newspaper's image and integrity at risk by associating it with the message.

George Cranberg, George Gallup professor of journalism at the University of Iowa, warns that a thin line separates news and advertising. "Major newspaper companies are describing advertisers as 'business partners' and editors at these companies are accompanying ad salesmen when they call on customers."[21] The recession in the early 1990s prompted newspapers to develop special sections tailored to advertisers; small newspapers have featured advertorials that profile hometown merchants and local shopping centers. Large newspapers run pseudo-travel sections that promote vacation resorts in Mexico and other areas around the world. Advertorials lure tourists with bright—but far from objective—copy about the beauty of the resorts. Major national papers including the *Washington Post, New York Times*, and *Los Angeles Times* have run advertorials praising repressive regimes, such as North Korea, Singapore, and Saudi Arabia, that violate human rights, censor news stories, or exercise tight control over media.

Although newspaper publishers argue they cannot publish without advertising, critics argue that exercising care with advertorials will not bankrupt newspapers and that they undermine the depth and content of news, and the newspaper as a whole, by diverting advertising away from other news and feature sections. When advertising in special sections pulls advertising from other sections of the paper, the newshole in those sections shrinks because the number of pages are reduced. By promoting advertorials, the critics argue, advertisers, instead of editors, are able to control the scope of the news. Taken to its logical conclusions, according to critics, advertorials will have supermarkets preparing the food sections, auto makers sponsoring car sections, and realtors sponsoring real estate sections to gain control of the editorial matter surrounding their advertisements. The harshest critics assert that reporters in the future may end up working for the advertising department, and their projections are not wild speculation. The *Los Angeles Times*, for example, has an advertorial staff that includes fifteen reporters and two special-section editors who operate independently of the editorial department and have siphoned off features for their special sections. The result is an enormous amount of advertorial material. In 1987 alone, the *Times* printed about 20,000 pages of advertorial material in 2,000 different sections.[22]

When advertorials cross the line into politics, the results can be especially distressing because the entire objectivity of the newspaper can be questioned. That's what happened to the *New York Times* in 1993 when the paper published a seven-page advertising section promoting the North American Free Trade Agreement (NAFTA). The section promoted the benefits of NAFTA at the same time the newspaper was editorializing in favor of the agreement. Vigorous criticism of the advertorial developed when the *Times* solicited advertisers who supported NAFTA, but denied space to opponents of the agreement. A pitch letter sent to advertisers by the *Times* clearly appealed to partisan interests. "In an effort to educate the public and influence Washington decision makers, the *New York Times* has planned a series of three special advertorials presenting the positive economic and social benefits of NAFTA." *Times* spokespersons later emphasized that the letter was expressing the view of the advertorial, not the paper as an institution, but the *Times* made no effort to produce an anti-NAFTA advertorial. A group of media critics and journalism professors charged that the *Times'* behavior involving the advertorials "created the appearance that editorial and advertising policy at the *Times* work together to exclude the views of those the paper disagrees with."[23]

Because of such problems, many publishers, advertising directors, and editors are reconsidering whether and how they will include advertorials in their papers. It is unlikely that many will refuse advertorials and special sections altogether because of their financial benefits, but the issues raised are forcing newspaper managers to confront the problems that have emerged from their increasing publication.

COST-CONTROLS, DOWNSIZING, AND LOWERED FINANCIAL EXPECTATIONS

Perhaps the most painful and nearly constant business and management issue faced by newspaper managers during the 1990s has been the financial pressure caused by the recession in the early part of the decade, corporate restructuring and downsizing, and the cost of newsprint at mid-decade. Although newspaper managers, particularly in group-owned papers, were required to operate under fiscal controls to achieve the high profits of earlier decades, the decline in profits in the 1990s forced even tighter controls and more difficult decisions.

Many publishers and editors initially responded to the difficulties by tightening cost controls, reducing spending on travel, office supplies, syndicated materials, and stringers. But because those costs are rather low in the overall budgets of newspapers, managers soon turned their attention to personnel, which is a major contributor to newspaper costs. During the early 1990s, those costs were tackled by forgoing raises, leaving empty positions unfilled, and then by offering early retirement to reduce the number of higher wage employees and finally offering buyouts of employees not yet close to retirement. Ultimately, layoffs followed in many newspapers.

By 1994, the effects of those cost-savings and the emergence from the recession could be seen in the financial reports of public companies, many of which posted record earnings and some of which achieved levels of profits not seen since the best years of the 1980s.[24] By mid-decade, rising newsprint prices forced newspapers nationwide to increase spending controls again and to cut operating expenses, but rising advertising revenue offset some of the effects of the increases in paper prices. Many public companies began reviewing their overall strategies and a number of the larger newspapers began significant restructuring programs in which they divested holdings in cable and broadcasting to concentrate their efforts on newspaper and electronic information divisions. Others began closing or selling less profitable newspaper operations. The costs associated with those restructuring efforts made for a difficult 1995, but many companies managed to increase their profitability.[25] Investors viewed the cuts favorably and responded by pushing the average stock price up 28 percent.[26]

A good part of the frustration felt in the newspaper industry has been the result of its history of high margins, according to Philip Meyer, Knight Chair in Journalism at the University of North Carolina and formerly news and circulation research director for Knight–Ridder. "The easy money culture has led to some bad habits that still haunt the industry. If the money is going to come in no matter what kind of product you turn out, you are motivated to turn it out as cheaply as possible," he says. "If newspapers are under pressure, you can cheapen the product and raise prices at the same time." Those strategies do not work now, however, because new competitive situations require newspapers to expend money to nurture and improve the content, while at the same time experiencing modest profit margins and lowering their financial expectations.[27]

Although some stability appears to be developing in the revenue picture for newspapers in the second half of the 1990s, uncertainties about costs, potential changes in advertisers' choices, and emerging competitors can be expected to keep the financial pressures a major issue for editors and publishers into the next century. Although financial issues have not been as constantly salient in the newspaper industry as in other industries in recent decades, the strength of and constancy of the issues will be equivalent in years to come and newspaper managers will need to become more adept at financial management and planning than in previous years.

ENDNOTES

1. Department of Commerce, *Statistical Abstract of the United States* (Washington, DC: U.S. Government Printing Office), 1994, 1–72.

2. Clint Wilson, III and Felix Gutierrez, *Race, Multiculturalism, and the Media: From Mass to Class Communication* (Thousand Oaks, CA: Sage Publications, 1995), 12.

3. Ted Pease, "Philosophical and Economic Arguments for Media Diversity" in *Pluralizing Journalism Education—A Multicultural Handbook* (Westport, CT: Greenwood Press, 1993), 12.

4. Quoted in Pease, 11.

5. Wilson and Gutierrez, 24.

6. Wilson and Gutierrez, 224.

7. Wilson and Gutierrez, 204.

8. Newspaper Association of America, *Seize It: Newspaper Minority Recruitment Kit* (Reston, VA: Newspaper Association of America, 1994).

9. Jonathan Kozol, *Illiterate America*, (Garden City, NY: Anchor/Doubleday, 1985), 4–5.

10 "Nearly Half in U.S. Can't Read Well," *San Jose Mercury News*, September 9, 1993, A1.

11. Elinor Kelley Grusin and Gerald C. Stone, "The Newspaper in Education and New Readers: Hooking Kids on Newspapers through Classroom Experiences," *Journalism Monographs*, No. 141 (October 1993).

12. Grusin and Stone, op. cit.; Edward F. DeRoche, "Newspapers in Education: What We Know," *Newspaper Research Journal* 2 (Spring 1981):59-61; Edward F. DeRoche and Linda B. Skover, "Newspapers in Teaching and Learning Reading," *Newspaper Research Journal* 4 (Winter 1983):23–30; Paul E. Beals, "The Newspaper in the Classroom: Some Notes on Recent Research," *Reading World*, May 1984.

13. Jonathan Weber "Stop the Presses; Papers Enter a Brave New World," *Los Angeles Times*, January 17, 1994, A1.

14. George Garneau, "L.A. Times Exits Prodigy, for Now," *Editor & Publisher*, December 2, 1995, 37.

15. Dave Mayfield, "Knight–Ridder Buys into Infinet," *Virginia Pilot*, June 8, 1995, D1.

16. Ibid.

17. Raymond Snoddy and Stephen McGookin, "Ridder Moves Back the Future," *Financial Times*, August 7, 1995, 10.

18. Mark Fitzgerald, "Interest in Electronic Delivery Continues to Grow, Survey Shows," *Editor & Publisher*, February 11, 1995, 30–31.

19. Leo Bogart, "Advertorials in Our Future," *Proceedings of the 1989 Convention of the American Society of Newspaper Editors* (Washington, DC: 1989), 82.

20. J. B. Wilkinson, Douglas R. Hausknecht, and George E. Prough, "Reader Categorization of a Controversial Communication: Advertisement versus Editorial," *Journal of Public Policy and Marketing* (Fall 1995), 12:245.

21. M. L. Stein "Advertorials and the First Amendment," *Editor & Publisher*, September 18, 1993, 24.

22. Neil Morgan, *Proceedings of the 1989 Convention of the American Society of Newspaper Editors* (Reston, VA: American Society of Newspaper Editors, 1989), 88.

23. Elizabeth Sanger, "Only One View That's Fit to Print," *Newsday*, July 26, 1993, 29.

24. George Garneau, "Profit Peaks Are Here Again," *Editor & Publisher*, March 18, 1995, 14–16+.

25. Tony Case, "Still Strong," *Editor & Publisher*, January 6, 1996, 15–25+.

26. "A Good Year for Newspaper Shares," *Newspaper Stocks Report Annual Review* (Riverside, CA: Carpelan Publishing Co., January 1996), 1.

27. Philip Meyer, "Learning to Love Lower Profits," *American Journalism Review* (December 1995), 40-44.p

9

Legal and Regulatory Issues and Concerns

Because of their commercial nature, newspapers face the same kinds of legal and regulatory issues that all businesses and employees encounter. In addition to those issues, the communication functions and specialized and unique manufacturing processes of newspapers force them to face issues that other businesses and industries typically do not face.

Newspapers are wrestling with a number of legal and regulatory issues involving advertising, libel, copyright, censorship, distribution regulations, employment law, environmental regulations, taxation, and antitrust problems.

ADVERTISING ISSUES

Because certain types of advertising are regulated by law, newspapers are increasingly being required to be the initial point of enforcement or they risk fines and other penalties for publishing advertising that violates the regulations. As a result, advertising departments must be aware of the legal requirements regarding specific ads and enforce them by means of acceptance policies and practices.

Specific regulations, for example, require complex disclosure information in advertisements regarding automobile sales and the terms of their financing, advertisements of stocks, bonds, and other financial instruments, advertisements regarding pharmaceuticals, and advertisements involving contests and lotteries.

In recent years, newspapers have encountered special difficulties complying with the Fair Housing Act, which restricts discrimination in housing and applies to advertisements for rental properties, roommates, and so on. Enforcement of the act has led to hundreds of words and phrases being found that discriminate on the bases of race, color, religion, sex, disability, national origin, or family status. Ads deemed discriminatory have included phrases such as "no kids," "no wheelchairs," "senior citizens only," "Christians only," and "whites only." Although most newspapers now regularly screen ads for clearly discriminatory content, other combinations of words, phrases, and their context have brought claims that they create discriminatory impressions on individuals seeking housing.

Enforcement of the law has brought numerous papers into conflict with authorities because ads they accepted from customers were judged to contain discriminatory words or phrases.[1] Papers have been fined and ad staffs forced to undergo training in the law as a result of complaints and suits brought against them by regulatory agencies. After complaints from newspaper associations about the vagueness of regulations and that they faced enforcement proceedings for ads that were not explicitly discriminatory, the U.S. Department of Housing and Urban Development in 1995 issued new enforcement procedures and stipulated a variety of phrases and contexts that it did not deem discriminatory.[2]

As more and more daily and nondaily papers have increased their personal advertising sections, often linking them with audiotext ads, they find themselves walking a fine line involving both taste and legal issues. Most newspapers reject sexually explicit ads, but many accept ads for adult services and matchmaking for heterosexuals, homosexuals, or bisexuals as well as couples seeking individuals and other couples for sexual activities. Because of laws involving prostitution and pimping, most newspapers will accept such ads only from individuals, not commercial firms, and many reject ads that offer anything of financial value, including trips, gifts, housing, or payments in exchange for companionship.

LIBEL ISSUES

Issues of defamation of public and private persons, and damages awarded for such libel, have been a great concern for newspapers throughout their history. The newspaper industry has long sought to reduce its liability, the size of awards, and the costs of defending against suits. Although there are some general principles in place throughout the country, there are great differences in laws regarding libel among the states and between the state and federal levels.

In the early 1990s, a new and significant effort to coordinate and rationalize libel law appeared in the form of the Uniform Defamation Act, intended to make libel laws conform to the same standards in all fifty states. Among its provisions, plaintiffs could have exchanged the right to seek punitive damages for a trial in which they engaged reporters in an attempt to determine whether information in a disputed story was true or false. Although many publishers and journalists support-ed the general idea of coordinating libel law, this provision was seen as opening the door for harassment of the media by public officials and disgruntled readers crusad-ing for truth with reckless disregard for the privileges and constitutional protections afforded to journalists. After protests by civil libertarians and leading press associa-tions and publishers' organizations, the proposed law was dropped and, in its place, the Uniform Correction or Clarification of Defamation Act (UCCDA) was intro-duced in the summer of 1995.

Proposed by the National Conference of Commissioners on Uniform State Laws and the American Bar Association, the UCCDA dropped the unseemly provi-sions for "truth trials" from the Uniform Defamation Act, yet it still strove to pro-vide a means to settle defamation actions without going to court, a concept that has strong general support among publishers because it will reduce legal fees.[3] Like other uniform acts, the proposed law, which can be modified by state legislatures, will have to be passed in one version or another by all fifty states for it to have impact. Major features of the law include: limiting libel awards to provable eco-nomic loss if the defendant publishes a timely correction and limiting damages if the plaintiff fails to request a correction or clarification within ninety days. But most importantly, a publisher may publish a correction prior to trial and, if the plaintiff accepts, the publisher then pays the plaintiff's legal fees and the lawsuit is dismissed.[4] The act aims at limiting the harsh punitive measures of libel suits and resolving issues of fact by stressing the importance of requesting corrections and clarifications and allowing the publisher the option of publishing corrections or clarifications without going through the questionable process of a truth trial. Publishers and industry associations are watching developments surrounding the uniform law to ensure that their interests are carefully protected as it is debated within state legislatures.

Although the Internet is in its infancy regarding regulations and laws govern-ing defamation and invasion of privacy, the newspaper industry is becoming increasingly aware that cyberspace offers no protection from a potential libel action. Publishers that put material on-line through an electronic version of a news-paper or by operating electronic bulletin boards, where subscribers can post infor-mation read by readers on the Internet, may find themselves liable to both defama-tion and invasion of privacy suits. As far as the law is concerned, information pub-lished electronically for mass consumption is regarded the same way as informa-tion published on paper. In the case of an electronic newspaper, the publisher clear-ly exercises editorial control of the newspaper's content because the electronic newspaper for the most part is a copy of the newspaper's editorial product. The case of whether a publisher exercises editorial control over a bulletin board operated by a newspaper presents greater difficulty because bulletin boards may or may not be monitored.

San Francisco attorney James F. Brelsford, who specializes in managing risk in cyberspace, has warned that in terms of libel publishers "may be viewed as exercising control over the contents" of on-line bulletin boards. To Brelsford, publishing opinions in a newspaper's bulletin board is akin to publishing opinions in a letters to the editor column. By exercising the right to edit the opinion section, the newspaper controls the content.[5]

The real-time delivery of messages in cyberspace poses a problem for on-line services, which act as information providers and links to the Internet and the World Wide Web. Whereas a newspaper publishes from one to three editions, which are edited and distributed in the early morning, bulletin boards can receive messages in real time from subscribers around the clock. And while editors check every word that is published in a newspaper, on-line services would be hard pressed to check every message posted on the Internet.

The question the courts will have to decide is whether on-line services should be looked on as conduits of information, similar to a telephone company, or as providers of information, such as newspapers. According to Brelsford, an on-line provider's function could be considered analogous to that of a phone company, a distributor, or a publisher, depending on how the on-line provider operates. A phone company has the most protection from libel and invasion of privacy suits because common law holds that it is not responsible for statements made over its wires. A distributor can be held liable for defamation only if it had reason to know the information distributed was defamatory, and a publisher is generally held to be responsible for all information disseminated in media it owns.

The first on-line libel case to reach the courts involved Prodigy, an on-line service that is a joint venture of Sears, Roebuck and IBM. In 1995, New York State Supreme Court Justice Stuart Ain ruled that Prodigy was a publisher and could be held liable for information on its bulletin boards. The ruling came after the New York investment firm of Stratton–Oakmont filed a $200 million libel claim against Prodigy. The suit was filed after an anonymous person posted a note on Prodigy's money talk bulletin board accusing the investment firm of criminal activity. After Prodigy apologized, the suit was dropped but the judge refused to throw out his ruling.[6]

The court ruled that Prodigy had acted as a publisher because the on-line service exercised editorial control over the content of its bulletin boards by writing content guidelines in subscriber agreements and using software to screen out offensive words. The content guidelines, for example, warned subscribers against using obscene words. Randolph May, a Washington attorney who represents on-line service providers, said the content guidelines represent at best a warning. In criticizing the Prodigy decision, May noted the impossibility of policing the Internet. "The decision reflects a failure to employ a functional analysis in evaluating how the major on-line services operate…it is not feasible for operators to review the content of the tens of thousands of subscriber messages before they are posted. Prodigy cannot control for defamation, which would require it to investigate the truth of all posted messages. The resource burdens imposed by such a regime would threaten the economic viability of the services."[7]

Until either the courts or Congress clarifies the issue, publishers must be cautious about material disseminated on the Internet. U.S. information law has yet to catch up with the information age. The nature of communication and responsibility for the content of communication on the Internet need to be defined. Because online services are circulated worldwide, a variety of jurisdictional problems occur in the international setting. Could, for example, a U.S. publisher be charged and tried for something that is not libelous in the U.S. but is regarded as libelous in Peru, Egypt, Thailand, or France because the material is distributed in those nations via the Internet?

COPYRIGHT AND TRADEMARK ISSUES

Copyright is an important issue to any creator of intellectual and artistic products because it provides the proprietary right to and protection for the product. In the case of newspapers, this means their stories, photographs, layout, and design. The basic issues of copyright involving newspapers themselves have long since been sorted out, for the most part, but a host of new copyright issues involving the electronic dissemination of information and newspapers have arisen. The newspaper industry is paying careful attention to the debate about copyright protection awarded to electronic information and is closely following the courts as they rule on whether Internet access providers can be held liable for copyright violations committed by one of their users. Publishers have already come under attack from writers who have filed suit against them demanding compensation for reprinting electronic versions of their work, saying existing employment agreements and rights purchased from other writers do not cover electronic delivery. In addition, a debate has ensued over the right to read and download information that has copyright protection on the Internet.

In the first case to examine copyright infringement on the Internet, U.S. District Judge Ronald M. Whyte of San Jose ruled, on Nov. 21, 1995, that Internet access providers can be held liable for copyright violations, if they know their users are engaged in illegal copyright activity. In a case that involved the publication of material belonging to the Church of Scientology on Netcom On-line Services, Whyte argued in a thirty-two-page decision that bulletin board operators can be held liable in some situations for copyright infringement. "The court is more persuaded by the argument that it is beyond the ability of a BBS operator to quickly and fairly determine when a use is not infringement where there is at least a colorable claim of fair use," Judge Whyte wrote. "Where a BBS operator cannot reasonably verify a claim of infringement, either because of a possible fair use defense, the lack of copyright notices on the copies, or the copyright holder's failure to provide the necessary documentation…the operator's lack of knowledge will be found reasonable and there will be no liability for contributory infringement."[8] Publishers must take notice if they know copyrighted information is being conveyed on a bulletin board. As in the libel case against Prodigy, the courts are determining that the role of an access provider more closely resembles that of a newspaper publisher than a telephone company.

The question of who owns the rights to electronic publications may also be settled in court. The National Writers Union (NWU) has filed a federal suit against the New York Times Co., Mead Data Central, and others, charging that articles were published on-line without permission from or compensation to authors.[9] The union alleges that publishing companies are unfairly taking advantage of writers by failing to provide compensation for the electronic use of their material. The writers want royalties for the use of their material, but publishers say that when they buy rights, they buy all the rights, including electronic dissemination, too. Such a practice would prevent writers from profiting from the Internet. Because magazines and newspapers are publishing electronically, the writers want to be compensated for both the electronic and print versions of their work. The publishers counter that when they buy rights to freelance articles for a magazine or newspaper travel section, the purchase of the rights includes the electronic version of the magazine or newspaper.

The practice of downloading copyrighted material on the Internet has been questioned. Just as it is a violation to copy material on a copy machine, it could be a violation to copy material on the Internet by downloading it into the memory of a personal computer. Information that appears on the Internet does not automatically belong to the public domain. Editors should be careful about journalists grabbing software programs and other information from on-line services. It may be wise to establish rules in the newsroom about copying information, especially information that is protected by copyright. All software should be licensed; some companies have paid major fines for unlicensed software and, with the introduction of personal computers in the newsroom, editors should check the programs staffers install by themselves.

Trademark issues also affect newspapers. Trademarks provide a limited monopoly over the use of a word, terms, or symbols for commercial purposes. Because journalists regularly use words that are trademarks and newspapers regularly publish such words, firms that own trademarks regularly work to ensure that they are used properly, either in uppercase or appearing with the symbols ® or ™ properly displayed. Publications that fail to comply receive warnings and threats of lawsuits if they do not use such symbols appropriately. Damages and legal fees for trademark infringement can run into the hundreds of thousands of dollars.

To help deal with the problem, major journalistic stylebooks, such as the *Associated Press Stylebook and Libel Manual*[10] and *United Press International Stylebook*,[11] carry words protected by trademarks. Holders of trademarks also regularly take out ads in journalistic publications urging proper use of the names. The major trade magazine *Editor & Publisher* annually publishes a special section devoted to trademarks and the press.[12] The International Trademark Association publishes a media guide and other materials about protected works, and on-line services listing registered trademarks are available.

Xerox, for example, urges journalists not to use the term as a verb to indicate photocopying. Similarly Muralo asks newspapers not to use the word Spackle as a verb to mean repairing a hole in a wall, and Kimberly–Clark reminds writers that Kleenex is a brand of tissues. To holders of trademarks the issue is not trivial because the trademarks can be lost if companies do not protect them.

Newspapers have also taken steps to protect their names in court. Although trademark infringement involving newspaper trademarks are unusual, they do occur and newspapers have gone to war over a nameplate or section title. In 1994, for example, the issue came to a head when two small Minnesota papers, the Mesabi *Daily News* and Hibbing *Daily Tribune,* decided to publish a Saturday edition named the *Saturday Daily News & Tribune.* The name of the Saturday paper infuriated the owners of the nearby Duluth *News-Tribune.* They claimed the nameplate infringed on their trademarked nameplate and that the new name was causing confusion among readers. The Duluth paper filed suit in federal court, but lost on summary judgment. The issue is being appealed. But the court cited differences between the color and typeface of the two nameplates and said one product was a daily and the other appeared only on Saturday. The court also pointed out that the Duluth paper used a hyphen, and the new paper, an ampersand.[13] Although the Duluth paper lost the suit, newspapers should keep an eye on potential trademark violations to protect their name in the community.

CENSORSHIP ISSUES

American newspapers have the unusually strong protection of the First Amendment against government censorship. Except in time of war, the press has been free from direct censorship by the state. The traditional definition of censorship as an activity conducted by agents of the state dates to ancient Rome when the emperor appointed "censors" to safeguard public morals. However, in recent years, scholars and journalists have attempted to expand the definition of censorship to include activities initiated by the press, including self-censorship and the suppression of news. The new definition expands the concept of censorship to include stories that the mainstream press pays little attention to or ignores. Media critics charge that pressure from attorneys, editors, publishers, and political figures as well as corporations, public relations firms, and interest groups has created an atmosphere of self-policing within the American press. The move to replace investigative and public affairs reporting with light features and reader-friendly news has raised concern that the press has abrogated its traditional watchdog role and responsibility to inform citizens about issues and social problems within society.

Carl Jensen, a communications professor at Sonoma State University in California, founded "Project Censored" in 1976 to call attention to important stories that have been missed or downplayed by the press. "For the purposes of this project," Jensen said, "censorship is defined as the suppression of information, whether purposeful or not, by any method—including bias, omission, under-reporting, or self-censorship—which prevents the public from fully knowing what is happening in the world." Not every authority agrees with Jensen. Newton Minnow, director of the Annenberg Program in Washington, believes Jensen has gone too far. In a speech before the Children Now Conference at Stanford University in March, 1995, Minnow said: "If ever a word were in need of rest, 'censorship' is that word. It is used as a cue to critics to shut up. But the word is used so often, and so casually, as to have lost its meaning. Every year, for example, a California university issues a list of the most underreported stories of the past year, which it calls "Project Censored." The list consists of events that have been ignored, underreported, inaccurately reported, unfairly reported, and even slanted—but by no means censored." Minnow would hold Jensen to the narrow definition of censorship as an act by government officials.[14] Jensen, on the other hand, believes the public is being shortchanged. Compelling stories uncovered by Jensen and the Project Censored group include the failure to report about corporate welfare cheats, violence against children, and the destruction of tropical rain forests. At the same time the media ignored and underreported important stories, Jensen and his colleagues have documented an alarming trend that coincides with "censorship"—the rise of trivial, sensationalized, celebrity-oriented junk food news that is personified by the plethora of ink squandered on Tonya Harding, Roseanne, Michael Jackson, and the British royal family.[15] As the control of information in a free society moves into the hands of large corporations that focus more on monetary rather than journalistic goals, the future of press freedom may be threatened, he argues. The question that has been raised by Jensen and others is: Does the media in a free society, because of the constitutional protection granted to the press, have an obligation to report political and social aspects of the news or do the owners of the media have the right to control the content of the news in a way they see fit? With the ownership of almost half of the nation's newspapers concentrated in the hands of twenty-five corporations, the question becomes all the more important for the twenty-first Century.

The Internet was believed to offer a solution for those who believe in the free exchange of information and ideas. For the price of a local phone call, users gain access to a universe of data. Speech on the Net has generally been unregulated, and it is for the most part impossible to police a network that has millions of users all over the world and was designed and engineered to withstand a nuclear attack. But efforts to control what is said and published on the Net have begun. Congress and political interest groups around the world have begun to demand regulation of the sex-oriented and offensive material on the Internet that could lead to rules restricting press freedom. Pressure has been mounting to keep minors from having access to sexually explicit information, but broader efforts would restrict access to discussions of topics some deem offensive and even books that have been banned by some libraries for reasons other than sexual content.

At the end of 1995, CompuServe bowed to pressure from the German government to cut off worldwide subscriber access to more than 200 sexually-oriented Internet news groups. To please German authorities, CompuServe blocked its 4 million subscribers around the world, marking the first time a government has successfully censored material on the Internet.[16]

That the action was undertaken by a foreign government sounds the alarm that U.S. news organizations may come under increasing pressure from foreign agents to censor news and information that is constitutionally protected in the United States. With about 100 U.S. newspapers already on-line, as well as eighty foreign newspapers, the possibility that a foreign government could censor and attempt to impose its laws on U.S. news organizations, and their parent companies, becomes all the more real. Could a nation with laws limiting coverage of trials halt coverage conveyed in another country's press if that paper was on-line? The issue is not pedantic because the democratically liberal nation of Canada recently censored U.S. newspapers and magazines imported into that nation, as well as television news carried on cable channels, that carried reports about sensational Canadian criminal trials.

U.S. newspapers that publish editions in other parts of the world have regularly run into censorship problems, but the ante was increased in May 1995 when Singapore forced the *International Herald Tribune* to pay a fine for an article published in the *Tribune* that offended Singapore's High Court. The judicial body charged the newspaper with contempt of court for printing a column in 1994 by an American professor that was allegedly critical of Singapore's judiciary.[17] The Singapore ruling could have a chilling effect on publications which are distributed worldwide. A government could take offense at a news story in *USA Today* or the *New York Times* and fine the newspaper, put pressure on correspondents, or close down its operation abroad. Reporters in China are used to having their phones tapped and have been followed by secret police.

Perhaps the most extreme form of censorship has come with attacks on journalists. Although attacks on newspapers and murders of journalists are all too common throughout the world, they are relatively rare in the U.S. and are normally the work of a lone, disgruntled individual. Despite the general safety of the industry as a whole, the immigrant press has been especially vulnerable in the U.S. and a significant number of attacks have occurred in recent years directed against ethnic journalists working in the United States. This is especially true when the papers and journalists represent groups for traditionally undemocratic regimes or without a tolerance for free expression.

At least ten immigrant journalists working for the non-English press have been killed in the United States since 1981. Five of the journalists worked for Vietnamese-language publications; three for Haitian radio stations; one for a Chinese-language newspaper; and one for a Spanish-language newspaper. The murders of these immigrant journalists received little attention in the mainstream press—no group of reporters rallied to find their assailants. There was hardly an outcry, unlike when *Arizona Republic* reporter Don Bolles was killed in 1976, and some thirty-six reporters from across the country descended on Arizona to help find Bolles's killer.

The attacks against ethnic journalists have had a chilling effect. Vietnamese-immigrant journalists, threatened by right-wing, anti-Communist members of the community, self-censor the news to keep themselves from being attacked. The Latino editor Manuel de Dios was shot in the back in a New York City restaurant by members of a Colombian drug cartel. De Dios had written about drug traffic in the community and the execution silenced him and intimidated other Latino journalists. Two years after de Dios was killed in 1992, five Colombians—all said to have been working for the Cali cartel—were arrested and convicted of the slaying.[18]

The de Dios case and the murder of Chinese American journalist Henry Liu in 1984 were the only murders of immigrant journalists in the U.S. that have been solved. Liu was killed in Daly City, California, by a Taiwanese government hit team that had connections to the Taiwanese military and organized crime.

The attacks against Vietnamese Americans have occurred across the country—in San Francisco, Boston, Houston, and Orange County, California, home to the largest Vietnamese community in the United States. Law enforcement has made little progress in identifying the right-wing terrorist groups that prey upon the Vietnamese-language press and consider it treason to print any favorable news about Vietnam. While the United States has established diplomatic relations with Vietnam, and mainstream American journalists have covered events in Vietnam, immigrant Vietnamese journalists remain wary of going back to their homeland. As a result, news about Vietnam is censored for members of the Vietnamese community who cannot read English. The murders remain under investigation.

DISTRIBUTION ISSUES

The means by which newspapers deliver papers to customers have been increasingly subject to regulation and legal activity. In recent years many cities and communities have begun regulating the types and placement of news racks in the community for aesthetic and safety purposes. Some regulations have specified the types of news rack models and colors that are permitted and others have limited the locations in which they may be placed or the number that may be placed in a given location. Newspapers and newspaper associations nationwide have challenged such regulations, but courts are beginning to accept such regulations as long as they are content-neutral and designed to serve community interests rather than to punish or prohibit newspapers.

The distribution of free newspapers has increasingly been the subject of concern, with some communities arguing that they are a source of litter. Some individuals also make similar complaints when unwanted shoppers or free community papers are thrown into their yards. Laws and suits regarding free distribution crop up occasionally and no definitive national ruling on the subject has emerged, although local and state rulings tend to uphold the right to distribute.

Special distribution problems are developing in gated communities and condominiums and apartments with strong security regulations in which entry by nonresidents is restricted. As a result newspaper carriers are sometimes not permitted to enter to make deliveries even to customers who want to subscribe. Because the regulations are private and not governmental, and the facilities are private property, traditional arguments of First Amendment protections of the newspapers do not necessarily apply and papers are sometimes forced to make alternative delivery arrangements.

EMPLOYMENT ISSUES

Newspapers wrestle with the same employment issues that all businesses encounter, and in recent years they have been spending a great deal of effort responding to issues involving sexual harassment, the status of reporters, and alcohol and drug abuse.

The problem of sexual harassment in newspapers has increasingly become a salient problem for the industry as the number of female employees has increased and laws regarding harassment have been strengthened and enforced over the past two decades. Most newspaper groups and many individual papers have adopted specific policies and taken disciplinary action against unwelcome sexual advances, requests for sexual favors, and other harassing verbal and physical conduct. Although some dismissed employees attempted to use union grievance procedures to halt their dismissals, arbitrators have upheld such dismissals.[19] Despite such actions, 60 percent of women employed in newsrooms responded to a recent survey indicating that sexual harassment remains a serious problem for them. Almost two-thirds reported they had experienced nonphysical harassment, and 17 percent indicated they had experienced physical harassment.[20]

Sexual harrassment complaints, although primarily brought against men by women, have also been made by men against women, by women against women, and by men against men. Because such harassment is primarily an exercise of power, its use is not limited to persons of any one gender or sexual preference and the intimidation and humiliation it causes can be experienced by anyone with less power in an organization.

A special area of concern for newspapers has been whether reporters should be classified as "professionals" under labor laws. The newspaper industry has preferred this definition because such a classification would exempt journalists from wage and hour laws, including requirements of overtime payment, but has not been successful in moving reporters to the ranks of recognized professionals. In 1993, for example, the Concord (New Hampshire) *Monitor* lost an effort to have photographers and reporters classed as professionals in an attempt to avoid the time-and-a-half payments required for work exceeding forty hours a week.[21]

Newspapers have also been wrestling with the employment status of newspaper carriers, particularly adult carriers, and are regularly encountering difficulties with state and federal authorities over their status. Although papers wish to have a great deal of control over the activities of carriers, newspaper managers want to maintain carriers as independent contractors so that they do not have to pay them salaries and other benefits. This issue, which will be discussed further in a subsequent section on taxation issues, has become one of the most expensive issues for newspapers as state and federal agencies look for additional tax revenues.

ENVIRONMENTAL ISSUES

Environmental issues are increasingly affecting all businesses as city, state, and federal agencies respond to growing public pressures, health dangers, and economic considerations with environmental regulations and enforcement. Newspapers are affected by the general regulations and face some environmental issues that are unique to the printing industries.

The primary environmental issues facing the industry involve material consumption, energy consumption, pollutant emissions, and waste production. Four primary activities are the focus of concern in the newspaper industry: paper production, printing, distribution, and waste (see Figure 9.1).

Paper production issues concern the problems involved in the use of wood fibers, including the sources of raw materials, which raise questions about forest preservation and management. Other problems involve wood pulping in the preparation of the wood fibers. Mechanical pulping, the primary form of pulping of newsprint worldwide, requires high energy consumption, which can be reduced by thermo-mechanical pulping equipment, a method that requires capital investment that can raise the price of newsprint. Chemical and chemo-mechanical pulping processes produce papers that are often used for newspaper advertising inserts and newspaper magazines. Such pulping produces wastes in the form of cellulose fibers, acids, and sulfide emissions that pollute air and water. Bleaching, a process used primarily for white papers, often used in newspaper inserts, involves the use of chlorine, chlorine dioxide, or peroxide, which also create air and water pollution.

Printing done by newspapers themselves involves the use of chemical substances that create pollutants. The primary problem occurs in the use of inks and related production and cleaning solvents. Inks used in newspaper printing are composed of pigments, resins, and solvents. The pigments provide the ink's color, the resins hold pigments together and bond the pigments to the press, and then the solvents dissolve the resins and transfer the pigment to paper.

FIGURE 9.1 **Environmental Concerns Involving the Newspaper Industry**

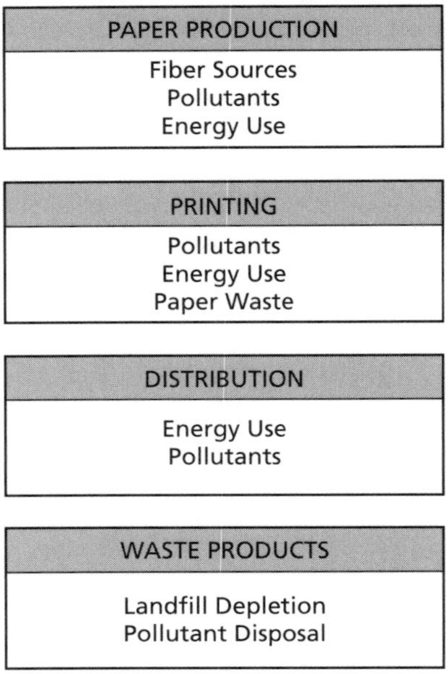

PAPER PRODUCTION
Fiber Sources
Pollutants
Energy Use

PRINTING
Pollutants
Energy Use
Paper Waste

DISTRIBUTION
Energy Use
Pollutants

WASTE PRODUCTS
Landfill Depletion
Pollutant Disposal

Pollution resulting from newspaper operations, or inappropriate handling of materials, can lead to sanctions by environmental agencies. In the early 1990s, for example, Knight–Ridder's San Jose *Mercury News* was fined by both the state of California and the Santa Clara County health authorities for violations relating to its silver-treatment system and disposal of waste ink.[22] More recently, groundwater contamination resulting from the use of trichloroethylene—a solvent used as a degreaser in the 1970s and 1980s before its use was restricted—by the Orlando, Florida, *Sentinel*, forced it to prepare an expensive cleanup project in conjunction with the state's Department of Environmental Protection.[23]

The standard solvents used in printing are petroleum-based; they emit compounds that cause air pollution. A great deal of effort has been made in the use of vegetable-based oils to replace petroleum in some printing, soy and linseed oils among them, and some water-based oils are being tested as well. The air and waste emission problems associated with the use of inks and maintenance and cleaning of related equipment are not the only difficulties in the printing process. Because newspapers rely on electrical power for printing presses and related production activities, issues of energy consumption and efficiency are increasingly important in the industry.

Inspection of newspaper premises and increased activities of monitoring agencies have led the newspaper industry to promote compliance and help ensure companies meet standards. The ANPA (now NAA), for example, set up an environmental assistance program to help papers comply, and environmental issues are regular topics at meetings of industry associations. The issue has become particularly important because regulatory agencies have begun cooperating and sharing information among themselves and the level of enforcement has increased.[24]

Newspaper distribution activities also raise environmental concerns, particularly for large metropolitan newspapers. Because newspapers must rely upon fleets of trucks for distribution to carriers, news racks, and newsstands, and many carriers use automobiles for distribution, issues of gasoline use and the subsequent pollutants emitted in the air by internal combustion engines come into play.

The industry is increasingly dealing with how customers dispose of newspapers. Paper of all types makes up about one-third of solid wastes in landfills and newspapers account for about 4.6 percent of that solid waste. Because the available space for waste is diminishing and the cost of landfills is high, government agencies have begun mandating recycling activities that will reduce and ultimately end disposal of newspapers and other paper products in landfills. One solution mandated by many government agencies is newspaper participation in paper recycling. Because used newsprint can be combined with coated papers and virgin wood pulp to produce newsprint that can be used again in the newspaper printing process, many agencies are requiring that a certain percentage of recycled newsprint be used by papers and that newspapers help operate or promote recycling operations. This recycling of paper fiber for paper production has the additional benefit of providing a new source of fiber for paper, thus reducing the demand for cutting forests.

Recycling programs have been growing and producing an increasing supply of old newspapers, and newspapers have actively supported such efforts. The Minneapolis, Minnesota, *Star-Tribune*, for example, prints the recycling symbol and the message, "Please Read and Recycle," on its front page. To help deal with the growing supply and difficulties in coordinating its exchange, the Chicago Board of Trade in 1995—through grants from the U.S. Environmental Protection Agency—opened an electronic Recyclables Exchange in which old newspapers and other recyclables will be traded.[25]

Although the amount of newspapers recycled has regularly increased since the 1980s, only 7.1 million metric tons of newsprint were recycled out of the 11.8 billion metric tons of newsprint consumed for all purposes in the United States in 1992. The daily newspaper industry claims, however, that nearly 60 percent of the newsprint it uses comes from the amount recycled, amounting to 6.9 million metric tons out of 11.8 million metric tons in 1994.[26]

In addition to the disposal problems posed by the paper itself, newspapers are increasingly facing pressures regarding the plastic bags used to protect papers from rain and snow. Although many newspapers have moved to the use of biodegradable polybags in recent years, time is revealing that even these products do not degrade very rapidly and pressures regarding their use may increase in the future.

Contamination issues in newspaper facilities are also significant. Asbestos used in flooring materials, as insulation, and in other construction in decades past creates health problems that are forcing newspapers and other businesses to remove the materials immediately, or whenever renovations are made, depending upon the level of threat. Newspapers that still use buildings in which production and printing using "hot type" methods and lead plates are sometimes found to be contaminated with lead residues that exceed permissible limits. In 1995 for example, the *Washington Post* was forced to temporarily move its photo department and editorial operations out of its third floor newsroom facilities to remove lead contamination left behind when the old production area was shut down and renovated into a newsroom.[27] Removal of asbestos, lead, and other contaminants is an expensive and time-consuming process because it must be done in a manner that does not endanger those doing the cleaning. In addition, all contaminated materials and materials used in the cleanup must be disposed of in special ways and cannot be handled as normal trash or construction wastes.

OTHER SAFETY ISSUES

Because newspapers employ personnel for a wide variety of activities involving the use of machinery and vehicles, newspapers face issues caused when employees, through accidents, misuse of equipment, or the actions of others or themselves, are injured or killed at work. When newspaper personnel are employees rather than contractors, issues of workers' compensation and disability payments arise.

Costs for workers' compensation tripled during the 1980s and early 1990s and newspapers and other employers began paying attention to preventing injuries through safety programs and a variety of other strategies designed to reduce cost. "Safety programs and loss prevention are the most important techniques for controlling costs," according to Daniel Free, president of a loss prevention firm.[28]

On-the-job injuries can happen to employees in any department of the newspaper and can range from repetitive stress injuries to an advertising clerk, to injuries sustained by a reporter driving to a news event, to a press operator whose hand is crushed in a press, or a mailroom worker who slips on concrete slippery from rainwater. Most injuries are not fatal, but even the more common injuries, such as strained hands and hurt backs, can be disruptive and expensive.[29]

Although the Occupational Safety and Health Administration inspects workplaces to ensure compliance with established safety regulations and procedures, most newspapers and other major employers work vigorously to ensure safety between inspections and to avoid the problems and costs caused by injuries. Larger newspapers often have full-time safety personnel, and smaller ones usually designate a part-time individual to handle the duties.

One difficult problem arises when newspaper personnel become victims of crime while carrying out their duties. Newspaper personnel have been robbed and injured or killed while trying to cover news, selling advertising, and delivering papers. In recent years, increasing attacks on carriers have led publishers to work to increase the safety of children and adults who deliver papers, especially if they are collecting money on their rounds.[30]

The problems and liabilities caused by attacks on newspaper personnel have led some papers to cease delivery to parts of town in which carriers are at high risk, to decrease the use of children as carriers, and to take a variety of steps to protect workers both in and outside of the newspaper buildings.

TAXATION ISSUES

Like all business enterprises, newspapers are subject to taxes but, because of their special role in society, embodied in the First Amendment and state constitutions, are protected against taxes that are punitive or discriminatory. States and various localities have taken different tacks in dealing with newspapers with regard to general sales and use taxes, taxes on production materials, supplies and equipment, sales taxes on circulation, and sales or service taxes on advertising.[31] In recent years, newspapers have faced a variety of changes regarding taxation as state and federal governments have attempted to increase tax revenues and begun reconsidering their traditional handling of newspapers under tax laws.

Newspapers have typically been exempted from sales taxes, and advertising sales have been exempted from service taxes by the legislatures of most states. These special interest exemptions have been given because the social and economic roles of newspapers benefit society. As states have attempted to increase tax revenues in recent years, removal of the exemptions have been proposed and enacted in a number of states.[32] Newspapers and newspaper organizations have nearly uniformly opposed these efforts on the grounds that they would increase their costs or reduce sales. Success at using this political and economic argument has varied.

In cases where the levy of taxes or removal of tax exemptions have dealt with newspapers' sales and services differently from other businesses or media and become punitive or discriminatory, newspapers have had both political and legal success in challenging the taxes on constitutional grounds. In Massachusetts, for example, a tax on newspaper equipment and supplies that did not apply to other manufacturers was struck down in 1991 by that state's Supreme Judicial Court because it singled out newspapers.[33]

Newspapers are also increasingly dealing with employment tax issues, usually relating to the role of newspaper delivery personnel. Both the Internal Revenue Service and state tax authorities have investigated newspapers' handling of carriers, and in a number of cases determined that, despite papers' claims that distributors were independent contractors, the distributors were employees because of noncontractual obligations or controls placed on them by newspaper managers that changed them from independent contractors to employees. Such findings can be very expensive because they require papers to pay employment taxes such as FICA, workers' compensation taxes, and so on, and can result in fines for avoiding those taxes. The IRS, for example, levied a $5.2 million fine against the Arlington Heights (Illinois) *Daily Herald* after it audited 1992 and 1993 tax returns and determined that carriers had not been properly classified as employees and employment taxes paid for them.[34]

A related concern involves stringers or correspondents who are not given regular employment status by newspapers, but are regarded as independent contractors or some other kind of worker. Because of investigations of their employment situations for tax purposes, many papers are reviewing their status and some are moving to make them part-time employees or else to ensure they are treated as independent contractors. The investigations have led to some unusual situations, however. The *Philadelphia Inquirer*, for example, which makes extensive use of such correspondents to work in suburban bureaus, recently fought with the IRS to win a ruling that makes these journalists neither employees nor independent contractors, thus saving the *Inquirer* tax money but simultaneously denying the employees the benefits of tax deductions normally afforded independent contractors.[35]

As a result of such issues the Newspaper Association of America and other associations are conducting educational campaigns to help newspapers avoid problems with tax authorities regarding the employment status not only of newspaper carriers but also of journalists who act as stringers, and are producing specialized educational materials for use by newspaper managers.[36]

ANTITRUST ISSUES

Although not an everyday concern for newspapers, antitrust issues regularly arise in the industry,[37] because of two major developments: increasing competition between daily newspapers and nondaily newspapers and acquisitions by newspaper groups that own nearby papers.

Antitrust laws have existed for a century and newspapers, like all business enterprises, are subject to their provisions. The primary purposes of antitrust law are to ensure that the marketplace can operate efficiently so that society and individuals can enjoy its benefits. Efforts to enforce antitrust laws can be undertaken by either government agencies or aggrieved parties and are normally pursued through lawsuits.

Antitrust laws prohibit actions that harm competition and deprive consumers of the benefits of the competitive economic system. They do not shield companies from competition or penalize firms that are successful in their competition. It is not illegal to engage in rigorous competition, but it is illegal to take action that tends to suppress competition and will result in a rise in prices in the long run or loss of other benefits of competition. Antitrust laws prohibit illicit efforts to gain a monopoly and harm competition, such as restraint of trade, efforts to monopolize, efforts to exclude competitors from markets, other actions that tend to harm competition and extend monopolies, and mergers and acquisitions that lessen competition.

The newspaper industry most often faces disputes involving efforts to monopolize or exclude competition, predatory pricing, price-fixing and issues involving mergers and acquisitions of newspapers or newspaper firms. One study of antitrust actions in the 1980s found that nearly two-thirds were brought by newspapers against other newspapers, and the remainder by advertisers, readers, and government agencies.[38]

Complaints that newspapers are engaging in efforts to monopolize and exclude competition, or engaging in predatory pricing designed to drive competitors out of business, have arisen regularly in courts in the past two decades. These disputes often involve complaints by publishers of weeklies and alternative papers against the publishers of daily papers, but they sometimes involve publishers of weeklies against other weeklies and dailies against other dailies.

It must be understood that the mere presence of monopoly power is not illegal, only anticompetitive acts that establish or increase monopoly power.

Competition Problems

Various activities in the newspaper industry involve competition in the marketplace, and four types have been the focus of antitrust problems in recent years: 1) competition between newspapers; 2) price competition between newspapers and advertisers; 3) price competition between newspapers and readers; and 4) price competition between newspapers and retailers and the degree to which newspapers can control retail prices.

When parties involved in these competitive actions have felt that other parties have acted unfairly to limit competition or engaged in illegal acts, antitrust litigation has occurred. Among the common types of antitrust complaints brought in newspaper cases have been price-fixing and predatory pricing.

Issues of price-fixing have arisen in a number of cases involving the prices that independent carriers charge for subscriptions and whether publishers can force a price on these and other retailers.[39]

Many cases involve charges that one publisher is attempting to drive another out of business by deliberately selling below cost for that purpose, a tactic called predatory pricing. These charges most often involve the pricing of advertising space. Antitrust cases based on such charges require clear cost-accounting and allocation of costs to advertising and circulation functions and activities.[40] That process becomes especially complicated when dealing with total market coverage papers and other free distributions of paid newspapers.[41]

Acquisition and Merger Problems

The acquisition of a competing newspaper or the merger of competing papers raises antitrust issues. Antitrust laws limit horizontal acquisitions and mergers involving firms that actually or potentially could compete in the same product and geographic market as a means of preserving competition and preventing monopolization through economic concentration and the gaining of monopoly power. In analyzing acquisitions or mergers, measurements of concentration are used to provide information on the degree of concentration in a market before and after an acquisition or merger. Using standard measures of competition, even the most competitive newspaper markets in the United States have been shown to be highly concentrated.[42]

In a 1995 application of antitrust laws to an acquisition, a competing paper—joined by the U.S. Department of Justice—successfully sued and rescinded the sale of the *Northwest Arkansas Times* to a subsidiary of the corporate owner of Donrey Media, which owned a newspaper in an adjacent town. The suit argued, and the court agreed, that the acquisition would monopolize the northwest Arkansas newspaper market to the detriment of consumers and the third daily newspaper in the region.[43]

If a newspaper is about to fold, antitrust authorities allow the acquisition of the paper by its competitor or its merger with its competitor under the "failing company" doctrine, which permits such acquisitions or mergers if no other company is willing to purchase the firm. It was under this mechanism that the *Houston Chronicle* bought out and closed the *Houston Post* and the Colorado Springs *Gazette-Telegraph* bought and closed the Colorado Springs *Sun*.

Although many critics of newspaper chains would like to see antitrust laws used to stop the growth of large newspaper groups, they have not been able to slow the growth of groups because of the local nature of newspaper markets and the ways that existing antitrust laws define and approach competition and markets.[44]

A unique antitrust element in the newspaper industry is that competing newspapers may apply for exemptions from antitrust laws under the Newspaper Preservation Act of 1970. Under the law, newspapers may combine their operations in ways not normally permitted by law in what are called joint operating agreements. These arrangements do not preserve unprofitable newspapers but give some short- and mid-term relief that allows their owners to withdraw their investments before the papers close.[45] Newspapers that recently entered such agreements include the *Detroit Free Press* and *Detroit News* and the Las Vegas *Sun* and Las Vegas *Review-Journal*. Papers that recently closed despite such agreements have included the *Miami News*, the Shreveport (Louisiana) *Journal*, and the Tulsa *Tribune*.

SUMMARY

The newspaper industry faces a wide variety of legal and regulatory issues and challenges and is one of the most active industries in lobbying efforts nationwide. State and national associations of publishers, editors, and journalists for all categories of papers regularly monitor developments and lobby legislators for positions supportive of the industry. The issues are often complex and technical, so associations hire or contract with specialists who monitor specific topics in various government agencies, help newspaper associations develop positions on the issues, and help present those views to relevant agencies and legislatures. The process and issues arise constantly, although there tend to be flurries of activity around certain topics as society and governments wrestle with specific problems and issues that develop.

ENDNOTES

1. "Housing Ads Draw Heightened Scrutiny," *Presstime*, November 1994, 17:13.

2. Dorothy Giobbe, "HUD Clarifies Its Classified Ad Language Policy," *Editor & Publisher*, February 4, 1995, 26, and "HUD Offers Relief," *Presstime*, February 1995, 128:13.

3. Debra Gersh Hernandez, "Uniform Correction Act Introduced," *Editor & Publisher*, July 22, 1995, 128:16.

4. Henry S. Hoberman, "Libel Reform Isn't Necessarily Bad for Nation's Media," *Quill*, March 1995, 83:14.

5. Judy Greenwald, "Publishers Cautioned on Risks of Online Publishing Ventures," *Business Insurance,* December 4, 1995, 68.

6. Susan Benkelman, "Online Services Seek Guidelines for Treks in Cyberspace, Legal and Moral Issues Remain Unidentified," *Commercial Appeal,* December 30, 1995, 8C.

7. Randolph J. May, "Online Libel and Cyberspace Porn," *Connecticut Law Tribune,* Dec. 4, 1995, 40.

8. Andrew Blum, "Internet Copyright Ruling," *National Law Journal,* December 11, 1995, 19:A6.

9. "Pulling and Pushing E-Rights: Publishers Negotiate for Content and Writers Follow the Money," *Digital Media,* Sept. 11, 1995, 19.

10. Associated Press, *Associated Press Stylebook and Libel Manual* (New York: Associated Press, annual).

11. United Press International, *United Press International Stylebook* (New York: United Press International, annual).

12. See, for example, "Trademarks and the Press," *Editor & Publisher*, vol. 128, Special Editorial Section, December 9, 1995.

13. James T. Borelli, "The Forgotten Peril; Trademark Infringement is One More Risk to Consider When It's Time to Name a Newspaper or Buy Insurance," *Editor & Publisher*, vol. 128, Special Editorial Section, December 9, 1995, 12T.

14. Newton N. Minnow, "The Communications Act: Our Children are the Public Interest," *Vital Speeches* 61, 13 (April, 15, 1995), 389.

15. Carl Jensen & Project Censored, *Censored: The News That Didn't Make the News— and Why* (New York: Four Walls Eight Windows 1994), 27.

16. Rex Weiner, "CompuServe Move Irks Netheads," *Daily Variety*, January 2, 1996, 3.

17. "Singapore Orders Newspaper to Pay," UPI, May 10, 1995, BC cycle.

18. Ana Arana, "The Chilling Effect is Palpable," *Silenced: The Unsolved Murders of Immigrant Journalists in the United States* (New York: Committee To Protect Journalists, 1994), 3.

19. Patricia P. Renfroe, "Sexual Harrassment," *Presstime*, May 1985, 17:14–15.

20. Carolyn Terry, "Sexual Harrassment: Old News," *Presstime*, September 1995, 17:63.

21. George Garneau, "Monitor Loses Overtime Case," *Editor & Publisher*, November 13, 1993, 126:26–27.

22. "California Daily Pays Fine for Hazardous Waste," *Editor & Publisher*, April 18, 1992, 125:45.

23. Mark Fitzgerald, "Accord Close in Groundwater Contamination Case," *Editor & Publisher*, June 24, 1995, 128:58+.

24. John Consoli, "Get Your Act Together: Newspapers Warned They Had Better Make Sure They are in Compliance with Environmental Regulations or Face Criminal Prosecution," *Editor & Publisher*, June 22, 1991, 124: 7–8.

25. Mark Fitzgerald, "Old Newspaper Now Traded on Chicago Exchange," *Editor & Publisher*, November 18, 1995, 128:36.

26. Newspaper Association of America, *Facts About Newspapers '95* (Reston, VA: Newspaper Association of America, 1995).

27. Bob Salgado, "Dealing with a Contamination Problem," *Editor & Publisher*, November 18, 1995, 128:26.

28. Phillip Perry. "12 Ways to Cut Your Workers Comp Costs," *Editor & Publisher*, December 25, 1993, 126:28–30.

29. Carolyn Terry, "Safety First," *Presstime*, July 1993, 15:60–63.

30. C. David Rambo, "Newspapers Seek New Ways to Increase Carriers' Safety," *Presstime*, September 1984, 6:6–7.

31. American Newspaper Publishers Association and International Federation of Financial Executives, *Taxes on Advertising, Circulation, Preprints, Production Materials, Supplies and Equipment Affecting Newspapers: A 50-State Compilation* (Reston, VA: American Newspaper Publishers Association, 1989).

32. Rosalind C. Truitt, "A Taxing Climate," *Presstime*, May 1995, 17:65–68

33. George Garneau, "Sales Tax on Newspaper Equipment Overturned," *Editor & Publisher*, June 8, 1991, 124:28ff.

34. Dave Martens, "When the IRS Knocks...," *Presstime*, August 1995, 17:53–56.

35. Kim Nauer, "Tax Attacks: How Newspapers Flirt with Evasion," *Columbia Journalism Review* (September/October 1993), 20–21.

36. Newspaper Association of America, *Newspaper Manual for Utilizing Independent Contractors* (Reston, VA: Newspaper Association of America, 1995).

37. S. Chesterfield Oppenheim and Carrington Shields, *Newspapers and Antitrust Laws* (Charlottesville, VA: Michie 1981).

38. John C. Busterna, "Antitrust in the 1980s: An Analysis of 45 Newspaper Actions," *Newspaper Research Journal* 9:25–336.

39. Herbert Hovenkamp, "Vertical Integration by the Newspaper Monopolist," *Iowa Law Review* 69 (1984), and Robert G. Picard, "Critical Assumptions in Arguments for Maximum Price Fixing of Newspaper Circulation," *Communications and the Law* (December 1990), 12:69–86.

40. Robert G. Picard, "The Relationship between Newspaper Costs and Predation Lawsuits," *Newspaper Research Journal* 10 (Winter 1990):112–125.

41. Robert G. Picard, "Cost Analyses of Predation Involving Free Circulation Subsidiaries of Paid Newspapers," *Journal of Media Economics* 4 (Summer 1991):19–34.

42. Robert G. Picard, "Measures of Concentration in the Daily Newspaper Industry," *Journal of Media Economics* 1 (Spring 1988):64–94.

43. George Garneau, "Return to Seller," *Editor & Publisher*, July 22, 1995.

44. John C. Busterna, "Application of US Antitrust Laws to Daily Newspaper Chains," *Journal of Media Law and Practice* 10:117–122, and John C. Busterna, "Newspaper Chains and Antitrust Laws," *Journalism Monographs*, No. 110, March 1989.

45. John C. Busterna and Robert G. Picard, *Joint Operating Agreements: The Newspaper Preservation Act and Its Application* (Norwood, NJ: Ablex Publishing, 1993).

Appendix
Major Newspaper
Groups, 1995

CAPITAL CITIES/ABC

This diversified media company operates daily and weekly newspapers, magazines, books, television and radio stations, and the ABC Television Network.

The nation's largest media company with significant daily newspaper holdings, Capital Cities/ABC had sales of $6.4 billion and assets of $6.8 billion in 1994. About 17 percent of its revenues came from newspaper operations. Stock in the firm is traded on the New York Stock Exchange under the symbol CCB.

Among its daily newspaper holdings are the *Kansas City Star*, Ft. Worth (Texas) *Star-Telegram*, and the Belleville (Illinois) *News-Democrat*.

Capital Cities/ABC is based at 77 W. 66th Street, New York, NY 10023. (212) 456-7777.

CENTRAL NEWSPAPERS

Based in the midwest, Central Newspapers was established by Eugene C. Pullium and grew out of his ownership of the *Indianapolis Star*. It had annual sales of $520 million and assets of $500 million in 1994. Some 99.5 percent of its revenues came from newspapers. Shares in the firm are traded on the New York Stock Exchange under the symbol ECP.

Central Newspapers operates daily and weekly newspapers in Indiana and Arizona, including the *Indianapolis Star* and *News* (of which it is the principal owner) and the *Arizona Republic* and Phoenix *Gazette.*

Central Newspapers, has its headquarters at 135 N. Pennsylvania, Suite 1200, Indianapolis, IN 46204-2400. (317) 231-9200.

CHRONICLE PUBLISHING

This California-based company publishes daily and weekly newspapers in California, Illinois, and Massachusetts, and operates book publishing and cable television subsidiaries. In 1994 its annual sales were estimated to be $188 million.

The private firm traces its history to the establishment of the *San Francisco Chronicle* by Charles and Michael De Young Jr. in 1849.[1] Today, its daily papers include the *San Francisco Chronicle*, Worcester (Massachusetts) *Telegram & Gazette*, and Bloomington (Illinois) *Pantagraph.*

The company is based at 901 Mission Street, San Francisco, CA 94103. (415) 777-7444.

COPLEY PRESS

This southern California-based company operates daily papers in California and Illinois, as well as a group of weekly newspapers.

This privately held company traces its history to the purchase of the Aurora (Illinois) *Beacon* by Ira C. Copley in 1905. It is known for its philosophy of autonomy for managers of its individual papers.

The flagship paper for Copley is the San Diego *Union-Tribune.* Among its other papers are the Santa Monica *Outlook*, Torrance (California) *Daily Breeze*, Aurora (Illinois) *Beacon-News,* and Springfield (Illinois) *State Journal-Register.*

The company's headquarters are located at 7776 Ivanhoe Avenue, La Jolla, CA 92038. (619) 454-0411.

COX ENTERPRISES

This diversified Georgia-based company operates newspapers and broadcasting stations nationwide and was one of the first newspaper companies to diversify into other media operations. The company had estimated sales of $2.9 billion in 1994.

The privately held company traces its history to the purchase of the Dayton (Ohio) *Evening News* in 1898 by James M. Cox. The firm began centering its operations in Georgia after the purchase of the *Atlanta Journal* in 1939.

It operates its newspapers through its Cox Newspapers subsidiary. The company's flagship papers are the *Atlanta Journal* and *Constitution*. Among other papers included in the group are the Tempe (Arizona) *Daily News Tribune*, Dayton (Ohio) *Daily News*, and Austin (Texas) *American-Statesman*.

The company offices are located at P.O. Box 105720, Atlanta, GA 30348. (404) 843-5000.

DONREY MEDIA GROUP

This Arkansas-based firm operates more than fifty daily newspapers nationwide, as well as television, cable television, and outdoor advertising operations. The company had estimated sales of $223 million in 1994. The group was established in 1940 by Donald W. Reynolds. After his death, the company was purchased by Jackson T. Stephens.

Included in the company's newspaper holdings are papers such as the Asheboro (North Carolina) *Courier-Tribune*, Ontario (California) *Inland Valley Daily Bulletin*, and Las Vegas (Nevada) *Review-Journal*.

Offices of the Donrey Media Group are located at 3600 Wheeler Avenue, Fort Smith, AR 72901. (501) 785-7810.

DOW JONES & CO.

Dow Jones & Co. is internationally recognized as a publisher of newspapers and business publications and as a provider of information services. It had annual sales exceeding $2 billion and assets of more than $2.5 billion in 1994. Its publishing activities account for about 53 percent of its revenues. Shares in the company are traded on the New York Stock Exchange under the symbol DJ.

The company was established in 1882 by Charles H. Dow, Edward D. Jones, and Charles M. Bergstresser to produce financial information and began publishing the *Wall Street Journal* in 1889. Today, that paper—along with Asian and European editions—remains the company's flagship paper.[2] The company operates daily and nondaily newspapers through its Ottaway Newspapers subsidiary, which includes papers such as the Santa Cruz *Sentinel*, Joplin (Missouri) *Globe*, and the *Pocono Record* in Stroudsburg, Pennsylvania.

The corporate headquarters of Dow Jones & Co. are located at World Financial Center, 200 Liberty Street, New York, NY 10281. (212) 416-2000.

FREEDOM COMMUNICATIONS

This southern California-based company operates daily and weekly newspapers nationwide, as well as television stations and magazines. Revenues for 1994 were estimated at $294 million.

Founded by R. C. Hoiles, Freedom Communications remains a privately owned family firm, although its managers are increasingly from outside the Hoiles family.[3] Among its daily newspaper holdings are the Santa Ana *Orange County Register*, Colorado Springs *Gazette-Telegraph*, the Greenville (Mississippi) *Delta Democrat-Times*, and the McAllen (Texas) *Monitor*.

The company has its main offices at 17666 Fitch, Irvine, CA 92714. (714) 553-9292.

GANNETT

Perhaps the most visible of newspaper groups, Gannett had revenues of more than $3.8 billion and assets exceeding $3.7 billion in 1994. The company has newspaper, advertising, and television and radio station operations nationwide. Its income from newspaper operations accounts for 78 percent of its revenue. The company is listed on the New York Stock Exchange under the symbol GCI.

The company was begun by Frank E. Gannett with the *Times-Union* in Rochester, New York. Today the firm owns more than eighty newspapers nationwide.[4] Major newspapers owned by the company include *USA Today*, *Des Moines Register*, and the Detroit *News*. Its other holdings include the Wilmington (Delaware) *News Journal*, Palm Springs (California) *Desert Sun*, and Honolulu (Hawaii) *Advertiser.*

The company's headquarters are at 1100 Wilson Blvd., Arlington, VA 22234. (703) 284-6000.

HARTE–HANKS COMMUNICATIONS

This Texas-based company operates daily newspapers and dozens of nondaily newspapers and shoppers nationwide, as well as a television station, and direct marketing and advertising operations. The company had sales of $514 million and assets of $497 million in 1994, with 27 percent of its revenues coming from newspaper operations. The company is traded on the New York Stock Exchange under the symbol HHS.

Among the firm's dailies are the Dedham (Massasschusetts) *Daily Transcript*, Corpus Christi (Texas) *Caller-Times*, and San Angelo (Texas) *Standard Times*.

Harte–Hanks Communications has its headquarters at P.O. Box 269, San Antonio, TX 78291. (210) 829-9000.

HEARST

A diversified media company, Hearst publishes daily newspapers, as well as operating consumer and business magazines, a news feature service, television and radio stations, book publishing firms, and television and cable programming services. In 1994, the company had revenues estimated at $1.8 billion.

Established in 1887 by William Randolph Hearst, this privately held company became one of the nation's first newspaper groups. Today, its principal daily newspapers are the *San Francisco Examiner*, Seattle (Washington) *Post-Intelligencer*, and San Antonio (Texas) *Express-News*.[5]

Hearst has offices at 959 8th Avenue, New York, NY 10019. (212) 649-2000.

HOLLINGER INTERNATIONAL (AMERICAN PUBLISHING)

A subsidiary of Hollinger Inc., the Canadian-based newspaper company, this firm based in the Midwest operates nearly 100 daily newspapers and more than 200 weekly and free distribution publications nationwide. In 1994, the company had sales of $423 million and assets of about $636 million. About 98 percent of its revenue came from newspaper operations. Shares of the public company are traded on NASDAQ, under the symbol HOLI.

The company was established as a wholly owned subsidiary of Hollinger Inc., the Canadian-based newspaper company. In 1994, the company went public under the name American Publishing, offering Class A shares to the public, but Hollinger maintained a majority equity ownership. In 1995, the firm was restructured and renamed Hollinger International.

Its papers include the *Chicago Sun-Times*, but the bulk of its holdings are smaller papers such as the Naugatuck (Connecticut) *Daily News*, Canton (Ill.) *Daily Ledger*, San Marcos (Texas) *Daily Record*, and Fort Morgan (Colorado) *Times*.

The company's headquarters are at 111–115 S. Emma Street, West Frankfort, IL 62896. (618) 932-2146.

KNIGHT–RIDDER

One of the most respected groups, Knight–Ridder is known for the quality of its newspapers and information services. It had annual revenues of $2.6 billion and assets of $2.5 billion in 1994. Newspaper operations account for about 80 percent of its revenues. The company is traded on the New York Stock Exchange under the symbol KRI.

The company was created in 1974 by the merger of Ridder Publications, founded by Herman Ridder, with Knight Newspapers. Knight traces its history to the purchase of the Akron (Ohio) *Beacon-Journal* by Charles L. Knight in 1903.

Today, the company publishes the *Miami Herald*, *Detroit Free Press*, *Philadelphia Inquirer* and *Daily News*, San Jose (California) *Mercury News*, and twenty-two smaller papers such as Charlotte (North Carolina) *Observer*, Macon (Georgia) *Telegraph*, Duluth (Minnesota) *News-Tribune*, and Boulder (Colorado) *Daily Camera*.

The company's corporate headquarters are located are One Herald Plaza, Miami, FL 33132-1693. (305) 376-3800.

LEE ENTERPRISES

Based in the Midwest, Lee Enterprises had annual revenues of $403 million and assets of $475 million in 1994. Its newspapers provide about 60 percent of the company's sales income. One of the smallest publicly traded newspaper companies, shares of Lee Enterprises are traded on the New York Stock Exchange under the symbol LEE.

Founded by A. W. Lee in 1890, the company today operates nineteen daily newspapers, nearly three dozen nondaily papers, and television stations in small and mid-sized markets nationwide, as well as printing supply and service companies. Its daily newspaper holdings include papers such as the *Quad-City Times* in Davenport, Iowa, the *Missoulian* in Missoula, Montana, and the *Herald & Review* in Decatur, Illinois.

The company's headquarters is located at 400 Putnam Building, 215 N. Main Street, Davenport, IA 52801-1924. (319) 383-2100.

MCCLATCHY NEWSPAPERS

Firmly based in the newspaper industry on the West Coast, McClatchy Newspapers had sales of $471 million and assets of $587 million in 1994. All of its revenue came from newspaper operations. McClatchy Newspapers is a public company and its shares are traded on the New York Stock Exchange under the symbol MNI.

The company began in 1857 with the establishment of the *Sacramento Bee* by James McClatchy. Today, the firm remains based in California's San Joaquin Valley, where it publishes the *Sacramento Bee*, *Fresno Bee*, and *Modesto Bee*, as well as smaller daily and weekly papers. The company also publishes daily and weekly newspapers in Alaska, Washington, North Carolina, and South Carolina, including the Anchorage (Alaska) *Daily News*, Tacoma (Washington) *News Tribune*, the Raleigh *News and Observer*, and Rock Hill (South Carolina) *Herald*.

McClatchy Newspapers has its corporate offices at 2100 Q Street, Sacramento, CA 95816. (916) 321-1846.

MEDIA GENERAL

A mid-Atlantic based company, Media General had annual sales of $626 million and assets of $787 million in 1994. Its newspaper operations accounted for about 52 percent of its revenues. Media General is a public company and its shares are traded on the American Stock Exchange under the symbol MEGA.

Media General traces its history to 1850 when it began publishing what is now its flagship, the Richmond (Virginia) *Times-Dispatch*. It also publishes the Tampa (Florida) *Tribune*, and the Winston-Salem (North Carolina) *Journal*. Its corporate offices are in Richmond. The company operates more than a dozen nondailies in Florida and also owns a minority interest in Garden State Newspapers, which publishes fourteen papers nationwide.

The company also owns television and cable television stations in Atlantic states and has significant holdings in newsprint production companies.

The firm's headquarters address is P.O. Box 32333, Richmond, VA 23293. (804) 649-6000.

MEDIANEWS GROUP

This Texas-based group is a tightly held group that operates sixteen daily newspapers nationwide and accounts for almost 2 percent of the newspaper circulation in the United States. Its daily newspaper holdings include the Denver *Post*, Oakland *Tribune*, Las Cruces (New Mexico) *Sun-Times*, and York (Pennsylvania) *Dispatch*.

MediaNews Group is headquartered at 4888 Loop Central Drive, Suite 525, Houston, TX 77801-2211. (713) 840-5633.

MORRIS COMMUNICATION

This Georgia-based firm operates thirty-one daily newspapers, as well as nondailies and magazines. A privately owned firm, it had estimated sales of $144 million in 1994. Its papers include the Juneau (Alaska) *Empire*, Jacksonville (Florida) *Times-Union*, and Lubbock (Texas) *Avalanche-Journal*.

The company has its headquarters at P.O. Box 936, Augusta, GA 30913. (706) 724-0851.

MULTIMEDIA

Multimedia operates daily and nondaily newspapers, television stations, and cable systems, primarily in the Midwest, South, and mid-Atlantic states, and is a producer of television and cable programming. It had annual sales in excess of $630 million and assets of more than $684 million in 1994. About 24 percent of its revenue resulted from newspaper publishing. Shares in Multimedia are traded on NASDAQ under the symbol MMEDC.

In late 1995, Multimedia agreed to be acquired by Gannett pending approval of shareholders and regulatory authorities.

Among its eleven daily newspapers are the Montgomery (Alabama) *Advertiser*, Asheville (North Carolina) *Citizen-Times*, Gallipolis (Ohio) *Daily Tribune*, and Greenville (South Carolina) *News*. It also operates more than four dozen nondailies including the Mountain Home (Arkansas) *Twin Lakes Shopper*, Columbia (South Carolina) *Fort Jackson Leader*, and Hendersonville (Tennessee) *Star News*.

Multimedia has its corporate offices located at 305 S. Main Street, Greenville, SC 29601. (803) 298-4873.

NEW YORK TIMES

Publisher of the nation's newspaper of record, the company also owns newspapers and broadcast stations nationwide as well as magazines, information services, and forest product companies. It had sales of $2.3 billion and more than $3.1 billion in assets in 1994. Eighty-four percent of its revenue came from newspaper publishing. A public company, its shares are traded on the American Stock Exchange under the symbol NYTA.

Begun in 1851 with the establishment of the *New York Times* by Henry J. Raymond and George Jones, the company has grown to include extensive newspaper holdings including the *Boston Globe* and smaller papers such as the Gainesville (Florida) *Sun*, the Houma (Louisiana) *Courier*, and the *Press-Democrat* in Santa Rosa, California.[6]

The offices of the firm are located at 229 W. 43rd Street, New York, NY 10036-3959. (212) 556-1234.

NEWHOUSE NEWSPAPERS

This privately held firm owns newspaper and magazines nationwide and had sales estimated at $421 million in 1993.

The company was established by S. I. Newhouse, beginning with his purchase of the *Staten Island Advance* in 1922. For most of its history, the company's newspaper operations were primarily based in New York state. The company's activities spread rapidly with its purchase of Booth Newspapers in 1976, a deal that was one of the largest buyouts of a media company in its day. Among the firm's newspapers are the Birmingham (Alabama) *News* and *Post-Herald*, the Ann Arbor (Michigan) *News*, the New Orleans (Louisiana) *Times-Picayune*, and the Portland (Oregon) *Oregonian*.

Newhouse Newspapers has its company offices at 485 Lexington Ave., New York, NY 10017. (212) 697-8020.

PARK COMMUNICATIONS

Founded by Roy H. Park, Sr., this company had estimated sales of $159 million in 1994. The company operates twenty-nine small and mid-sized dailies, as well as weeklies, shoppers, and television stations, primarily in the Eastern and Midwestern United States.

Following the death of its founder, the firm was purchased for $711 million and privatized in 1995 by an investment group owned by Gary Knapp and Donald Tomlin. Among its daily newpspaers are the Effingham (Illinois) *Daily News*, Bemidji (Minnesota) *Pioneer*, Hudson (New York) *Register-Star*, and the Rockingham (North Carolina) *Daily Journal*.

The company's headquarters are at Terrace Hill (P.O. Box 550), Ithaca, NY 14851. (607) 272-9020.

PULITZER PUBLISHING

This midwestern company had sales exceeding $486 million dollars and $468 million in assets in 1994. Newspaper operations account for nearly 68 percent of its sales. Shares of Pulitzer Publishing are traded on the New York Stock Exchange under the symbol PTZ.

The company was founded by Joseph Pulitzer in 1878 with the acquisition of the St. Louis *Dispatch* and its merger with the *Post* to form the *Post-Dispatch*. He turned it into one of the nation's first newspaper groups with the purchase of the now-defunct New York *World* in 1883.[7] Today, the St. Louis *Post-Dispatch* continues as the hub of the company's activities, along with the *Arizona Daily Star* in Tucson, Arizona. In addition, the company operates television and radio stations nationwide·

The Pulitzer Publishing offices are located at 900 N. Tucker Blvd., St. Louis, MO 63101. (314) 340-8000.

E. W. SCRIPPS

E. W. Scripps is one of the oldest newspaper companies in the United States with total sales exceeding $1.2 billion and more than $1.7 billion in assets in 1994. The company operates newspapers, news and feature services, television and radio stations, and cable systems, and its publishing division contributes about 50 percent of its total revenue. Shares in the firm are traded on the New York Stock Exchange under the symbol SSP.

The history of the E. W. Scripps Company began in 1878 with the establishment of the Cleveland (Ohio) *Penny Press* by Edward W. Scripps. In 1890, he entered a partnership with Milton McRae, establishing the Scripps–McRae League, the first newspaper group in the United States This became Scripps–Howard Newspapers, in a partnership with Roy W. Howard, in the early 1920s.[8] The John P. Scripps Company, which operated primarily in California, was merged into the company in 1986.

The company operates twenty-one daily newspapers in ten states, with its largest concentration (nine) in California. Its largest paper is the *Rocky Mountain News* in Denver, Colorado, which has a daily circulation of more than 350,000. Other well-known papers in the company include the Cincinnati (Ohio) *Post*, the Knoxville (Tennessee) *News-Sentinel*, and *The Commercial Appeal* in Memphis, Tennessee.

The offices of E. W. Scripps Co. are located at 312 Walnut Street, Cincinnati, OH 45201. (513) 977-3825.

THOMSON

This Canadian firm had sales of $5.9 billion (U.S.) in 1993 and was created through the 1989 merger of Thomson Newspapers and International Thomson Organisation. The firm includes 160 daily and 70 weekly newspapers in the United States and Canada as well as specialized information services.

The group traces its founding to the purchase of a radio station in 1931 and a small Canadian newspaper in 1934 by Roy Thomson. The firm expanded to become a major group operating in eight countries including Canada, the United Kingdom and the United States.[9]

U.S. papers owned by the company include the Dothan (Alabama) *Eagle*, Sheboygan (Wisconsin) *Press*, Mexico (Missouri) *Ledger*, and Pasadena (California) *Star-News*. The firm began restructuring its U.S. operations in 1995 by agreeing to sell dozens of its papers to other newspaper groups.

Thomson has its offices at Toronto-Dominion Centre, Toronto, Ontario, Canada M5K 1A1. (416) 360-8700.

TIMES MIRROR

One of the most recognized and diversified media companies, Times Mirror operates nationwide and had sales exceeding $3.3 billion annually on assets of $4.3 billion in 1993. Newspaper publishing accounts for slightly more than 60 percent of its revenue. This public company is traded on the New York Stock Exchange under the symbol TMC.

The Times Mirror began with the establishment of the *Los Angeles* (California) *Times* in 1881 by General Harrison Gray Otis and was incorporated in 1884. It became the Times Mirror Co. after it established the *Mirror* as an afternoon tabloid in 1948.[10]

Today the company owns newspapers nationwide, including *Newsday*, the *Baltimore Sun*, and the Hartford *Courant*, and is a leader in publishing professional and educational books and materials. It is also active in the magazine and consumer book markets, as well as in multimedia and cable programming.

Times Mirror Company operates from its headquarters at Times Mirror Square, Los Angeles, CA 90053. (213) 237-3700.

TRIBUNE

One of the nation's leading media firms, the Tribune Company operates daily newspapers, television and radio stations, and produces syndicated programming. It had annual sales of nearly $2.1 billion and assets totaling more than $2.7 billion in 1994. Nearly two-thirds of its revenue comes from its publishing activities.

The *Tribune* was established in 1847, but did not become an important paper until after it was purchased by Joseph Medill and his partners in 1855.

Today the company's papers include the *Chicago Tribune*, Fort Lauderdale (Florida) *Sun-Sentinel*, Orlando (Florida) *Sentinel*, Escondido (California) *Times-Advocate*, and the Newport News (Virginia) *Daily Press*.

The Tribune offices are located at 435 N. Michigan Avenue, Chicago, IL 60611. (312) 222-3238.

WASHINGTON POST

The company had annual sales of about $1.6 billion with assets of about the same level in 1994. Its newspaper operations contribute about 45 percent of the company's revenues. A public company, its shares are traded on the New York Stock Exchange under the symbol WPO.

Its flagship *Washington Post* is the company's primary newspaper operation, but it also owns the *Herald* in Everett, Washington. It has a half interest in the

International Herald Tribune and owns more than one-fourth of Cowles Media, which publishes the Minneapolis *Star Tribune*. It is also the majority owner of a weekly newspaper group in suburban Maryland.

In addition, Washington Post owns news services, television stations, cable television systems, *Newsweek* magazine, and interests in newsprint manufacturing.

Its main offices are located at 1150 15th Street, N.W., Washington, DC 20071. (202) 334-6000.

ENDNOTES

1. John P. Young, *Journalism in California* (San Francisco: Chronicle Publishing Co., 1915).

2. E. Schraff, *Worldly Power: The Making of the Wall Street Journal* (New York: New American Library, 1988).

3. J. L. Sullivan "Not Quite All in the Family: Outside Directors Signal Change in Register Empire," *Orange County Business*, March 27–April 2, 1995, 1+.

4. J. Donald Brandt, *A History of Gannett, 1906–1993* (Arlington, VA: Gannett, 1993).

5. James F. O'Donnell, *100 Years of Making Communications History: The Story of the Hearst Corporation* (New York: The Hearst Corporation, 1987); Lindsay Chaney and Michael Cieply, *The Hearsts: The Family and Empire—The Later Years* (New York: Simon and Schuster, 1981); and W. A. Swanberg, *Citizen Hearst* (New York: Charles Scribner's Sons, 1961).

6. Meyer Berger, *The Story of the New York Times, 1851–1951* (New York: Simon and Schuster, 1951); Gay Talese, *The Kingdom and the Power* (New York: World, 1969).

7. George Juergens, *Joseph Pulitzer and the New York World* (Princeton, NJ: Princeton University Press, 1966); W. A. Swanberg, *Pulitzer* (New York: Scribner's, 1967).

8. Jack Casserly, *Scripps, the Divided Dynasty: A History of the First Family of American Journalism* (New York: Donald I. Fine, 1992); Charles R. McCabe, ed. *Damned Old Crank: A Self Portrait of E. W. Scripps,* (New York: Harper and Brothers, 1951).

9. R. Bradden, *Roy Thomson of Fleet Street* (New York: Walker, 1965).

10. Robert Gottlieb and Irene Wolt, *Thinking Big: The Story of the Los Angeles Times, Its Publishers, and Their Influence on Southern California* (New York: G. P. Putnam's Son's, 1976).

Glossary

Advance Term used to designate a story written in advance of an anticipated event and held for release. Also used to indicate a story written to play up an upcoming event.

Advertising Information for which a fee has been paid for its publication. It is usually intended to notify or inform individuals about goods or services for sale, but is also used to provide legal notification of certain events or plans, and to promote social and political ideas or personalities.

Advertorials Advertising material presented in the form of editorial material, resembling news. Advertorials are sometimes published as special sections or supplements, but may be included on regular pages within the newspaper.

All-day paper A paper that publishes editions several times in one day, for example, morning, noon, and evening.

All other zones Portions of a newspaper market outside the primary commercial and residential area.

Alternative papers Nondaily newspapers supporting social or political views or lifestyles outside of the mainstream. Originally used to designate counterculture papers, the term now includes a broader variety of weeklies and monthlies that are well funded and have large circulations.

Angle The main point or slant used in a news or feature story.

Art A graphic design, photo, or visual composite used in conjunction with editorial or advertising material or alone in the paper.

Audio text Information services that provide information or advertising via telephone. Services can be provided without charge or for a fee.

Audit A study, usually by a neutral party, that examines and verifies information. In the newspaper industry audits are used for circulation figures and financial information.

Audit Bureau of Circulation The primary newspaper industry organization that provides standardized, audited circulation data, which permits reliable comparisons of daily newspaper circulation.

Audited circulation Circulation data that has been subjected to verification. Primary firms conducting newspaper industry audits are the Audit Bureau of Circulation, Certified Audit of Circulation, and Verified Audit of Circulation.

Average net paid circulation A figure of circulation sales that averages sales over a period, normally a five-day work week, to account for traditional fluctuations experienced in single copy sales due to content factors.

B

Banner The main headline on the first page or section of a newspaper, usually across the entire width of the page.

Beat An area of news coverage to which a journalist is primarily assigned, such as police and fire, city hall, or education.

Body copy The editorial material in a story, excluding its headline and the *lead*.

Breaking news Information on a news event that is just occurring. News on such events is typically incomplete and, sometimes, unverified because of its immediacy.

Broadsheet Originally a term for news sheets printed only on one side and concentrating on a single event, it now designates a newspaper of traditional size as opposed to a tabloid.

Byline The name of the author of an article, typically printed under the headline just before the story begins.

C

Caption A display line used above art, such as a photograph. Sometimes confused with *outline*.

Cartoons Drawings used as a form of commentary about political and social issues and figures. Primarily published on editorial pages.

Certified Audit of Circulation A firm that provides circulation audits primarily for free circulation newspapers.

Chain A company that includes two or more newspapers operated separately in different locations. Such companies are also called a *group*.

Churn A measure of the percentage of customers that are replaced in a given period to maintain a stable level of circulation.

Circulation 1) The number of papers distributed to customers; 2) The department responsible for sales and distribution.

City zone A circulation area that includes the central portion of a city and its contiguous suburbs.

Classified advertising A type of advertising, primarily using only type, divided into classifications of products or services for easy use by readers. Typically found in the final section of a newspaper.

Cold type Production of material for printing using phototypesetting techniques.

Columns Editorial material providing the comments or advice of an identifiable person on political or social developments or personal interests.

Column inch A standard measurement indicating a depth of one inch of space in whatever column width is used in a paper.

Columnist A writer who produces a personalized column of opinion or feature material rather than news and general feature material.

Comics Stories and jokes, usually humorous, illustrated with drawings.

Cold type Phototypesetting, which replaced the hot type method of creating type for printing.

Co-op Advertising A type of advertising in which the manufacturers and retailer split the cost of advertising because it is beneficial to both.

Copy Written material prepared for stories or advertising.

Copydesk The work area in a paper where copy produced by others is edited, given a headline, and prepared for publication.

Copyright An exclusive right to use, publish, or distribute intellectual and artistic products that is given by government to those who create the works. All or part of the rights can be sold or purchased.

Crossword puzzles Word puzzles that are among the most popular features in newspapers worldwide.

Cutline Information accompanying a photograph that is used to describe and explain the contents of the photo.

D

Daily newspaper In the United States a daily newspaper is one published at least five days a week. No internationally accepted definition for a daily paper exists; each nation chooses its own definition.

Dateline An indicator at the beginning of a story that indicates the city and country from which the story originated. In years past, datelines also indicated the date on which the story was written because news moved more slowly around the world than it does today and datelines indicated the currency of the information.

Delivery The transportation of newspapers from printing facilities to locations where subscribers receive their copies and single-copy sales are made.

Display advertising Advertising that includes visual material, such as illustrations, and is usually purchased in units of space required rather than lines of type.

Double-truck Two connecting pages of advertising used as a single advertisement.

Drop head A second-level headline, normally in smaller and different typeface than the headline, that provides additional information about the contents of a story.

Duplicate readership Readers who read more than one newspaper available in a market.

Duplicate subscribership Refers to individuals who pay for subscriptions to more than one newspaper available in a market.

E

Edition An issue of a paper. Some papers produce more than one edition daily, such as home delivery and newsstand editions or local and state editions.

Editor A person who manages and reviews the work of reporters and has responsibility for one or more sections of a paper.

Editor-in-chief The individual with responsibility for overseeing all editorial operations of the newspaper.

Editorial 1) The opinion of the newspaper or its publisher published on the opinion page; 2) material in the paper that is not advertising.

Extra A special or "extra" edition of the paper that is produced when news events warrant extra coverage or distribution is desired at times between the normally scheduled editions.

F

Fax services Information and advertising sent by facsimile transmission through a telephone system. Newspapers offer fax services as a supplemental service, typically by subscription.

Feature Editorial information that does not contain the characteristics chiefly associated with news.

Feature services Organizations that act like news agencies but provide feature materials rather than news.

Flag The area of the first page of the newspaper in which the name of the paper is published.

Flagship The primary paper in a newspaper group. Flagships are typically the first paper in the group, the largest in the group, or the most prestigious in the group.

Free circulation Circulation of a newspaper made without charge to the reader. Free circulation newspapers may be either delivered to homes or made available through news racks and other distribution locations.

Full run A a particular story, feature, or advertisement that appears in all editions of a newspaper rather than in selected or zoned editions as in part-run material.

G

Gathering The assembling of folded signature sheets into proper order or sequence.

Graphics Art and other materials used to illustrate and improve the appearance of printed material in newspapers.

Group A company that includes two or more newspapers operated separately in different locations. Groups are sometimes called *chains*.

Gutter The margin between two facing pages.

H

Headline Words in large type at the beginning of a story used to summarize it and to attract reader interest.

Hot type Systems for creating lines or plates of type by casting them in molten lead or another metal.

Household penetration A measure of the number of occupied housing units that receive a newspaper in a market area.

I

Impression The result of the contact made by printing plates or type on paper.

Infographics The presentation of information through art and graphs designed to make it more comprehensible.

Internet A loose system of worldwide computer networks linked together to facilitate communications and data transfer.

Investigative reporting Journalism that focuses on problems and issues through extensive research not normally conducted when covering day-to-day news events.

J

Joint operating agreement An agreement between two papers to pool resources and equipment in a single market. Usually characterized by the establishment of a production, advertising, and business arrangement used by both newspapers. When many of these agreements were found to violate antitrust laws, Congress exempted them from the laws in 1970.

Journalese The writing style characterized by short paragraphs and a lead paragraph that sums up the story being reported, followed by information in descending order of importance. Also used to describe stilted or cliched writing.

Jumpline In stories appearing on more than one page, a jumpline is use to indicate the page on which the next portion of the story is printed ("jumped").

Justification The alignment of lines of text in relation to a margin. Text is typically justified to the left margin, the right margin, or to both.

K

Kerning The reduction of space between pairs of characters in type so they are displayed in a more aesthetically pleasing manner. Certain combinations of letters are more likely to require kerning, including AV, VA, WA, and YA. Some computerized layout software is now including automatic kerning functions.

Kicker A small line of headline type placed above the main headline.

L

Lead The first paragraph (or paragraphs) of a story that summarizes its facts or angle. The term is also used to indicate the main story of the day or a news tip that a journalist is investigating.

Leading The space between lines of type, measured from baseline to baseline of each line.

Letterpress printing Printing method in which paper is pressed onto raised type on which ink has been placed, thus transferring the ink to the paper.

Lineage A measure of lines of material printed, usually advertising, calculated by number of column inches.

Linecaster Typesetting machine that sets single slugs of justified movable type or lines of type created by using melted lead. Generally replaced by phototypesetting, but still found in some small newspapers.

Localize Taking a general story or one that originates away from the city in which a paper is located and adding material to provide a local angle.

M

Market The area in which a firm conducts business for a specific type of newspaper product and services.

Marketing The process of selling and promoting the sales of the newspaper or newspaper advertising through direct and indirect activities designed to make the paper more salable.

Masthead The area, usually on the editorial page, where the official name of the paper, its office location, its top managers, and subscription information is published.

Metric ton Standard weight measurement used for newsprint. A metric ton is approximately 2,205 pounds.

Movable type Individual letters of type that made mass printing possible. First created in China using clay and later wood and metal. An integrated system of movable type was introduced by Johann Gutenberg in Germany in the 1450s. Although still used by some printers, movable type has been replaced by hot and cold type in most newspaper operations.

Mug shot A photograph featuring the head and bust of an individual.

N

Nameplate The area of the first page of the newspaper in which the name of the paper is published.

National advertising Advertising, usually display advertising, that comes from national advertisers outside the market of the newspaper.

Net paid circulation A standardized circulation sales figure that adjusts figures to account for discounted sales.

News Information about events and occurrences that includes elements of timeliness and proximity or import to the audience.

News agency An organization that provides news to clients written by its own employees. Distribution may be made by mail or telecommunication services.

News exchange An arrangement between two or more papers in which news produced by each is exchanged for potential use by the other(s).

Newshole The amount of space available for news and features.

Newspaper designated market area The primary commercial and residential portion of a newspaper market.

Newspaper rack An unattended stand from which newspapers are distributed. Paid circulation newspapers use racks in which coins must be deposited to receive a paper and free circulation newspapers are available in racks without charge.

Newsstand A retail sales establishment specializing in the sales of newspapers and other periodicals, typically kiosk or storefront operations.

Nondaily A paper published fewer than five times a week.

Nonduplicating coverage (NDC) A shopper produced by a paid circulation paper to give advertisers total market coverage. The shopper is delivered to households that do not subscribe to the paid newspaper.

Nuggets Brief news items, typically presented in a group, that allow readers to quickly scan news and other developments.

O

Official newspaper A newspaper designated by a government agency as being the official location in which public and legal notices should be published.

Offset printing Printing method by which an inked image is transferred to paper without the paper ever coming into actual contact with the printing plate.

On-line services Computer-based services that permit customers to access a newspaper's databanks to receive information or advertising through a telephone modem linked to their personal computers.

P

Pagination The process of creating newspaper pages on a computer, drawing together page design, text, and graphics.

Pass along rate A figure that includes the purchaser and additional readers of an average newspaper copy.

Pasteup The process of pasting copy and graphics onto a layout board to be photographed in the platemaking process. Pasteup is being increasingly replaced by computer pagination throughout the newspaper industry.

Penetration A measure of the percentage of households in a market area receiving a newspaper.

Perfecting press A printing press that prints on two sides of paper at the same time. Nearly all modern newspapers use perfecting presses.

Photocomposition The transfer of a film image to a metal printing plate using photochemistry techniques; this method replaced composition based on linecasting and movable type.

Photoengraving Halftone process by which photographs and other illustrations are prepared for printing by rephotographing the object through a grid pattern to create dots of varying sizes that reproduce the original image on the press. Currently being replaced by digitized computer methods.

Photojournalism The use of photography to record events and occurrences as news rather than for artistic purposes.

Play The emphasis given a story by its size, position, or length. A story can be played up or played down.

Post-press Activities including, folding, gathering, and bundling, which take place after a paper leaves the printing press.

Pre-press Preparatory activities that take place before actual printing occurs.

Preprint advertising Advertising material prepared by advertisers and inserted into a newspaper.

Pressrun The number of copies of an edition of a newspaper that are actually printed, whether distributed or not.

Printing The act of creating copies of information on paper by transferring it with ink through letterpress or offset technology.

Promotion   Activities designed to support marketing and sales of subscriptions or advertising and to otherwise bolster the image or position of the newspaper.

Put to bed   Period after all changes or additions to the paper have been made, plates have been put on the presses, and the paper cannot be changed without stopping the presses.

R

Readers per copy   A figure that includes the purchaser and additional readers of newspaper copy.

Readership   The number or percentage of individuals who actually read a newspaper, headline, news story, advertisement, or other portion of a newspaper. Often broken down by a variety of demographic characteristics.

Replate   To change the metal page plates on the presses. Done to change pages for different editions or to correct significant errors.

Reporter   A person who writes news and feature stories.

Retail advertising   Display advertising from retail merchants such as department, appliance, hardware and grocery stores. Sometimes used interchangeably with the phrase *display advertising.*

Retail trading zone   The area surrounding a city from which customers for the central city are drawn.

Run-of-paper advertising   Ads that have no stipulated preferred or agreed-on position and can be run anywhere in the paper.

Run-of-press advertising   Advertising produced on a newspaper's press and contained in the pages of a newspaper as opposed to preprint advertising.

S

Saddle-stitch   A form of binding in which a paper is joined, often by staples, at its major fold.

Scoop   To cover or publish a story that no competing news organization has developed.

Section   A portion of the paper covering a specific topic that is set off from other content by a separate banner or logo for that section, for example: "Business," "Style," and "Sports."

Sensationalism   A reporting and editing technique that emphasizes coverage of events and issues designed to elicit emotional responses from readers, and typically uses stories about sex, violence, and social deviance.

Shopper   A free circulation newspaper available through home delivery or in newspaper racks.

Sidebar   A shorter, related story placed adjacently to a main story.

Signature   A folded sheet of paper that creates four pages for a newspaper.

Single-copy sales Copies sold not by subscription, but by news rack, newsstand, or some other retail outlet.

Slugline A short identifying word or phase used to identify a story for planning purposes and for storage and retrieval purposes.

Stringer A part-time correspondent.

Subhead An internal headline—normally only one line in length and in body copy typeface—used as an organizational device within a story to indicate a new section or shifting emphasis within the story.

Subscription A newspaper purchase covering all editions published within a specified period, typically quarterly.

Stereotyping Process of making duplicate metal plates of pages in hot type production of a newspaper so several presses can produce the same paper simultaneously.

Syndicate A feature or art service.

Syndication The creation of editorial materials and their sale to newspapers in different markets.

T

Tabloid A reduced-size paper designed for readability that targets a mass audience. Although tabloid papers tend to emphasize popular topics, the term primarily refers to the size of the paper.

Tearsheet A full page containing an advertisement that is provided to advertisers as proof of publication.

Total market coverage (TMC) A newspaper or free distribution portion of a newspaper that is delivered to all or nearly all homes in a market to satisfy the household penetration needs of advertisers.

U

Umbrella competition A competitive situation in a metropolitan area in which dailies and weeklies compete under the umbrella of a large metropolitan paper.

V

Verified Audit of Circulation A firm that conducts circulation audits primarily for nondaily newspapers.

Video display terminal A computerized device that produces an on-screen display.

Videotext The transmission of information in written form through a broadcast or cable system so that it can be read on television screens.

Voluntary pay newspaper A paper, often a shopper, that is delivered free of charge but for which payment is later requested. Delivery continues whether or not a payment is received.

W

Web A roll of paper that is fed through a printing press.

Web offset press The most common type of newspaper. It uses a roll of paper that is passed through the press and then folded into signatures, gathered, and trimmed.

Weekly A paper published once a week.

Workstation A desktop computer system linked to a computer network from which it can access shared network resources.

Z

Zoned edition An edition of a newspaper produced for a distinct region that includes content for that "zone" that does not appear in other editions of the paper.

Bibliography

Adler, Jerry. "Typing Without Keys," *Newsweek,* December 7, 1992, 63.

The Age of Indifference. Los Angeles, CA: Times Mirror Center for The People and The Press, June 1990.

Albers, Rebecca Ross. "Back to Boca," *Presstime*, April 1995, 27-30.

The American Media: Who Reads, Who Watches, Who Listens, Who Cares. Los Angeles, CA: Times Mirror Center for The People and The Press, 1990.

American Newspaper Publishers Association and International Federation of Financial Executives. *Taxes on Advertising, Circulation, Preprints, Production Materials, Supplies and Equipment Affecting Newspapers: A 50-State Compilation.* Reston, Va.: American Newspaper Publishers Association, October 1989.

American Society of Newspaper Editors. *Marginal and At-Risk Readers—Findings of Two New ASNE Studies. Proceedings of the American Society of Newspaper Editors.* Reston, VA: American Society of Newspaper Editors, 1991, 69–86.

Arana, Ana. "The Chilling Effect is Palpable," *Silenced: The Unsolved Murders of Immigrant Journalists in the United States.* New York: Committee to Protect Journalists, 1994, 3.

Associated Press. *Associated Press Stylebook and Libel Manual.* New York: Associated Press, annual.

Bagdikian, Ben. *The Media Monopoly,* 4th ed. Boston: Beacon Press, 1993.

Baker, Bob. "NIOSH Study Backs Claims of Stress Injury," *Los Angeles Times,* October 29, 1992, D1.

Balen, Amy, and William Glaberson. "A Tablet Moses Just Couldn't Have Dreamed of," *Business Times,* February 8, 1994, 13.

Barlett, Donald L., and James B. Steele. *America, What Went Wrong? Kansas City:* Andrews and McMeel, 1992.

Barry, Dave. "Newspapers Pulling Up Their Dockers," *Dayton Daily News,* November 14, 1994, B6.

Beals, Paul E. "The Newspaper in the Classroom: Some Notes on Recent Research," *Reading World,* May 1984.

Benjaminson, P. *Death in the Afternoon: America's Newspaper Giants Struggle for Survival.* Kansas City, MO: Andrews, McMeel, & Parker, 1984.

Benkelman, Susan. "Online Services Seek Guidelines for Treks in Cyberspace, Legal and Moral Issues Remain Unidentified," *Commercial Appeal,* December 30, 1995, 8C.

Bennett, Charles O. *Facts without Opinion.* Chicago: Audit Bureau of Circulation, 1965.

Berger, Meyer. *The Story of the New York Times, 1851–1951.* New York: Simon and Schuster, 1951.

Black's Law Dictionary. St. Paul, MN: West Publishing, 1968.

Blankenburg, William B. "Determinants of Pricing of Advertising in Weeklies," *Journalism Quarterly* 57 (1980): 663–666.

_____ "Newspaper Ownership and Control of Circulation to Increase Profits," *Journalism Quarterly* 59 (Autumn 1982):390–398.

Blankenburg, William B., and Gary W. Ozanich. "The Effects of Public Ownership on the Financial Performance of Newspaper Corporations," *Journalism Quarterly* 70 (1993):68–75.

Bleyer, Willard. *Main Currents in the History of American Journalism.* Boston: Houghton Mifflin, 1927.

Blum, Andrew. "Internet Copyright Ruling," *National Law Journal,* December 11, 1995, A6.

Bogart, Leo. "Advertorials in Our Future," *Proceedings of the 1989 Convention of the American Society of Newspaper Editors.* Washington, DC: American Society of Newspaper Editors, 1989, 82.

Bogart, Leo. "The State of the Industry," *The Future of News.* Washington, DC: Woodrow Wilson Center Press, 1992.

Borelli, James T. "The Forgotten Peril; Trademark Infringement is One More Risk to Consider When It's Time to Name a Newspaper or Buy Insurance," *Editor & Publisher,* Special Editorial Section, December 9, 1995, 12T.

Bradden, R. *Roy Thomson of Fleet Street.* New York: Walker, 1965.

Brandt, J. Donald. *A History of Gannett, 1906–1993.* Arlington, VA: Gannett, 1993.

Busterna, John C. "Antitrust in the 1980s: An Analysis of 45 Newspaper Actions," *Newspaper Research Journal* 9:25–336 (1988).

_____ "Application of US Antitrust Laws to Daily Newspaper Chains," *Journal of Media Law and Practice* 10:117–122 (1989).

_____ "The Cross-Elasticity of Demand for National Newspaper Advertising," *Journalism Quarterly* 64 (Summer–Autumn 1987), 346–351.

_____ *Daily Newspaper Chains and the Antitrust Laws. Journalism Monographs* No. 110, March 1989.

Busterna, John C., and Robert G. Picard. *Joint Operating Agreements: The Newspaper Preservation Act and Its Application.* Norwood, NJ: Ablex Publishing, 1993.

"California Daily Pays Fine for Hazardous Waste," *Editor & Publisher*, April 18, 1992, 45.

"California Paper Promotes Good News," *Editor & Publisher*, February 11, 1995, 15.

Cameron, Glen T., Glen J. Nowak, and Dean M. Krugman. "The Competitive Position of Newspapers in the Local Retail Market," *Newspaper Research Journal* (Summer/Fall 1993):70–81.

Case, Tony. "A Rocky Road Predicted for Newspaper Ads," *Editor & Publisher* September 23, 1995, 128:27.

_____ "Still Strong," *Editor & Publisher*, January 6, 1996, 15–25+.

Casserly, Jack. *Scripps, the Divided Dynasty: A History of the First Family of American Journalism*. New York: Donald I. Fine, 1992.

Chaney, Lindsay, and Michael Cieply. *The Hearsts: The Family and Empire—The Later Years*. New York: Simon and Schuster, 1981.

Christopher, L. Carol. "Closing the Gap," *Quill*, January/February, 1994, 27.

Clark, Jeff. "Circulation Increase Despite Higher Subscription Rates," *Editor & Publisher,* February 4, 1976, 32.

Cobb, Chris. "A No-Paper Paper in a Future Near You," *Ottawa Citizen,* April 9, 1994, B1.

Cole, David M. "Pagination, Page by Page," *Presstime*, February 1995, 27–32.

Compaine, Benjamin M. *The Newspaper Industry in the 1980s: An Assessment of Economics and Technology*. White Plains, NY: Knowledge Industry, 1982.

Compaine, Benjamin C., Christopher H. Sterling, Thomas Guback, and J. Kendrick Noble, Jr. *Who Owns the Media? Concentration of Ownership in the Mass Communication Industry*. White Plains, NY: Knowledge Industry, 1982.

"Computer Users Suffer Ailments, UC Study Finds," *San Francisco Chronicle,* November 21, 1992, A2.

Consoli, John. "Get Your Act Together: Newspapers Warned They Had Better Make Sure They are in Compliance with Environmental Regulations or Face Criminal Prosecution," *Editor & Publisher*, June 22, 1991, 7–8.

Cunningham, Richard. "Ombudsman Gives High Marks to Washington Post," *Quill,* September, 1995, 17.

Demers, David P., and Daniel Wackman, "Effect of Chain Ownership on Newspaper Management Goals," *Newspaper Research Journal* 9 (1988):59–68.

DeRoche, Edward F. "Newspapers in Education: What We Know," *Newspaper Research Journal* 2 (Spring 1981):59–61.

DeRoche, Edward F., and Linda B. Skover, "Newspapers in Teaching and Learning Reading," *Newspaper Research Journal* 4 (Winter 1983):23-30.

Dertouzous, J. N., and T. H. Quinn. *Bargaining Responses to the Technology Revolution: The Case of the Newspaper Industry*. Santa Monica, CA: Rand, 1985.

Dertouzous, J. N., and K. E. Thorpe. *Newspaper Groups: Economies of Scale, Tax Laws, and Merger Incentives*. Santa Monica, CA: Rand, 1982.

Devitt, James. "The Daily Newspaper," *The Future of News*. Washington, DC: Woodrow Wilson Center Press, 1992.

Dewey, John. *Democracy and Education.* New York: Macmillan, 1915.

Doig, Stephen K. "The Big One," *Quill,* September, 1993, 26.

Emery, Edwin, and Michael Emery. *The Press and America: An Interpretive History of the Mass Media*, 5th ed. Englewood Cliffs, NJ: Prentice–Hall, 1984.

Ferguson, James M. *The Advertising Rate Structure in the Daily Newspaper Industry.* Englewood Cliffs, NJ: Prentice–Hall, 1963.

Fink, Conrad. *Strategic Newspaper Management.* New York: Random House, 1988.

____ "Old Newspaper Now Traded on Chicago Exchange," *Editor & Publisher*, November 18, 1995, 36.

Fost, Dan. "Newspapers Enter the Age of Information," *American Demographics,* September 1990, 14.

Furhoff, Lars. "Some Reflections on Newspaper Concentration," *Scandinavian Economic History Review* 21 (1973):1–27.

Ghiglione, L. *The Buying and Selling of America's Newspapers.* Indianapolis, IN.: R. J. Berg, 1984.

Giobbe, Dorothy. "HUD Clarifies its Classified Ad Language Policy," *Editor & Publisher*, February 4, 1995, 26.

____ "Study: Classified Ads Remain Most Popular Source for Finding a Job," *Editor & Publisher*, August 5, 1995, 20.

Gottlieb, Robert, and Irene Wolt. *Thinking Big: The Story of the Los Angeles Times, Its Publishers, and Their Influence on Southern California.* New York: G.P. Putnam's Son's, 1976.

Goulden, Joseph C. *Fit to Print, A. M. Rosenthal and His Times.* Secaucus, NJ: Lyle Stuart, 1988, 103–104.

Greenwald, Judy. "Publishers Cautioned on Risks of Online Publishing Ventures," *Business Insurance,* December 4, 1995, 68.

"50,000 Records Analyzed for Series," *Indianapolis Star,* September 24, 1995, A11.

Field, Robert W. "Circulation Price Inelasticity in the Daily Newspaper Industry," M.A. thesis. Norman:University of Oklahoma, 1978.

Fitzgerald, Mark. "Accord Close in Groundwater Contamination Case," *Editor & Publisher*, June 24, 1995, 58+.

____ "Interest in Electronic Delivery Continues to Grow, Survey Shows," *Editor & Publisher*, February 11, 1995, 30–31.

Flanigan, James. "Pixar Makes a Great Story, but the Big Picture Belongs to Computers," *Los Angeles Times,* December 3, 1995, D-1.

Francese, Peter. "Newspapers and the Future," *Proceedings of the 1988 Convention of the American Society of Newspaper Editors,"* 1988, 239.

Gannon, James P. "Warning: Entertainment Values Threaten Journalism's Health," *Editor & Publisher,* August 27, 1994, 48.

Garneau, George. "L.A. Times Exits Prodigy, for Now," *Editor & Publisher*, December 2, 1995, 37.

____ "Monitor Loses Overtime Case," *Editor & Publisher*, November 13, 1993, 26–27.

____ "Profit Peaks Are Here Again," *Editor & Publisher*, March 18, 1995, 14–16+.

____ "Return to Seller," *Editor & Publisher,* July 22, 1995.

____ "Sales Tax on Newspaper Equipment Overturned," *Editor & Publisher*, June 8, 1991, 28+.

"A Good Year for Newspaper Shares," *Newspaper Stocks Report Annual Review.* Riverside, CA: Carpelan Publishing Co., January 1996, 1.

Grotta, Gerald. "Consolidation of Newspapers: What Happens to the Consumer," *Journalism Quarterly* 48 (Summer 1971):245–250.

_____ "Daily Newspaper Circulation Price Inelastic for 1970–75," *Journalism Quarterly* 54 (Summer 1977):379–382.

Grusin, Elinor Kelley, and Gerald C. Stone. "The Newspaper in Education and New Readers: Hooking Kids on Newspapers through Classroom Experiences," *Journalism Monographs* No. 141 (October 1993).

Gustafsson, Karl Erik. "The Circulation Spiral and the Theory of Household Coverage," *Scandinavian Economic History Review* 28 (1978):1–14 .

Hale, F. Dennis. "An In-Depth Look at Chain Ownership," *Editor & Publisher,* April 28, 1984, 117:30ff.

Heath, Shirley Brice, and Sar Dewitt. *Truths to Tell Youth and Newspaper Reading: A Special Report for the American Society of Newspaper Editors Literacy Committee.* St. Petersburg, FL: Poynter Institute for Media Studies, 1995.

Hartman, John K. *The USA Today Way: A Candid Look at the National Newspaper's First Decade.* Bowling Green, OH: John K. Hartman, 1993.

Hernandez, Debra Gersh. "Uniform Correction Act Introduced," *Editor & Publisher,* July 22, 1995, 16.

Hirsh, Fred, and David Gordon. *Newspaper Money.* London: Hutchinson, 1978.

Hoberman, Henry S. "Libel Reform Isn't Necessarily Bad for Nation's Media," *Quill,* March, 1995, 14.

"Housing Ads Draw Heightened Scrutiny," *Presstime*, November 1994, 13.

Hovenkamp, Herbert. "Vertical Integration by the Newspaper Monopolist," *Iowa Law Review* 69 (1984):451–459.

"How Scary Are You?" *Los Angeles Times*, October 2, 1995, View Section, 1.

"How We Did It," *St. Petersburg Times,* October 22, 1995, 7A.

"HUD Offers Relief," *Presstime*, February 1995, 13.

Hume, Ellen. *Tabloids, Talk Radio, and the Future of News: Technology's Impact on Journalism.* Washington, DC: Annenberg Washington Program in Communication Policy Studies, Northwestern University, 1995, 20.

Institute Of Newspaper Controllers and Finance Officers. *Standard Chart of Accounts for Newspapers.* Morristown, NJ: Institute of Newspaper Controllers and Finance Officers, 1979.

International Federation of Newspaper Publishers. *World Press Trends.* Paris: International Federation of Newspaper Publishers, 1995.

International Newspaper Promotion Association. *Promoting the Total Newspaper.* Reston, VA: International Newspaper Promotion Association, 1984.

Jensen, Carl, & Project Censored. *Censored: The News that Didn't Make the News— and Why.* New York: Four Walls Eight Windows 1994, 27.

Johnson, J. T. "Newspapers Slow to Embrace Advances in Computer World," *Quill,* September, 1995, 20.

_____ "The Unconscious Fraud of Journalism Education; Failure of Journalism Schools to Teach Database Skills," *Quill,* June, 1992, 31.

Johnson, Scott. "Newsroom Circles," *Quill,* March, 1993, 28.

Jones, Tim. "Newspapers Struggle to Read between the Lines; Publishers Seek Right Definition of 'Content' as Circulation Slides," *Chicago Tribune,* May 1, 1994, B3.

Juergens, George. *Joseph Pulitzer and the New York World.* Princeton, NJ: Princeton University Press, 1966.

"Jury finds for Atex, IBM," *National Law Journal,* May 8, 1995, B2.

Kozol, Jonathan. *Illiterate America.* Garden City, NJ: Anchor/Doubleday 1985.

Kurtz, Howard. "For Nation's Newspapers, the News Isn't Good," *Messages 2: The Washington Post Media Companion.* Boston: Allyn & Bacon, 1993, 48.

Lacy, Stephen, and Frederick Fico. "Newspaper Quality and Ownership: Rating the Groups," *Newspaper Research Journal,* 11 (Spring 1990):42–56.

Lacy, Stephen, and Todd F. Simon. *The Economics and Regulation of United States Newspapers.* Norwood, NJ: Ablex Publishing, 1993.

Lail, Jack D. "Newspaper On-line," *Quill,* January/February, 1994, 40.

Lambeth, Edmund. "Gene Roberts: Leading the Way to the Standard for Contemporary Prize-Winning Journalism," *Quill,* June, 1991, 14.

Landau, Edmund, and John Scott Davenport, "Price Anomalies of the Mass Media," *Journalism Quarterly* 36 (Summer 1959):291–294.

Landau, George. "Computer Journalism Takes Off," *Columbia Journalism Review,* May, 1992, 61.

Lee, Alfred McClung. *The Daily Newspaper in America.* New York: Macmillan, 1937.

Lewis, Regina. "Relation between Newspaper Subscription Price and Circulation, 1971–1992," *Journal of Media Economics* 8 (1995):25–41.

Liebman, Hanna. "A New Breakfast Serial. Think That You Can't Believe What the Papers Say? Newspapers Publish Fiction to Increase Readership," *Media Week,* October 11, 1993, 12.

Louv, Richard. "Extra, Extra! Tell Me All about It!" *Christian Science Monitor,* June 27, 1991, 19.

"Lower Circulation Lifts Readership, NAA Chief Asserts," *Editor & Publisher,* May 20, 1995, vol. 128.

Lynch, Stephen. "O.J. Response Means Online Media Guilty," *Orange County Register,* October 23, 1995, B24.

Martens, Dave. "When the IRS Knocks...," *Presstime,* August 1995, 53–56.

Mauer, Richard. "I was a Mac Agitator," *Quill,* September, 1993, 24.

May, Randolph J. "Online Libel and Cyberspace Porn," *Connecticut Law Tribune,* December 4, 1995, 40.

Mayfield, Dave. "Knight–Ridder Buys into Infinet," *Virginia Pilot,* June 8, 1995, D1.

McCabe, Charles R., ed. *Damned Old Crank: A Self Portrait of E. W. Scripps.* New York: Harper and Brothers, 1951.

McClure, Leslie. *Newspaper Advertising and Promotion.* New York: Macmillan, 1950.

McKinney, John. *How to Start Your Own Community Newspaper.* Port Jefferson, NY: Meadow Press, 1977.

Meyer, Philip. "Learning to Love Lower Profits," *American Journalism Review,* December 1995, 40–44.

_____ *The Newspaper Survival Book: An Editor's Guide to Marketing.* Bloomington: Indiana University Press, 1985.

Meyers, P., and S. T. Wearden. "The Effect of Public Ownership on Newspaper Companies: A Preliminary Inquiry," *Public Opinion Quarterly* 48 (1984):564–577.

Minnow, Newton N. "The Communications Act: Our Children are the Public Interest," *Vital Speeches* 61, 13 (April, 15, 1995), 389.

Moran, Michael. "Downcast News," *Evening Standard,* November 23, 1994, 62.

Morgan, Neil. *Proceedings of the 1989 Convention of the American Society of Newspaper Editors*. Washington, DC: American Society of Newspaper Editors, 1989, 88.

Morton, John. "Farewell to More Family Dynasties," *American Journalism Review* (October 1995), 17:68.

_____ "Worried Publishers Enter the Information Age," *San Francisco Examiner*, April 24, 1994, A15.

Mott, Frank Luther. *American Journalism*, rev. ed. New York: Macmillan, 1962.

Nauer, Kim. "Tax Attacks: How Newspapers Flirt with Evasion," *Columbia Journalism Review* (September/October 1993), 31:20-21.

"Nearly Half in U.S. Can't Read Well," *San Jose Mercury News*. September 9. 1993, A6.

"Newspaper Industry Making Headlines with Comeback in 1994 and 1995," *Standard and Poor's Emerging & Special Situation*, No. 4, April 17, 1995, 3.

Newspaper Association of America. *Facts About Newspapers*, Reston, VA: various years.

Newspaper Association of America. *NAA Subscriber Churn Management Handbook*. Reston, VA: Newspaper Association of America, 1995.

Newspaper Association of America. *Newspaper Manual for Utilizing Independent Contractors*. Reston, VA: Newspaper Association of America, 1995.

Newspaper Association of America. *Seize It: Newspaper Minority Recruitment Kit*. Reston, VA: Newspaper Association of America, 1994.

Newspaper Association of America. *Why Newspapers? They Add Value for Advertisers*. New York: Newspaper Association of America, 1994.

"Neuharth Urges Higher Newspaper Prices," *Editor & Publisher,* October 26, 1985, 118:20.

O'Donnell, James F. *100 Years of Making Communications History: The Story of the Hearst Corporation*. New York: Hearst Corporation, 1987.

Oppenheim, S. Chesterfield, and Carrington Shields. *Newspaper and Antitrust Laws*. Charlottesville, VA: Michie, 1981.

Owen, Bruce M. *Economics and the First Amendment: Media Structure and the First Amendment*. Cambridge, MA: Ballinger, 1975.

Paterno, Susan. "The Way to Do It," *American Journalism Review (*March, 1995), 17:29.

Paul, Nora. *Computer Assisted Research*. St. Petersburg, FL: Poynter Institute,

Payne, George H. *History of Journalism in the United States*. New York: Appleton–Crofts, 1920.

Pease, Ted. "Philosophical and Economic Arguments for Media Diversity," *Pluralizing Journalism Education—A Multicultural Handbook*. Westport, CT: Greenwood Press, 1993.

Picard, Robert G. "Cost Analyses of Predation Involving Free Circulation Subsidiaries of Paid Newspapers," *Journal of Media Economics* 4 (Summer 1991):19–34.

_____ "Critical Assumptions in Arguments for Maximum Price Fixing of Newspaper Circulation," *Communications and the Law* (December 1990), 69–86.

_____ "The Effect of Price Increases on Newspaper Circulation: A Case Study of Inelasticity of Demand," *Newspaper Research Journal* 12 (Summer 1991): 65–75.

_____ "Gender Representation in Corporate Management of Public Newspaper Companies," Research Report. Fullerton, CA: California State University, 1995.

_____ "Institutional Ownership of Publicly Traded U.S. Newspaper Companies," *Journal of Media Economics* 7 (1994): 49–64.

_____ "Measures of Concentration in the Daily Newspaper Industry," *Journal of Media Economics* 1 (Spring 1988):64–94.

_____ *Media Economics: Concepts and Issues.* Newbury Park, CA: Sage Publications, 1989.

_____ *The Press and the Decline of Democracy: The Democratic Socialist Approach in Public Policy.* Westport, CT: Greenwood Press, 1985.

_____ "Pricing Behavior of Newspapers." In Picard, Robert G., James P. Winter, Maxwell McCombs, and Stephen Lacy, eds. *Press Concentration and Monopoly: New Perspectives on Newspaper Ownership and Operation.* Norwood, NJ: Ablex Publishing, 1988, 55–69.

_____ "Pricing in Competing and Monopoly Newspapers, 1972–1982," *LSU School of Journalism Research Bulletin* (1986).

_____ "Rate-Setting and Competition in Newspaper Advertising," *Newspaper Research Journal* 3 (April 1982):23–33.

_____ "The Relationship between Newspaper Costs and Predation Lawsuits," *Newspaper Research Journal*, 10 (Winter 1990):112–125.

Picard, Robert G., James P. Winter, Maxwell McCombs, and Stephen Lacy, eds. *Press Concentration and Monopoly: New Perspectives on Newspaper Ownership and Operation.* Norwood, NJ: Ablex Publishing, 1988.

"Pulling and Pushing E-Rights: Publishers Negotiate for Content and Writers Follow the Money," *Digital Media,* September 11, 1995, 19

Rambo, C. David, "Newspapers Seek New Ways to Increase Carriers' Safety," *Presstime,* September 1984, vol 6, 6–7.

Randolph, Eleanor. "Extra! Extra! Who Cares?; Newspapers Face the Incredible Shrinking Reader," *Washington Post,* April 1, 1990, C1

Remnick, David. "Last of the Red Hots," *New Yorker,* September 18, 1995, 82.

Renfroe, Patricia P. "Sexual Harrassment," *Presstime*, May 1985, 14–15.

Roberts, Gene. "Suicide Hangs over Our Heads," *Quill,* November/December 1995, 63.

Rosse, James N. "Economic Limits of Press Responsibility," discussion paper. Palo Alto: *Stanford University Studies in Industry Economics*, No. 56, 1975.

Rucker, Frank W., and Herbert Lee Williams. *Newspaper Organization and Management*, 5th ed. Ames, IA: Iowa State University Press, 1978.

Salgado, Bob. "Dealing with a Contamination Problem," *Editor & Publisher*, November 18, 1995, 26.

Salmon, Lucy Maynard. *The Newspaper and Authority.* New York: Oxford University Press, 1923.

Sandstrom, Karen. "PD Attuned to Readers' Diverse Interests," *Cleveland Plain Dealer*, June 5, 1994, S30.

Sanger, Elizabeth. "Only One View That's Fit to Print," *Newsday*, July 26, 1993, 29.

Schiller, Herbert I. *Who Knows? Information in the Age of the Fortune 500.* Norwood, NJ: Ablex Publishing, 1981.

Scott, Jeffrey. "The Next Generation Newspapers Pursue the Young with Special Features, Sections," *Atlanta Journal and Constitution,* February 2, 1993, C1.

Schudsen, Michael. *Discovering the News: A Social History of American Newspapers.* New York: Basic Books, 1978.

Schraff, E. *Worldly Power: The Making of the Wall Street Journal.* New York: New American Library, 1988.

Shaw, David. "The Story That Hijacked America," *Los Angeles Times,* October 9, 1995, S1–12.

"Silicon Valley Nerds Herald Newspapers of Tomorrow," *South China Morning Post,* March 2, 1994, Media Supplement.

"Singapore Orders Newspaper to Pay," UPI, May 10, 1995, BC cycle.

Skrycki, Cindy. "OSHA Abandons Rules Effort on Repetitive Injury; Opposition by GOP, Business Cited," *Washington Post,* June 13, 1995, D1.

Smith, Anthony. *Goodbye Gutenberg.* New York: Oxford University Press, 1980.

Snoddy, Raymond, and Stephen McGookin. "Ridder Moves Back the Future," *Financial Times,* August 7, 1995, 10.

Spring, Greg. "Disney Eyes Launch of Kid-Themed Newspaper," *Los Angeles Business Journal,* April 17, 1995, 8.

Soloski, John. "Economics and Management: The Real Influence of Newspaper Groups," *Newspaper Research Journal* 1 (November 1979):19–28.

Stein, M. L. "Advertorials and the First Amendment," *Editor & Publisher,* September 18, 1993, 24.

_____ "Re-Establishing Relevance for Readers; Panelists Examine Concepts Aimed at Stopping Erosion of Readership," *Editor & Publisher,* March 5, 1994, 16.

Sullivan, J. L. "Not Quite All in the Family: Outside Directors Signal Change in Register Empire," *Orange County Business,* March 27-April 2, 1995, 1+.

"Survey: Newspapers Need Better Content," *Legal Intelligencer,* April 26, 1994, 11.

Swanberg, W. A. *Citizen Hearst.* New York: Charles Scribner's Sons, 1961.

Swaneberg, W. A. *Pulitzer.* New York: Charles Scribner's Sons, 1967.

Swisher, Kara. "Post Co., 7 Media Firms Enter On-Line Alliance," *Washington Post,* April 20, 1995, B10.

Talese, Gay. *The Kingdom and the Power.* New York: World, 1969.

Teinowitz, Ira. "Newspapers Rethink Their Eroding Position; 'Endangered As a Mass Medium,' Papers Fight Back," *Advertising Age,* August 12, 1991, S1.

Terry, Carolyn. "Breaking Through. Or Are They? Women in Newspaper Management Assess their Progress" *Presstime,* March 1995, 31–36.

_____ "Sexual Harrassment: Old News," *Presstime,* September 1995, 63.

Thorn, William J. (with Mary Pat Pfeil). *Newspaper Circulation: Marketing the News.* New York: Longman, 1987.

"Trademarks and the Press," *Editor & Publisher,* Special Editorial Section, December 9, 1995.

Truitt, Rosalind C. "A Taxing Climate," *Presstime,* May 1995, 65–68.

Udell, John G. *The Economics of the American Newspaper.* New York: Hastings House, 1978.

Underwood, Doug. *When MBAs Rule the Newsroom.* New York: Columbia University Press, 1993.

United Press International. *United Press International Stylebook.* New York: United Press International, annual.

United States. 4 Op. Attys. Gen. 10.

United States. Public Law 233, 65 Stat. 672.

United States. Public Law 91–353, 84 Stat. 466, 15 U.S.C. sections 1801–1804 (1970).

United States Department of Commerce. *Statistical Abstract of the United States.* Washington, DC: U.S. Government Printing Office, 1994.

Walker, Jerry. "Computer Helps AP Reporters Get News," *Jack O'Dwyer's Newsletter,* October 4, 1995, 4.

Weber, Jonathan. "Stop the Presses; Papers Enter a Brave New World," *Los Angeles Times,* January 17, 1994, A1.

Weinberg, Steve. *The Reporter's Handbook, An Investigator's Guide to Documents and Techniques.* New York: St. Martin's Press 1996..

Weiner, Rex. "CompuServe Move Irks Netheads," *Daily Variety,* January 2, 1996, 3.

Welles, Chris. "Is the Gray Lady Slipping?" *Business Week,* March 7, 1994, 19.

Wilkinson, J. B., Douglas R. Hausknecht, and George E. Prough. "Reader Categorization of a Controversial Communication: Advertisement versus Editorial," *Journal of Public Policy and Marketing* (Fall 1995), 12:245.

Willis, Jim. *Surviving in the Newspaper Business: Newspaper Management in Turbulent Times.* New York: Praeger, 1988.

Wilson, III, Clint, and Felix Gutierrez. *Race, Multiculturalism, and the Media: From Mass to Class Communication.* Thousand Oaks, CA: Sage Publications, 1995.

Young, John P. *Journalism in California.* San Francisco: Chronicle Publishing, 1915.

Index